CREATING CHARACTERS

This is a book about beginnings, and it is dedicated to every creative writer who has ever faced a blank sheet of paper with sometimes only a vague notion about some fictional characters and the story that will house them.

CREATING CHARACTERS

A Writer's Reference to the Personality Traits That Bring Fictional People to Life

by HOWARD LAUTHER

McFarland & Company, Inc., Publishers
Jefferson, North Carolina, and London

British Library Cataloguing-in-Publication data are available

Library of Congress Cataloguing-in-Publication Data

Lauther, Howard, 1935–
    Creating chararacters : a writer's reference to the personality
traits that bring fictional people to life / by Howard Lauther
      p. cm.
    Includes index.
    ISBN 0-7864-0569-4 (library binding : 50# alkaline paper) ∞
    1. Fiction — Technique.   2. Characters and characteristics in
literature. I. Title.
PN3383.C4L37   1998
808.3'97 — dc21   98-8073
                                             CIP

Manufactured in the United States of America

*McFarland & Company, Inc., Publishers
  Box 611, Jefferson, North Carolina 28640*

Table of Contents

Introduction	1
1. What Are the Character's Internal Traits?	3
2. What Are the Character's External Traits?	33
3. What Does the Character Want, Not Want, or Need?	83
4. What Does the Character Like or Dislike?	97
5. What Does the Character Fear?	104
6. What Does the Character Believe?	116
7. What Are the Character's Strengths, Weaknesses, and Habits?	124
8. What Is the Character's Background?	127
9. What Is the Character's Self-Assessment?	134
10. What Is the Character's "Type"?	147
11. Does the Character Have a Nickname?	189
12. What Is the Character's Job?	202
13. Will the Character Face a Nonhuman Adversary?	212
14. What Plot Drivers Will Affect the Character?	222
Index	235

Introduction

This is not a how-to book. It is not a step-by-step, paint-by-the-numbers kind of reference guide that, if carefully followed, will lead you to create an audience-pleasing novel or script. Instead, *Creating Characters* was developed for the writer who wants to know as much as possible about a fictional character before putting one word on paper. To help the writer achieve that end, it asks a series of questions. What are the character's internal and external traits? What are his or her needs, fears, and beliefs? What does the character do for a living? The answers to these and other questions are vital parts of the biography that brings a fictional character to life.

For each question, *Creating Characters* provides either a wide array of possible answers or a series of further questions. Either way, the material provided is designed to encourage considerable thought about who will be charged with driving the plot. Mind you, sometimes all it takes to create an interesting hero or heroine is the answer to just one question. But even that single answer can be elusive, and the writer can waste a lot of time if he or she jumps headlong into a story with only a vague notion about the people who are in it.

Creating Characters is like a tool box. It contains hammer, saw, nails, screwdrivers, braces, levels, rulers, and other paraphernalia necessary for construction, but only the writer's skilled use of them can build something great in literature. Indeed, the tools in this book are useless without the writer's unique insight, raw talent, and ability to organize disparate parts into a coherent whole. A whopping good tale, filled with enchanting characters, is a magical act of creation — and the magic comes from within.

Ultimately, this reference book has been developed to help the writer find something that may otherwise be overlooked — crucial character traits that are too often missing, leaving only stereotypes and overworked stories in their absence. It has been developed for that writer who appreciates complexity and who knows that interesting characters make interesting stories — not the other way around.

The traits, types, fears, beliefs, and so forth discussed in this book are intended to apply to characters of either gender. For simplicity's sake, however, I have chosen to use the pronoun "he" and its related forms in all character descriptions. I hope this does not offend the reader, or the female fictional character who is now waiting in the wings to be discovered.

Creating Characters is simple to use, but it does not take a simplistic approach, for it looks at character development from a great many angles. The best approach is always to launch your search from the Table of Contents, for it lists all the primary questions. The Table of Contents is the writer's springboard into much greater depth of detail.

Again, however, this book makes no attempt to dictate precise steps that will lead to three-dimensional characters and thumping-good stories. That is a journey you must take on your own.

1. What Are the Character's Internal Traits?

A fictional character's internal traits are not always visible to the others in the story. While fellow characters might easily spot one who is adventurous because that trait will bleed through to the outside and affect his manner, it is not always going to be readily apparent to all of the other characters if, say, the hero is intuitive or keenly observant. The author should let the reader in on the secret, but at the same time he may well choose to keep at least one internal trait hidden from the other characters in the story.

Some internal traits are *inborn* or inherited. These are the traits determined by a character's genetic makeup. They remain constant throughout his life, sometimes increasing or decreasing in intensity, depending upon his social environment, the prevailing situation, and so on.

Other internal traits are *acquired* over time depending on the character's experience — for example, his education and social environment, or specific incidents that have occurred in his life. A character who is distrustful or cynical will usually not be born that way; instead, it is the result of what he has seen, heard, or endured.

Some acquired internal traits are strictly *transitory*. One or more of them may be present within the character at the beginning of the story, or they may not become a part of his inner nature until later. In either case they have the potential to disappear quickly, depending upon what turn the plot takes. Discontent, for instance, can become a character's inner trait, yet it can vanish almost immediately when he or she becomes satisfied in some way.

Here is a list of internal traits, one or more of which may be used to help formulate a fictional character.

INTELLIGENT

Related Traits:
All-knowing, analytical, astute, brainy, bright, brilliant, clever, cunning, discerning, keen-witted, logical, omniscient, perceptive, philosophical, quick, quick-witted, rational, reasonable, sharp, shrewd, smart, understanding.

Character Possibilities:

Discerns things quickly and grasps concepts with better-than-average speed.

Tends to divide problems and concepts into individual parts, not only seeing their relationships but observing other factors as well.

Ability to identify "gray areas" is particularly sharp.

While viewing elements that seem identical, can discern what sets one apart from the other.

Tracks the ascending or descending parts of an argument and finds fault lines within them.

Sees the cause and effect of things that are often hidden from others.

Explores the sections and sub-sections of an argument as if each were a passageway that held secrets.

Has a mind like a highly polished diamond.

Through the power of thought, able to encircle the truth of a matter.

UNINTELLIGENT

Related Traits:

Addlebrained, backward, birdwitted, blockheaded, brainless, dense, dizzy, doltish, dopey, dull, dull-witted, dumb, empty-headed, featherbrained, foolish, fuddlebrained, ignorant, lean-witted, mindless, oafish, obtuse, rattlebrained, shallow, shallow-brained, simple-minded, stolid, stupid, superficial, thick, thick-headed, undiscerning, unperceptive, unwise, vacuous, witless, woodenheaded.

Character Possibilities:

Lags behind the average person in learning something new.

His mind contains only the thinnest layer of knowledge.

Intellect has been severely impaired since birth.

Slow to catch the meaning of a joke, and therefore may not know that he is the butt of it.

Cannot grasp complexities.

Sees only what is directly in front of him.

Implications, hints, hidden meanings, ambiguities, and all the subtleties that often enter human conversation are likely to pass him by without his ever noticing them.

Notions enter his mind with only the greatest of difficulty.

His thoughts are heavy-footed and move slowly.

Each drop of learning that penetrates his brain creates an echo there.

CERTAIN

Related Traits:

Believing, cocksure, confident, convinced, fixed, overconfident, persuaded, positive, self-assured, self-confident, undoubting.

Character Possibilities:

Satisfied that something is true, even if it isn't.

Has no doubt that something has happened or will happen.

Accepts something as being true, because that is what he has always been taught.

Has drawn a conclusion about something, as a result of what he has experienced.

Within his conviction there is no room for doubt.

Regarding something, someone, or himself, is in possession of an unshakable conviction.

Accepts someone's word without questioning it, possibly because it is preceded by trust.

Feels perfectly safe surrounded by his assumptions.

Has come to accept something because he has been heavily influenced by someone's arguments.

UNCERTAIN

Related Traits:

Confused, doubtful, confounded, daunted, hesitant, indecisive, indefinite, irresolute, irresolved, unconvinced, undecided, undetermined, unfixed, unsettled, unsure, vacillating.

Character Possibilities:

Tormented by doubt when no clear course presents itself.

When faced with something he knows little about, or when several competing developments take place, his thoughts invariably become chaotic.

More than one option tends to overwhelm him.

Generally lives in a world that daily adds to his confusion about what is right or wrong, what should or should not be done.

Tossed into a dilemma each time a decision has to be made between at least two things.

The slightest disturbance to the status quo becomes unnerving.

The unpredictability of life frequently leaves him in a quandary.

Fearful of ambiguities and all things equivocal.

Lacks the nerve to act; thus, he tends to wait and see what others do.

OPEN-MINDED

Related Traits:

Detached, equitable, fair-minded, flexible, free-thinking, impartial, impressionable, influenceable, movable, neutral, nonpartisan, objective, persuadable, pliant, responsive, suggestible, swayable, uncommitted, undogmatic, unopinionated.

Character Possibilities:

Has an interest in what other people have to say about things.

In the light of new or contradictory information, he quietly readjusts his own thoughts regarding a matter.

Tries to remain aloof from any tightly held convictions.

Changes his mind easily when he sees a line of reasoning that makes more sense.

Always open to suggestion.

The road to persuading him is not cluttered with the junk that causes fair reason to wreck.

CLOSED-MINDED

Related Traits:

Bullheaded, dogmatic, firm, hardheaded, hardened, hard-shelled, headstrong, immovable, impenetrable, inelastic, inflexible, intractable, intransigent, obstinate, opinionated, pigheaded, reactionary, rigid, stiff-backed, stubborn, unalterable, unchangeable, uncompromising, unmalleable, unpersuadable, unyielding, willful.

Character Possibilities:

Silently holds fast to his conclusions, no matter what.

Tends to tune out any view that is opposite from his own.

Locks out any notion that he could be wrong about something or someone.

Not even the most persuasive argument can bend him.

Resistant to any kind of compromise, even one that would allow most of his opinion to stand.

Hears nothing that is not in harmony with what he believes.

Slams the door in the face of anything that would intrude upon his certainty.

Refuses to consider another's appeasement.

His opinions are aligned within him like an army preparing for battle.

TOLERANT

Related Traits:

Broad-minded, dispassionate, forbearing, indulgent, lenient, liberal, long-suffering, magnanimous, nonpartisan, permissive, unassuming, unbiased, unbigoted, understanding, unjaundiced, unprejudiced.

Character Possibilities:

Allows no one's race, religion, or background to bend his thoughts unfairly toward them.

Strives to be fair in his judgment of what people do or don't do, as well as what is expected of them.

Nonjudgmental regarding the beliefs and customs that are central to the lives of others.

Patiently endures offenses against himself.

Attitude is decidedly liberal, in that he believes everyone deserves to be heard.

Socially, sees others as being equal to himself.

Able to withstand nonphysical abuse over an extended period of time.

INTOLERANT

Related Traits:

Biased, bigoted, fanatical, hidebound, illiberal, jaundiced, mean, narrow-minded, one-sided, partial, parochial, petty, prejudiced, priggish, sectarian, self-righteous, small, snobbish, nonindulgent, unreasonable, unsympathetic.

Character Possibilities:

Because the acts, beliefs, or customs of one or more person(s) are different than his own, views them as vastly inferior.

Thinks his social status, *i.e.,* birth and wealth, is superior to those who belong to another group and believes it would be unbecoming of him to mix with them.

Sees others as corrupting influences and wants nothing to do with them.

Assumes he is more virtuous or knowledgeable than any member of another group.

Unable to reason effectively and cannot see the entanglements of all human beings and their ultimate dependency upon one another.

Sees himself as traveling the main road in the universe and forbids everything to the right or left of himself.

His lack of tolerance is a result of jealousy or envy.

INTUITIVE

Related Traits:
Anticipative, apprehensive, foreknowing, foresighted, insightful, perspicacious, precognizant, prescient, sagacious, second-sighted.

Character Possibilities:
Because of a sixth sense beyond the rim of logic, able to perceive a hidden truth about something or someone.

Frequently anticipates what will happen, as a result of what has either already occurred or is occurring.

Senses the presence, or the intended visit, of good or evil.

Often able to see misfortune's approach long before it ever becomes visible to anyone else.

Can immediately and clearly see through the most heavily veiled and complex situation.

Possesses an understanding about that which is yet to be, or which is clouded over in the present, thus simply defying explanation.

Able to see the results of today's action long before it happens.

UNPERCEPTIVE

Related Traits:
Myopic, shortsighted, unanticipative, unexpectant.

Character Possibilities:
Cannot ascertain anything other than what his five senses tell him.

Disconnected to the future and is only able to see what is close at hand.

Prone to make a judgment based solely upon first appearances.

Unable to see the consequences of his, or someone else's, action.

Deaf to the voices of caution.

IMAGINATIVE

Related Traits:
Artistic, creative, enterprising, fanciful, gifted, improvisational, ingenious, innovative, inventive, notional, original, resourceful, talented, visionary, whimsical.

Character Possibilities:
Able to create images in his mind, which may or may not have practicality.

Has the skill to turn his mental-picture power into actual forms that others can either appreciate and perhaps even use, affecting such areas as art, science, etc.

Concocts mental images that are decidedly odd and not rooted in any current reality.

Has the power to develop things on the spur of the moment.

Possesses the skill to bring a freshness to something by somehow changing one or more of its elements.

Cannot only see something that may have a practical use but is able to fabricate it as well.

Sees possibilities within the realm of impossibility.

Envisions bold departures from the norm.

UNIMAGINATIVE

Related Traits:

Barren, dull, imitative, practical-minded, pragmatic, prosaic, realistic, unfanciful, uninspired, uninventive, unromantic.

Character Possibilities:

Not only unable to produce mental abstractions but cannot improvise, innovate, or see anything that is not already in existence.

Copies what has already been proven to work.

Dislikes theory and speculation.

Measures the value of something by the extent to which others use it.

His thoughts dance with the commonplace.

Lacks the skill to court fresh images.

If he owned a horse, he would not understand the coming of the automobile; if he owned a radio, he would scoff at the idea of television; if he owned a typewriter, he would be unable to see the promise of the computer age.

Tied to what works and does not entertain any thoughts about what might work better.

Takes pride in having both feet anchored solidly to the ground.

CURIOUS

Related Traits:

Absorbed, engaged, enthusiastic, examining, fascinated, immersed, inquiring, inquisitive, interested, interrogative, intrigued, investigative, involved, meddlesome, nosy, open-eared, preoccupied, probing, prying, questioning, quizzical, searching, snoopy.

Character Possibilities:

Always searching to learn more about something or someone.

Eagerly follows the scent of information, whether it is narrow or broad in scope and whether it has any redeeming value or not.

His mind is greatly occupied with the who, what, where, or why of something.

Enthusiastic, if his interest becomes a burning passion.

Has become irresistibly and unexplainably attracted to find out more about someone or a particular thing.

Titillated by, and subsequently pursues, information that concerns the privacy of others and which is frankly none of his business.

His ears are consistently cocked to find out something he didn't know before.

His mind grows questions.

INCURIOUS

Related Traits:

Aloof, apathetic, blasé, bored, detached, disconnected, disengaged, disinterested, indifferent, jaded, nonchalant, uncaring, unconcerned, uninterested, uninvolved, unmindful, unmoved.

Character Possibilities:

The possibility of learning more about a particular subject or some individual does not intrigue him.

Has almost no interest in something because he sees it as being unimportant.

His interest regarding a matter has diminished, if not exhausted, since his original curiosity has produced no results.

Tends to let things slip by without noticing them.

Hardened by experience, he no longer has the exuberance that paves the way for curiosity.

Tends to think "So what?" rather than "Why?"

Because something does not immediately affect him personally, has virtually no interest in its implications.

Views matters in a most casual way.

OBSERVANT

Related Traits:

Alert, astute, attentive, aware, heedful, keen, mindful, open-eyed, perceptive, ready, thoughtful, vigilant, wary, watchful.

Character Possibilities:

Without being spurred by curiosity, he is habitually attentive to almost all things that happen.

A symphony of eyes and ears.

Tries not to be caught off guard.

Constantly prepared for an emergency.

Poised to stop the intrusion of peril or to welcome the advance of opportunity.

By paying close attention to the words and actions of people, attempts to determine their motives.

UNOBSERVANT

Related Traits:

Disregardful, heedless, inattentive, neglectful, oblivious, unalert, unaware, unconscious, undiscerning, unmindful, unperceptive, unvigilant, unwary.

Character Possibilities:

Tends not to see that which may be clearly obvious to almost everyone else.

Ignores that which he deems not worthy of serious attention.

His attention span is always narrowly focused; thus, he will fail to take note of something if he is immersed in something else.

Will allow a crisis to develop because he will overlook the elements that contributed to it.

Matters slip by him as if he sat blindfolded on the double yellow line of a busy highway.

Finds it hard to see what is obviously staring him in the face.

OPTIMISTIC

Related Traits:

Anticipative, blithe, bullish, buoyant, cheerful, confident, encouraged, enthusiastic, forward-looking, heartened, hopeful, jaunty, light-hearted, reassured, rosy, sanguine, sunny, upbeat.

Character Possibilities:

Believes that everything happens for the best and that something good must eventually follow that which is bad.

Fully expects something pleasurable is going to happen.

His hope is accompanied by certainty.

Entirely focused upon the future and is far more interested in where he's going than where he's been.

Even in the worst of situations, he clings to the expectation that things will soon get better.

His expectation is as light as a feather in the wind.

Looks at the future with an incurable sprightliness.

PESSIMISTIC

Related Traits:

Apprehensive, captious, cynical, defeated, dejected, despairing, despondent, disconsolate, discouraged, disheartened, dispirited, downhearted, funereal, gloomy, glum, low-spirited, lugubrious, misanthropic, solemn, spiritless.

Character Possibilities:

Looks at the future through dark-colored glasses.

Finds no justification in romancing hope.

Has abandoned all expectations that things will get better.

Believes that the possibility of a better world is a complete fantasy.

Convinced that everything man touches becomes corrupted.

His sense of hopelessness has crippled his desire to do something positive.

Distrusts all signs of virtue and is skeptical of the apparent superior motives of others.

His courage to withstand all that is mean and destructive in the world has become threadbare.

Defeated, he now sits immovable, wrapped tightly in a gray shroud.

REFLECTIVE

Related Traits:

Contemplative, deliberative, meditative, museful, pensive, ponderous, ruminative, speculative, thoughtful.

Character Possibilities:

Thinks before acting.

Ponders the future or past in a constructive manner, to either circumvent potential problems or to gain wisdom.

Takes considerable care in examining his options before deciding upon what to do.

Prone to weigh something in his mind for a long time.

Mulls things over like a cow chewing its cud.

Looks at things from all sides before making up his mind.

IMPULSIVE

Related Traits:

Eager, hasty, heedless, impetuous, imprudent, incautious, precipitate, rash, spontaneous, thoughtless, undeliberative, unreflective.

Character Possibilities:

Even when presented with a situation that does not demand immediate attention, has a tendency to initiate action rather than examine the matter closely.

Rarely weighs the pros and cons.

There are no stop signs or caution lights in his mind.

To him, consequence is a foreign language.

IMPASSIONED

Related Traits:

Amorous, ardent, bold, carnal, careless, concupiscent, daring, debauched, eager, emotional, enthusiastic, fervent, fevered, fiery, hasty, hearty, horny, hot-blooded, intense, lascivious, lecherous, licentious, lustful, profligate, prurient, salacious, sensual, spirited, temperamental, undisciplined, warm-blooded, wholehearted, zealous.

Character Possibilities:

His emotions simmer over a low fire, with first one and then another bubbling hot to the surface.

Has a propensity to fall in love quickly.

Once he becomes interested in something or someone, that thing or that person can consume him.

His appetite for sex is beyond the norm.

His enthusiasm for a cause can become overly enflamed.

Possesses a gluttonous desire for sensual pleasure, which in turn corrupts those thoughts unrelated to it.

Rare is the thought that lies cool in his mind.

His attraction to vice is underwritten by recklessness.

RESTRAINED

Related Traits:

Abstinent, ascetic, bridled, circumspect, composed, controlled, discreet, dispassionate, frigid, guarded, inhibited, judicious, moderate, monkish, non-indulgent, repressed, reserved, reticent, self-controlled, self-denying, self-disciplined, self-governing, self-regulating, stolid, temperate, tethered, unde-monstrative, unemotional, unimpassioned, unsexual, virginal.

Character Possibilities:

Emotions are imprisoned behind a cold demeanor.

Guards his thoughts and feelings as though he did not trust them.

Maintains calm over all his emotions and does not allow any to become agitated.

Has a low sexual urge.

Intimidated by his own sexual desires and, thus, suppresses them.

Only adopts an extreme view when there is nothing left to satisfy him, but refuses to become its mouthpiece.

It is impossible for him to generate any no-holds-barred enthusiasm for something or someone.

Never allows passion to get the better of him.

CALM

Related Traits:

Collected, composed, cool, coolheaded, equable, even-tempered, impassive, imperturbable, level-headed, pacific, peaceful, placid, poised, relaxed, sedate, self-possessed, serene, staid, tranquil, undisturbed, unflappable, unruffled.

Character Possibilities:

The candle within the core of his soul does not flicker.

Faces the challenges of adversity with a steady eye and refuses to be intimidated by them.

Subdues his feelings of excitement and prepares to do the job that needs to be done.

Usually resigns himself to doing battle and is willing to accept the consequences that follow.

Free of anxiety.

Not nibbled to his wishbone by life's incessant disturbances.

In the presence of danger, brings all thoughts and feelings under his strict command.

Feels superior to the storms that gather to rage upon him.

Sits above the fray like a bored monarch.

TURBULENT

Related Traits:

Aggravated, agitated, aroused, choleric, confused, disquieted, distraught, disturbed, excitable, flustered, fuming, high-strung, inflamed, nervous, perturbed, quick-tempered, stormy, tense, troubled, unstable, upset.

Character Possibilities:

Consistently buffeted by life's ill winds, some of which may be of his own making.

In the grip of a restlessness or uneasiness that he is unable to identify.

Feels his emotions being pulled in different directions.

His mind seems halved and then quartered by conflicting obligations.

His burdens bump into one another, each demanding more of his attention than he knows how to allow.

He is at the vortex of all things gone wrong.

His temper has a hair-trigger.

SENTIMENTAL

Related Traits:

Connected, emotional, homesick, longing, nostalgic, romantic, wistful, yearning.

Character Possibilities:

Harbors an affectionate image of something or someone that may, in fact, be far from what is true.

Aches for another time, *e.g.* the "good ol' days," and perhaps another place, such as the neighborhood in which he grew up.

Prone to romanticize about something and, in turn, possibly give it far more value than it deserves.

As time provides distance between him and that which he remembers fondly, his idealization becomes crisper, stronger, and more unrealistic.

His collection of things that remind him of the past are the roads that let him travel backwards through time.

UNSENTIMENTAL

Related Traits:

Disconnected, indifferent, realistic, unemotional, unromantic.

Character Possibilities:

Finds no value in romanticizing the past.

Exclusively interested in what the future holds rather than what has been lost within years that are irretrievable.

Prone to remember people and things as they *were* rather than idealize them over time.

Refrains from raising things to the level where they suck the tears out of one's affections.

AFFECTIONATE

Related Traits:

Attached, caring, cherishing, compassionate, constant, cordial, dedicated, devoted, doting, enamored, faithful, fond, loyal, lovelorn loving, maternal, nurturing, paternal, protective, regardful, sheltering, solicitous, tender, treasuring, true, true-blue, warm.

Character Possibilities:

Feels a soft, delicate connection with someone or something.

Desires to shield another from harm.

Wraps his thoughts around another as if they were a snowsuit.

Smiles at the music which another soul makes.

A massager of hearts, and would wag his tail if he could.

UNAFFECTIONATE

Related Traits:

Angry, antagonistic, averse, begrudging, choleric, cold, cool, distant, enraged, fuming, furious, hate-filled, hostile, ill-disposed, incensed, indignant, inflamed, infuriated, inimical, irate, irritated, mad, opposed, removed, sore, uncaring, unfeeling, unfriendly, uninterested, unprotective, venomous, vindictive, virulent, wrathful.

Character Possibilities:

Feels a deep antagonism toward at least one person.

His aversion to another has deep roots.

Stands opposed, the reason being clear or unclear to him.

Dislikes someone because that person has something that he wishes belonged to him.

His negative attitude toward another is sharp and is born out of some real or imagined injustice he believes he has suffered at the hands of that person some time ago.

Does not want to be anywhere near a particular individual.

Feels extreme hostility toward someone, and he would like to harm that person if he could do it without anyone finding out.

Takes the view that someone's actions are contrary to what he sees as the socially correct thing to do.

Cannot let go of a painful memory.

Has an ongoing desire to consistently annoy and exasperate someone.

Houses an anger that is not only long-lasting but is also moments away from erupting.

His animosity is such that he feels no pity for a certain individual when he learns of his or her misfortune; indeed, he is pleased.

Unable to feel any warmth toward a certain individual, possibly because there is nothing about that person that really interests him.

HAPPY

Related Traits:

Appeased, blissful, buoyant, carefree, cheerful, chipper, comfortable, complacent, contented, delighted, entranced, ecstatic, elated, exhilarated, exultant, gay, glad, gleeful, gratified, high-spirited, jaunty, jolly, joyful, jubilant, lighthearted, lightsome, merry, mirthful, mollified, overjoyed, pacified, placated, pleased, relaxed, relieved, rewarded, sanguine, satisfied, self-satisfied, serene, smug, sunny, transported, triumphant, unconcerned, untroubled, vindicated.

Character Possibilities:

Relatively free of worry and troubles.

His desires have been realized and life's prospects seem to give him reason to be optimistic.

Has the insight to appreciate and enjoy practically everything that he encounters.

Has suddenly, and possibly unexpectedly, become the recipient of prosperity's blessing.

Has gained peace of mind because someone has either granted concessions or given in to his demands.

Has been freed of suffering.

His spirit has been uplifted by a feeling of joy and hope.

Pleased with himself and does not ponder the possibility that there may be room for improvement.

Satisfied with the way things are and has no anxieties to nag him.

Has received the apology or payments that he believes is due him.

His spirit seems to have wings.

Has been cleared of all accusations, and others wait for his forgiveness.

His anger has been attended to by others, and they have erased it through their words or action.

All his concerns, which have laid heavy upon him, have slipped away like a school of fish.

Carried away on the shoulders of blind delight.

UNHAPPY

Related Traits:

Abashed, agitated, anguished, annoyed, anxious, apprehensive, bewildered, bored, bothered, careworn, concerned, confounded, confused, crushed, daunted, defeated, dejected, depressed, desolate, despairing, despondent, disaffected, disappointed, discomposed, discontented, discouraged, disheartened, disgusted, displeased, disquieted, dissatisfied, doleful, dour, downcast, embarrassed, exasperated, fearful, fretful, frustrated, gloomy, glum, grief-stricken, heart-broken, heavy-hearted, humiliated, hurt, insecure, irritated, low-spirited, melancholic, miserable, mortified, morose, mortified, mournful, offended, restless, sad, shamed, somber, sorrowful, staid, subdued, sulky, sullen, tormented, troubled, uncomfortable, vexed, worried, wretched.

Character Possibilities:

Has reached a point where his life is missing one or more key elements, thus darkening his spirit and possibly crippling his will.

Unhappiness arises out of a sense of inferiority, as a result of comparing himself with those who seemingly have more.

Feels surrounded by dilemmas, which poke at him.

Pained by what he has said or done.

Has seen an unfortunate part of his nature suddenly exposed, which he is not proud of and would rather have kept hidden.

His thoughts are in a turbulent state, with perhaps two or more of them colliding.

Something in the past endlessly eats away at him.

Someone keeps doing something, or something continues to occur, which in turn bites deeply into his nerves.

Cannot help but speculate about what tomorrow might bring, and the prospects make him fearful rather than hopeful.

The monotony makes him feel as though his life is a road too often traveled.

Shoulders a great weight of worries and troubles, unable to cast any aside.

Has reached a point where losing seems to be his destiny.

Feels he has no friends and that he has been cast adrift from the world.

Believes there is not one molecule of hope to which he can cling.

Has become frustrated in his bid to accomplish something.

Something or someone has not lived up to his expectations.

In the throes of a dissatisfaction that is not only accumulative but elusive.

Believes that someone or something is regularly thwarting his desires.

Overcome by the suffocating loss of someone he liked or loved.

Has suffered a great psychological wound as a result of what someone has said or done to him.

Greatly dissatisfied with the world in general.

His discontent is mixed with resentment.

HONORABLE

Related Traits:

Admirable, chaste, chivalrous, commendable, conscientious, constant, correct, decent, dependable, dignified, dutiful, duty-bound, elevated, equitable, estimable, ethical, evenhanded, excellent, exemplary, faithful, faultless, fine, good, high-minded, honest, illustrious, incorruptible, just, knightly, laudable, lofty, loyal, meritorious, moralistic, noble-minded, praiseworthy, princely, principled, proper, pure, puritanical, respectful, righteous, right-minded, scrupulous, staunch, steadfast, sublime, superior, true, truehearted, trustworthy, truth-loving, undefiled, unimpeachable, unspoiled, upright, upstanding, veracious, virtuous, wholesome, worthy.

Character Possibilities:

Has a splendid moral constitution and is careful not to disobey its tenets.

His attitude with respect to others glistens with idealism and it far exceeds that of the great majority.

Has a keen sense of right and wrong, and places a high value on doing right; indeed, his sense of duty prompts him to align his action with the principles that regularly guide him.

Does not waver in his aim to stand by others when he is needed.

Filled with a strong need to do what is expected of him.

Strives to treat others fairly.

Believes he should try to fulfill any promises or obligations he makes.

Not tempted to do something that would benefit himself at the expense of others.

Religiously maintains his impartiality in an effort to do what is reasonable and proper in relation to others.

Will not curtail his friendship with someone based upon what he hears or because the relationship may be socially restrictive.

Has been exposed to temptation but has not succumbed to it.

Lives by a code of conduct that most would consider worthy.

Careful to regard the rights of others before taking action.

Respects the wounds that others carry and refrains from aggravating them.

Places truth on a pedestal.

DISHONORABLE

Related Traits:

Amoral, base, brutish, contemptible, corrupt, corruptible, crooked, debauched, deceitful, despicable, dishonest, disloyal, false, false-hearted, guileful, ignoble, immoral, improper, impure, indecent, knavish, loose, low-minded, mean-spirited, mercenary, perfidious, petty, promiscuous, scheming, sinister, traitorous, treacherous, undependable, underhanded, unethical, unfaithful, unjust, unprincipled, unscrupulous, untrustworthy, venal, wanton, wicked.

Character Possibilities:

Sense of right and wrong is so lacking that his soul is deprived of grace.

Has no inner quality that sparkles.

Instincts are better compared to the animal world.

Believes his own wants and needs should supersede those of others.

His "code of conduct" is always self-serving and does not take anyone else into consideration.

Has a willful disregard for authority, whether it is God's or the government's.

Sees truth as something expendable and will reshape even the smallest fact to better serve his greater purpose.

Ruled by his loins instead of by reason.

Sits smiling upon an aggregation of unborn deceits.

His allegiance is a sickly thing that suffers relapses.

Finds amusement in toying with the unsuspecting.

To him, justice must accompany convenience.

Sells his services to the highest bidder.

COMPASSIONATE

Related Traits:

Clement, considerate, empathetic, humane, lenient, merciful, soft-hearted, sympathetic, tender-hearted.

Character Possibilities:

When witnessing the misfortune of others, has the capacity to feel pity, perhaps because he can imagine their misery or possibly because he knows from his own experience.

Does not even want the meanest thing alive to suffer.

To prevent needless pain, would attempt to reduce the punishment of a guilty person — given the opportunity.

Has tears for every sad thing that has happened and will happen.

UNCOMPASSIONATE

Related Traits:
Callous, case-hardened, hardened, hard-hearted, heartless, inconsiderate, insensitive, merciless, pitiless, stone-hearted, thick-skinned, unfeeling, unsympathetic.

Character Possibilities:
Cannot muster sympathy for any living thing that endures pain and suffering.

Not even the harshest treatment of another living thing is able to penetrate his emotional austerity.

Has the power to reduce the suffering of others, but sees no reason to use it.

Has been exposed to man's wickedness for so long that his feelings are encased in a hard shell, and he is no longer able to see or respond to those instances when compassion is required.

FORGIVING

Related Traits:
Conciliatory, generous, indulgent, unresentful, unrevengeful.

Character Possibilities:
Unable to sustain a grudge toward someone.

Excuses the wrongs committed against him.

Believes it is self-destructive to render punishment for injuries suffered.

Feels that it is not within his power to pass judgment and that he must overlook the sins of others, even though they might have been directed against himself.

Would much rather make up than tear down.

UNFORGIVING

Related Traits:
Acrimonious, bitter, embittered, envenomed, grudgeful, implacable, rancorous, resentful, retaliatory, retributive, revengeful, spiteful, unappeasable, vindictive.

Character Possibilities:
In the grip of strong displeasure, owing to a wrong he believes has been committed against himself or someone else.

Not only is he unable to forgive a transgression but feels compelled to answer it with some degree of punishment of his own.

Has the capacity to carry a thirst for retaliation over an exceptionally long period of time.

Ponders how he might inflict more injury than what he suffered at the outset.

Once wounded, tends to reject all attempts at reconciliation.

BENEVOLENT

Related Traits:

Altruistic, beneficent, big-hearted, bountiful, caring, charitable, clement, considerate, extravagant, generous, good-natured, gracious, helpful, kind, kind-hearted, large-hearted, liberal, magnanimous, mindful, munificent, open-handed, selfless, unselfish, unstinting.

Character Possibilities:

Consistently devoted to the interests of others and wants what is best for them.

Regards someone highly and, to prevent that person from suffering any misfortune, acts as a kind of sentry.

Spirit has no sharp corners, and he reaches out to others softly.

Holds affection in his heart toward almost everyone.

More interested in providing others with what they do not have than simply acquiring more of what he has already enjoyed.

Would, as they say, "give the shirt off his back."

More likely to say, "What do you need and how can I help?" rather than simply "Good luck."

MALEVOLENT

Related Traits:

Bloodthirsty, bloody-minded, cold-blooded, cold-hearted, cruel, devilish, diabolical, evil, fiendish, fierce, harsh, heartless, hostile, insidious, ill-natured, ill-disposed, ill-intentioned, inhuman, inhumane, invidious, maligning, mean-spirited, misanthropic, murderous, nasty, pernicious, ruthless, savage, stern, truculent, unbenevolent, uncharitable, unfeeling, unkind, unmerciful, vicious, vile, virulent, wicked.

Character Possibilities:

His attitude toward others is principally evil in nature, in that he takes pleasure in contemplating how he might deliberately inflict harm on one or more person(s).

Without the prodding of revenge, has an unquenchable need to see the blood of someone else flow.

His mind toys with the possibilities of how he could imperceptibly harm another.

His propensity to injure others is so malignant that only the death of those he opposes could temporarily provide satisfaction.

His hatred of the human race consumes him.

His heart is so poisonous that it would run shivers through vultures.

Ponders the ways he may render destruction, and takes pleasure in the contemplation.

His attitude toward others is so loathsome that he would even endanger his own life to do harm to them.

Has an addiction to evil that is astonishingly creative.

Spurns compassion as a needless plaything.

Would pluck a live chicken of all its feathers.

Adventurous

Related Traits:

Audacious, bold, bold-spirited, daring, devil-may-care, enterprising, exploratory, fearless, game, gutsy, hardy, indomitable, madcap, mettlesome, questing, rash, reckless, speculative, thrill-seeking, unafraid, unfrightened, spirited, venturesome, zestful.

Character Possibilities:

Irresistibly attracted to the unknown and wants to experience it, even though it may threaten his life, reputation, or livelihood.

Wears courage like a top hat.

Has a natural defiance toward any restraint.

Tends to ignore the obvious dangers that await him.

Does not become disheartened by obstacles.

Has an insatiable curiosity about what lies just around the bend, over the hill, within the woods, and on the other side.

Has the soul of a gambler, the stamina of a soldier.

Finds it almost impossible to say, "I give up."

His primary objective is to push his emotions to their limit by engaging in daring exploits.

He is likely to not only become seduced by the potential excitement of the unknown but to meet it head on with great enthusiasm.

Cautious

Related Traits:

Alert, awed, careful, circumspect, discreet, guarded, hesitant, intimidated, judicious, leery, politic, prudent, reluctant, reticent, suspicious, uneasy, unsure, vigilant, wary.

Character Possibilities:

Habitually self-protective in that he is more concerned about saving his neck than risking it.

Carefully previews each step in his life before actually taking it, always making sure to place his foot on something solid in order to not imperil himself.

Sees danger lurking behind every corner and eyes everything with suspicion.

Intensely watchful, a creator of routines.

Never sets out to have fun; if that occurs, he feels it must be a by-product of a well-executed plan.

Risk intimidates him, for the unknown is filled with goblins.

More concerned about dying than he is about living.

COURAGEOUS

Related Traits:

Brave, dauntless, doughty, gallant, great-hearted, gritty, heroic, intrepid, lionhearted, plucky, spunky, stalwart, stout-hearted, undaunted, unflinching, valiant, valorous.

Character Possibilities:

In spite of what either looms before him or he is forced to endure, possesses the strength of mind that consistently allows him to continue onward, fearful or not.

When in the presence of danger, usually believes he will prevail.

Upon encountering great trouble, his nerves become inextricably calm.

Accepts and performs the commonplace dregs of duty that others need accomplished, but which they do not want to do themselves.

Can move among those feeling pain and misery, and, with a breaking heart, push back a wall of tears and replace it with a smile.

Able to find, in the depths of his soul, that iridescent quality that helps to light his way.

TIMID

Related Traits:

Afraid, apprehensive, chicken-hearted, dastardly, gritless, cowardly, craven, faint-hearted, fearful, jittery, lily-livered, nervous, qualmish, scared, shrinking, spunkless, timid, timorous, tremulous, uncourageous, undaring, unheroic, wavering, weak-kneed, white-livered, yellow.

Character Possibilities:

Trembles at the thought of trouble.

So lacking in self-confidence that he keeps his opinions to himself.

Regarding practically everything he does, or is expected to do, he fears the unknown repercussions.

A cataloguer of exits.

A collector of misgivings.

The keeper of humankind's fears.

When challenged, searches for ways that he might agree with the challenger.

Lacks strength of purpose.

Beset with doubt each time he prepares to choose one course of action over another.

Unable to buck the status quo.

Dreads or distrusts what is yet to happen and may not even occur.

Imagines how he might blame others for the weakness that is only his.

AMBITIOUS

Related Traits:

Acquisitive, aspiring, competitive, contentious, desirous, determined, focused, emulative, goal-oriented, motivated, purposeful, single-minded, tenacious, upward-looking, wishful.

Character Possibilities:

Desires to attain something that will lead to his acquiring wealth, power, fame, or something else that he does not now have, and thus sets his attention toward achieving it.

Primary aim is to achieve overall excellence rather than reach a specific social plateau.

Motivated by a desire to equal or surpass what someone else has already attained.

Has a gnawing need to be recognized for his abilities and knowledge.

Sees the barriers and ponders how he might surmount them.

Never has enough of whatever he has.

AIMLESS

Related Traits:

Adrift, apathetic, causeless, content, desultory, goal-deficient, lethargic, purposeless, satisfied, unambitious, uncompetitive, unconcerned, unfocused, unmotivated.

Character Possibilities:

Floats across the months and years without either a compass or sail unfurled.

His attention swings abruptly from one thing to the next, like a monkey going nowhere in particular.

Does not have a climbing instinct.

His capacity to care about his future has been deadened.

The goal he has is so broad and poorly defined that it might as well not even exist at all.

Resents the prodding of others.

Accepts what he has and what he is, and is the flip side of the dreamer.

RESOLUTE

Related Traits:

Assiduous, constant, decided, determined, diligent, dogged, enduring, fixed, indefatigable, iron-willed, obstinate, persevering, persistent, pertinacious, purposeful, resolved, sedulous, steadfast, strong-minded, strong-willed, tenacious, tireless, uncompromising, unfaltering, unrelenting, unswerving, unwavering, unyielding.

Character Possibilities:

Once it becomes clear to him what must be done, he will not entertain any detours that will compromise his objective.

In his mind, maps out the route he will take.

The inability of others to stay the course perplexes and saddens him.

Has an extraordinary capacity to accept defeat and yet think he is getting closer to victory.

Unable to recognize the folly of his purpose.

An unbreakable marriage occurs between his mind and the thing to be achieved.

In terms of pursuit, he is tireless.

IRRESOLUTE

Related Traits:

Changeable, doubtful, fluctuating, half-hearted, hesitant, indecisive, purposeless, uncertain, undecided, undetermined, unsettled, vacillating, weak-willed.

Character Possibilities:

Lacks the necessary conviction that initiates action, even when it may be obvious to others that he should do so.

Pestered incessantly by uncertainty.

Approaches decision-making as if it were a two-headed monster.

Always waiting for that last shred of proof , so that he might be certain.

Today he is positive; tomorrow he will not be.

His ear is forever scanning the air to hear some key words of reassurance.

"What to do" and "what not to do" play Ping-Pong in his head.

Lacks the will that gives conviction its wind.

SELFISH

Related Traits:

Avaricious, covetous, envious, grasping, gluttonous, greedy, grudging, hoggish, mean, miserly, piggish, rapacious, self-absorbed, self-centered, self-interested, self-seeking, stingy, tight, uncharitable, wolfish.

Character Possibilities:

Principally concerned about those things that either bring him pleasure or provide him with comfort, whether it is to the detriment of someone else or not.

Resents the fact that someone has what he believes he alone deserves.

Would, if he could, keep all the good things for himself.

His motto: Get it from others before they have a chance to get it from you.

Has an appetite for self-satisfaction that is boundless.

Charity baffles him.

He is the altar upon which others should bestow their sacrifices.

UNSELFISH

Related Traits:

Altruistic, big-hearted, charitable, generous, giving, liberal-minded, munificent, selfless, self-denying, self-sacrificing.

Character Possibilities:

Willing to share with others.

Thinks it is better to deprive himself of something than to have someone else go without.

Views greed as being detrimental to the soul.

More concerned about the welfare of others than he is with his own comfort.

When choices are to be made between one thing or another, always intends to give the other person the biggest portion, the softest place, the better view, the nicest compliment, etc.

MODEST

Related Traits:
Constrained, diffident, humble, self-conscious, self-depreciative, unpretentious.

Character Possibilities:
Thinks it is unbecoming to advertise his virtues to others.

Abhors glowing recognition.

Locks out all thoughts of superiority, even though he may even excel in a specific area.

Distrusts his own abilities and puts almost no stock in the praises that fill up the plate before him.

Convinced that others have more to offer than he.

Consistently underestimates his own worth.

IMMODEST

Related Traits:
Arrogant, conceited, disdainful, egocentric, egotistic, imperious, lordly, narcissistic, prideful, proud, secure, self-esteeming, self-important, shameless, vain, vainglorious.

Character Possibilities:
He is the center of his own universe.

When comparing himself to others, he is often disdainful of them and proud of himself.

His capacity for contempt goes undiminished.

The word "we" is often a stranger to him, for he is much more comfortable with "I."

Fully expects others to not only recognize his superiority and to compliment him but also to comply with his wishes.

Has an ongoing love affair with himself.

Having accomplished something, raises it to a level far beyond what it truly deserves.

His vanity is either groundless or completely out of proportion to that on which it is based.

PATIENT

Related Traits:
Forbearing, imperturbable, indulgent, lenient, long-suffering, passive, tolerant, understanding.

Character Possibilities:

Calmly endures all the annoying adversities, delays, and setbacks that naturally occur.

Tends to spurn retaliation.

Sits on his temper, though it squiggles for expression.

Stifles the urge to complain.

Able to endure distress over long periods.

Believes that things will get better tomorrow.

Accepts small and great disappointments with resignation.

Knows that things rarely happen the way he would like and that people only occasionally behave as he would prefer.

IMPATIENT

Related Traits:

Agitated, antsy, anxious, disquieted, edgy, fidgety, fretful, high-strung, intolerant, jittery, jumpy, nervous, restive, restless, skittish, strained, taut, tense, uneasy, nonindulgent, uptight, worried.

Character Possibilities:

Delay picks at the sores of his composure.

His nerves are the strings strummed by Anticipation.

Being under the control of someone or something is suffocating to his peace of mind.

More afraid that something won't happen.

Finds no comfort in the saying, "All things come to those who wait."

RESPECTFUL

Related Traits:

Adoring, admiring, awe-struck, deferential, esteeming, idolatrous, obeisant, regardful, reverential, worshipful.

Character Possibilities:

Sees a characteristic in another person that he admires and which he may wish he had, whether his estimation is misplaced or not.

His high regard for someone is also tempered by a degree of fear.

His appraisal of another is supported by a strong approval of that person's moral standards.

His respect for another takes on a hallowed nature.

Psychologically, he bows deeply toward another.

Feels mute in the presence of a certain person's accomplishments.

DISRESPECTFUL

Related Traits:
Class-conscious, contemptuous, disdainful, disregardful, irreverent, prejudicial, scornful.

Character Possibilities:
Observes one or more characteristics in someone that he views as offensive; thus, in his eyes, that person's worth is significantly devalued.

Mentally separates groups of people into categories and views those who do not measure up to his standards as being undeserving of his attention.

Toward one or more people who are held in high regard by others, he mentally scoffs at their so-called merit.

Unable to esteem one of the following: an idea; a principle; an achievement; a set of assumptions; an argument; an accepted truth; a prediction; a form of art; a belief; or, in fact, one of perhaps hundreds of possibilities that involve what people do or say.

GRATEFUL

Related Traits:
Appreciative, beholden, bound, gratified, indebted, obligated, thankful.

Character Possibilities:
Because of what has been done for him, feels an obligation to somehow repay the kindness at some time in the future.

Feels blessed because he has been on the receiving end of good luck.

UNGRATEFUL

Related Traits:
Forgetful, indifferent, oblivious, unappreciative, unaware, ungrateful, unmindful.

Character Possibilities:
Never burdens himself with the responsibility of having to repay someone for a kindness.

Views a favor as an intrusion.

Believes the help he received is something he deserved and sees no reason to express his appreciation.

Accepts any assistance that comes his way, but at the same time places no value on the spirit in which it was given.

Forgets the help he receives almost as soon as he accepts it.

REMORSEFUL

Related Traits:

Anguished, ashamed, chagrined, compunctious, conscious-stricken, contrite, distressed, embarrassed, guilt-ridden, heavy-hearted, mortified, penitent, regretful, repentant, rueful, self-accusing, self-condemning, self-convicting, self-reproachful, sheepish, sorry, tormented.

Character Possibilities:

Weighted with guilt, as a result of something he has either done or thinks he has done.

Desires to make amends for the wrong he committed.

Condemns himself for engaging in what he believes to be a mortal sin.

Greatly embarrassed to learn that he, of all people, should do or say such a thing.

In the name of justice, chooses a method by which to punish himself.

UNTROUBLED

Related Traits:

Callous, guiltless, impenitent, shameless, unashamed, uncontrite, unembarrassed, unregretful, unrepentant, unsorrowful.

Character Possibilities:

Unable to see that what he has said or done is very wrong, possibly hurtful to another.

Because he has become emotionally hardened by injustice, unable to shoulder any guilt for the injustices he renders.

Whatever harm he brings to another, it's his opinion that the individual had it coming to him.

The words "I'm sorry" never come together in his mind.

TRUSTING

Related Traits:

Believing, deceivable, deludable, dupable, exploitable, gullible, indubious, ingenuous, innocent, näive, simple-hearted, undoubting, unguarded, unquestioning, unsuspecting, unwary, unworldly.

Character Possibilities:

Tends to accept things as being truthful without carefully examining them.

More liable to take someone's word than not.

Likely to fall for something hook, line, and sinker; one could sell him the Brooklyn Bridge.

Doesn't believe a particular individual would lie to him.

Places far more value in someone's words than they actually deserve.

Gobbles up the first thing he hears.

Does not know how to test veracity by attacking it with questions.

Believes what he reads, or what the gossip mill churns out, or what the voices of authority tell him.

DISTRUSTFUL

Related Traits:

Cynical, disbelieving, doubting, inconvincible, incredulous, jealous, leery, mistrustful, questioning, skeptical, suspecting, suspicious, vigilant, wary.

Character Possibilities:

Rarely does he accept something to be true without first examining its value like a jeweler.

Intuition tells him that what he sees or hears is not an accurate reflection of what is being presented.

Experience has installed roadblocks in his mind and almost nothing he hears or sees can circumvent them.

Doubts the weightiest of evidence.

Believes that someone is receiving the love or attention that he is convinced should be his alone.

Guards his trust as if it were his life's savings.

Investigates motives; seeks the parents of conclusion.

2. What Are the Character's External Traits?

How do the other people in the story see the character?

This has nothing to do with a physical description of the character, *e.g.*, the way he looks and dresses; instead, the question refers specifically to the character's behavior pattern. Now, whether another character in the story is observant enough to notice the behavior, or whether he has been placed in a situation that would *allow* him to see it, is of course another matter altogether. It is the writer who, in the name of plot development, must make that decision.

For example, the author may want only one character to know that another person in the story has been physically violent, leaving all the others ignorant of the fact. Or he or she may choose to let nearly everyone else in on the knowledge while keeping it hidden from at least one character. Whichever the case, at least one person in the story has seen the behavior at least once. Or thinks he has.

There are two other important questions to consider when deciding on a character's external traits:

Whatever one character sees in another, is it correct?

That is, is he laboring under a misconception? For example, one or more characters in a story could be led to believe that someone is brave, when in fact he is cowardly. Thus external behavior may veil a character's true nature. If that is the case, is it by the character's own design, or has action on his part been misinterpreted by another?

Is the character's external trait an extension of an internal trait?

While it is certainly true that some external traits extend from those classified as "internal" (in fact, they may bear the same name), there are nevertheless a great many instances in which a character's external nature deserves separate attention.

Here is a list of external traits from which you, the author, may extract something that will assist you in the development of a major or minor character. There is, of course, no limit to the number that may be selected. Moreover, even exact opposites can become a part of a fictional character. For example, he or she may be sociable in one regard and unsociable in another. Likewise, a character may be both complimentary and faultfinding, skillful and unskillful, and so on. Just keep this in mind: all external traits are visible to other characters in the story, though not necessarily to *all* other characters.

SOCIABLE

Related Traits:

Affable, amiable, approachable, companionable, congenial, cordial, folksy, fraternal, genial, gregarious, hail-fellow, hearty, homey, hospitable, ingratiating, neighborly, outgoing, pleasant, sunny, warm.

As Seen by Others:

Seeks the company of others.

Enjoys conversations, telling or hearing jokes.

Likes to entertain.

Treats everyone like a friend.

Has a pleasing nature that is irresistible.

Always ready to talk.

Presence often seems to brighten a room.

A slapper of backs, a firm shaker of hands.

Gravitates toward a room full of people like a moth is attracted to a light bulb.

A walking welcome mat.

Rarely meets a stranger that he can't get to talk.

UNSOCIABLE

Related Traits:

Aloof, brusque, chilly, cold, cool, glowering, haughty, hostile, inaccessible, inhospitable, snobbish, sour, sullen, unapproachable, unfriendly, uncongenial, uncordial.

As Seen by Others:

Doesn't care much for chit-chatting.

His "hellos," when he has any, are like icebergs.

Not easily approached.

Keeps his distance from almost everyone.

Has forgotten how to smile.

Treats people as if he were better than them.

Has the face of someone who looks like he's expecting someone to ask him for a donation.

More likely to be seen alone than with others.

He's a slam-the-door-in-your-face kind of person.

Has a bad case of the grims.

RESERVED

Related Traits:

Bashful, constrained, constricted, controlled, correct, detached, distant, guarded, formal, inhibited, introverted, repressed, restrained, reticent, retiring, rigid, starched, stiff, subdued, unassuming, undemonstrative, withdrawn.

As Seen by Others:

Goes out of his way not to be noticed.

Acts like he's afraid to do or say the wrong thing.

Seems to be holding something back all the time.

The proverbial stuffed shirt, ramrod, starched back.

At first glance, appears to be snooty.

Looks like he's all wound up in a ball, with no thread hanging loose.

Not a joke teller or a slap-on-the back kind of person.

Never gets excited about anything.

Won't hug anyone; in fact, he'll turn stiff as a poker if you try to embrace him.

Has probably never done anything on the spur of the moment, just for the heck of it.

Sits apart from everyone else.

Actions appear to be a little too precise and correct, almost mechanical.

Has good manners, but it's as if they've been drilled into him.

If he gets mad, he keeps it to himself.

UNRESERVED

Related Traits:

Approachable, bold, casual, cocky, confident, demonstrative, direct, extroverted, folksy, forward, informal, open, outgoing, rambunctious, self-assertive, spirited, spontaneous, uninhibited, unrestrained.

As Seen by Others:

Two whoops and a holler are always waiting to come out of him.

He'll run his feelings out there for everyone to take a peek.

Says what he thinks and does what he wants, without worrying about how others will react.

If there's only one person in a restaurant, chances are he'll go over and sit down at the same table.

Not afraid to make a fool of himself.
Doesn't stand on formality.
He can talk to almost anyone.
He makes you feel like you're important.

CONSIDERATE

Related Traits:
Accommodating, attentive, caring, civil, comforting, complaisant, concerned, consoling, courtly, diplomatic, discreet, gracious, helpful, judicious, kindhearted, obliging, polite, politic, respectful, sensitive, solicitous, soothing, tactful, tenderhearted, thoughtful.

As Seen by Others:
Tries not to inconvenience people.
Does his best not to hurt someone's feelings or become annoying.
Obeys the Golden Rule.
He'll give up what's best for him, just to make it easier on someone else.
Listens to people's opinions and won't make fun of them if they're different than his own.
He'll do everything in the world to make you comfortable.
Won't become rude, even when he's prompted.
If something's bothering you, he'll try to talk to you about it and maybe take the edge off your mood.
Shows a sincere desire to please others.
To prevent misunderstanding or hurting someone's feelings, he chooses his words carefully.
He's the kind of person who does favors that people really need.
Seems to possess some advance knowledge of what someone needs or desires.

INCONSIDERATE

Related Traits:
Aggravating, annoying, discourteous, disobliging, harsh, impolite, inhospitable, mocking, nagging, nasty, pesky, rude, sarcastic, tactless, taunting, thoughtless, unaccommodating, uncivil, unfeeling, unhelpful, unkind.

As Seen by Others:
Never shows that he has a clue about what someone needs or wants, and he doesn't seem to care.
If he finds out something irritates you, he'll keep doing it.
Ridicules people.

Doesn't apologize if he's late.

Never makes you feel at home.

Has a sharp tongue, which he uses to cut people up when they fail to meet his expectations.

Doesn't have the slightest idea about what is the proper thing to do or say in delicate situations, and so he's likely to blurt out anything that comes to his mind.

Insults and sarcasm are his stock in trade.

Doesn't know what kind of assistance someone might need, and he wouldn't supply it even if he did.

He'll nag you to death.

Acts like no one's important except him.

COOPERATIVE

Related Traits:

Collaborative, compromising, contributive, cooperative, harmonious, helpful, mediatory, participatory, noncompetitive.

As Seen by Others:

He'll work with you rather than against you.

Takes the attitude that we're all in this thing together.

Won't try to outdo you.

Prefers to get along rather than get ahead.

He'll give up something, to get something.

Put him in the middle of a dispute and he won't take sides; instead, he'll want to know what they agree upon and then try to work out their differences from that point.

If you need a helping hand, he's the one you want.

UNCOOPERATIVE

Related Traits:

Autonomous, competitive, individualistic, rivaling, separated, solitary, uncollaborative, uncompromising, vying.

As Seen by Others:

If you want to reach a goal, you'll have to get there without him.

Once he stakes out a position, that's where he stays.

Doesn't know the meaning of give and take.

Keeps his ideas to himself.

Works independently of everyone else, even when he is among them and they're engaged in the same thing.

Acts like people are going to steal his ideas.

Put him in a group and he'll try to do something better, faster, longer, etc. than everyone else.

Seems as if he's not happy unless he has a rival.

Incapable of surrendering one of his principles or desires for the benefit of a group.

Partnership is a word he does not understand or appreciate.

SOPHISTICATED

Related Traits:

Aristocratic, courtly, cultivated, cultured, delicate, dignified, elegant, finished, genteel, grand, graceful, punctilious, polished, refined, urbane, well-bred.

As Seen by Others:

There is an unmistakable aristocratic air about him, and yet it is not pretentious.

Appears to be well-educated or well-mannered.

His image suggests aristocracy, without his actually being an aristocrat.

There's a polish to him.

There is a special excellence about him that can be observed, if not explained.

Has displayed a keen appreciation of beauty.

Movements are graceful, even refined.

Possesses an unmistakable nobility that demands one's respect.

Knows the rules of etiquette and obeys them.

Absent from him is any sign of crudity or coarseness.

UNSOPHISTICATED

Related Traits:

Boorish, bourgeois, coarse, clownish, common, graceless, hickish, ill-behaved, ill-bred, ill-mannered, indelicate, inelegant, loutish, low-born, primitive, raw, rustic, uncouth, uncultivated, unpolished, untaught, untutored, vulgar.

As Seen by Others:

Manners are rough.

Dresses badly.

Language is coarse.

Reminds one of lumber that needs sanding.

Hasn't had the education that would fine-tune his mind.

Seems as ordinary as an unpainted picket fence.
Has none of the qualities that turns heads.
He's an outside toilet kind of person.
Knows almost nothing about a lot of things.
A raisin among strawberries.

SKILLFUL

Related Traits:

Accomplished, adept, competent, efficient, experienced, expert, gifted, handy, ingenious, inventive, masterly, practiced, professional, proficient, qualified, talented, trained, versatile, versed, well-trained.

As Seen by Others:

In a certain area, his ability is of such magnitude that little is left for him to master.

In his area of expertise, rarely makes a mistake — if ever.

God gave him a talent that you just can't just sit down and explain.

He's a jack-of-all-trades.

Give him a problem and he'll give you a solution.

Adept at using his hands to either build or repair something.

Practice and more practice have been always been his mistresses.

Exceptional at generating new ideas.

There's little he can't do, and he does it well.

He's among the best at what he does.

UNSKILLFUL

Related Traits:

Amateurish, deficient, green, incompetent, inefficient, inept, inexperienced, inexpert, neophytic, unable, unaccomplished, unpolished, unpracticed, unqualified, unschooled, unseasoned, untalented, untrained, untutored.

As Seen by Others:

Has little or no ability in a particular area.

Lacks the experience.

He could botch a cup of coffee.

Gives amateurs a bad name.

Regularly proves he is unable to do the job expected of him.

Mistakes roll off him like sweat.

Still a beginner, after all these years.

He practices and practices, but never gets any better.

Has no dexterity, no understanding of the thing.

POWERFUL

Related Traits:

Absolute, arbitrary, authoritative, autocratic, bossy, commanding, controlling, despotic, dictatorial, dominant, domineering, dynamic, forceful, high-handed, high-powered, imperious, indestructible, influential, invincible, invulnerable, ironfisted, masterful, mighty, omnipotent, oppressive, overbearing, peremptory, ruling, strong, superior, supreme, totalitarian, tyrannical, unassailable, unconquerable.

As Seen by Others:

Has the upper hand (because of his wealth, position, influence, achievements, talent, knowledge, physical strength, or mental skill).

Has been challenged and has excelled.

Defies anyone or anything to restrict him.

Perhaps to amuse himself, he will suddenly use his strength in a capricious and unreasonable manner.

Uses power in a severe and suffocating way.

Sees himself as being above the law.

Won't let anyone do anything unless he sanctions it.

There is a spiritual forcefulness that radiates from him.

When ordering something to be done, he doesn't tolerate any refusal or excuse for inaction.

He can get others to take action by simply suggesting that it might be in their best interest to do so.

Others are afraid of him.

Appears to be unconquerable.

Acts as if he were a god.

Will neither allow his decisions to be debated nor endure any opposition.

If he wants something done, it gets done.

INEFFECTUAL

Related Traits:

Defenseless, disenfranchised, dominated, inferior, insignificant, powerless, subjugated, subordinate, weak.

As Seen by Others:

Has no ability to either make things happen or to get people to act.

Few, if any, pay any attention to his requests.

His judgment is questioned and challenged.

Has no discernible means of retaliation.

Deprived of any special privilege that would help lend weight to his decisions.

Totally at the mercy of someone's beck and call.

Lacks authority because of his official classification within a group or organization.

Few, if any, pay any attention to him.

INDEPENDENT

Related Traits:

Individualistic, inner-directed, nonaligned, self-governing, self-reliant, self-sufficient, self-supporting, self-sustaining, sovereign, unallied, unattached, unconstrained.

As Seen by Others:

Relies upon no one but himself to make his way in the world.

Insists on doing things his way.

Forms his own opinions without having to wait to see what someone else says on the matter.

Openly resentful of other people telling him what he must or must not do.

Unhesitant about acting on his inner-instincts.

Does not solicit advice.

Never depends on anyone else.

DEPENDENT

Related Traits:

Bloodsucking, controlled, dominated, freeloading, governed, leechlike, manipulated, mooching, parasitic, regulated, restrained, restricted, sponging.

As Seen by Others:

A follower rather than a leader.

Leans upon the friendship or kindness of others.

Gets all of his ideas from other people.

He's a clinging vine.

Never acts on his own.

A puppet on a string.

Attaches himself to the good will of another, to ensure he is provided with shelter, food, and other side benefits.

What he wants to do is always the handmaiden to what he is expected to do.

When he dies, the words "May I?" should be chiseled into his gravestone.

SUCCESSFUL

Related Traits:

Acclaimed, accomplished, affluent, blessed, celebrated, distinguished, decorated, eminent, esteemed, famous, flourishing, flush, fortunate, glorified, honored, illustrious, important, lionized, loaded, lucky, moneyed, notable, noteworthy, preeminent, privileged, prominent, prosperous, renowned, rich, thriving, triumphant, victorious, wealthy, well-fixed, well-heeled, well-known, well-off, well-to-do.

As Seen by Others:

His social status is high as a result of his wealth, position, fame, accomplishment — and others admire him.

No one gave him anything; he got to the top through his talent and hard work, or so it seems.

There's a lot more people who know *who* he is than those who don't.

He's been given awards for what he has done.

Stands at the top of his profession.

Has turned good luck into a lifelong friend.

Born into money and has multiplied it.

Success is based on a victory he has achieved.

UNSUCCESSFUL

Related Traits:

Anonymous, bankrupt, beaten, broke, defeated, deprived, destitute, disadvantaged, downtrodden, failed, hapless, ill-fated, ill-starred, impoverished, indigent, insignificant, insolvent, luckless, needy, nondescript, penniless, poverty-stricken, second-rate, unaccomplished, underprivileged, unfortunate, unimportant, unknown, unlucky, unrecognized.

As Seen by Others:

Has yet to achieve what he set out to do.

Hasn't lived up to his promise.

Lacks those things by which one measures success.

He was born poor and he'll die poor.

Always winds up being second- or third-best.

Has never risen above his original life's station.

Opportunity has passed him by again and again.

He simply can't get a break.

He's never been able to take advantage of a situation, because he's either too early or too late.

Seems to have a love affair with disappointment.

There is nothing about him that distinguishes him from the crowd.
Has never had the ability to make something of himself.

LEARNED

Related Traits:

Bookish, cerebral, educated, enlightened, erudite, highbrow, intellectual, knowledgeable, lettered, literary, literate, pedantic, professorial, scholarly, schooled, schoolmarmish, schoolmasterish, self-taught, studious, trained, tutored, versed, well-educated, well-read.

As Seen by Others:

Knows a lot about a great number of things.
Always got his nose in a book.
A bona fide expert.
Has spent most of his life trying to find out the who, what, where, why, and how of things.
Knows more about that subject than anyone else.
Has spent his life studying, and it shows.

UNLEARNED

Related Traits:

Ignorant, illiterate, incognizant, semi-literate, uneducated, unenlightened, uninformed, uninstructed, unintellectual, unlettered, unschooled, untrained, unversed.

As Seen by Others:

What he knows doesn't amount to very much.
Unable to read or write.
His knowledge is elementary — enough that he can get by.
Has probably never read a book from cover to cover.
His education has been the school of hard knocks.
Dropped out of school.
Doesn't know enough to realize that there are two sides to every question and answer.
Reads trash and thinks trash.

COMPLIMENTARY

Related Traits:

Adulatory, bootlicking, congratulatory, extolling, fawning, flattering, glorifying, honeyed, laudatory, mealy-mouthed, obsequious, praising, smooth-spoken, sugary, sycophantic, uncritical, unctuous.

As Seen by Others:

For every praise he utters, he's got ten more in reserve.

Plays upon other people's vanity like they were violins.

Never finds fault with anyone.

Acts sweet enough to give you a toothache.

What he says to your face is probably a hundred miles away from what he's thinking.

Puffs up people's virtues that they didn't even know they had.

Never lets an opportunity pass when he can pet someone's feathers.

FAULT-FINDING

Related Traits:

Acrimonious, aspersive, backbiting, bitchy, belittling, bitter, calumnious, captious, carping, caustic, caviling, censorious, condemning, critical, cutting, defamatory, denigratory, denunciatory, deprecating, detractive, derisive, derogatory, discrediting, disparaging, hurtful, hypercritical, impugning, injurious, libelous, maligning, nagging, nasty, nit-picking, querulous, rancorous, ridiculing, scoffing, scornful, slanderous, uncomplimentary, unflattering, vilifying.

As Seen by Others:

He's never seen anyone's virtue that he has liked.

Would find fault with the tilt of an angel's wing.

What he says behind your back would melt your shirtfront.

If he can't say anything bad about you, he would rather not say anything at all.

Has standards that not even a saint could meet.

Always dropping little hints about someone's indiscretion.

Maintains a running complaint about some mistreatment he thinks he has suffered at the hands of another.

Openly attempts to reduce someone's worth in the eyes of others.

His complaints are as constant as air.

His "compliments" are carefully seeded with reservation or misgiving.

Attacks someone's character like it was a spider.

PERSUASIVE

Related Traits:

Affecting, agitative, arousing, assuring, bolstering, commanding, compelling, convincing, eloquent, encouraging, enlightening, exciting, forceful, galvanizing, goading, impassioned, impressive, incendiary, incitive, inflammatory, influential, inspiring, instigative, logical, manipulative, motivating, moving, rabble-rousing, reassuring, seductive, sensible, stirring, supportive, uplifting.

As Seen by Others:
Able to make other people take action.
He can keep the fire boiling beneath your interest.
He can get others to believe something despite their initial doubts.
Using words, he can maneuver you into a corner.
He can make you believe in yourself.
He's able to elicit tears, cheers, and fears, when in fact none are warranted.
Could make you believe water is wine, and vice versa.
Knows how to inflame your interest or passion, by saying just the right thing.
Plays on your ear like a lover.
He can twist arguments around to where you forget which side you favor.
Has the ability to lead one astray.

UNPERSUASIVE

Related Traits:
Discouraging, dissuasive, illogical, inexpressive, tongue-tied, unaffecting, uncompelling, unconvincing, unimpressive, uninspiring, unprovocative.

As Seen by Others:
Couldn't motivate someone to move if the two of them occupied the same phone booth.
Will put you to sleep before he puts you on the road to doing something.
His reasoning is about as inspiring as an income tax form.
His arguments are so insipid that you're inclined to believe that the opposite approach must be better.
When he talks, his logic is scattered all over the place.
Couldn't get a hungry dog to eat.
Legions have collapsed unconscious over his pleas.
Talks like he doesn't believe it himself.

CHARISMATIC

Related Traits:
Absorbing, alluring, appealing, bewitching, captivating, charming, compelling, delightful, electrifying, enchanting, engrossing, entertaining, enthralling, enticing, entrancing, fascinating, interesting, irresistible, magnetic, mesmerizing, pleasing, pleasurable, provocative, stimulating, thrilling.

As Seen by Others:
> You may not agree with him, but he can rivet your attention.
> When he walks into a room, heads turn.
> He could charm the skin off a snake.
> He puts a charge into whatever group he belongs or visits.
> Curiosity follows after him like a trained dog.
> If you've got a smile in you, he'll find it.
> He is a light toward which everyone gravitates.

UNINTERESTING

Related Traits:
> Bland, boring, humdrum, prosaic, tedious, tiresome, unappealing, uncompelling, unenticing, uninteresting, unmagnetic, unprovocative, wearisome.

As Seen by Others:
> Has nothing that draws you to him.
> He is the color gray.
> His conversation is as sparkling as a box of dry oats and there is no prospect for wetness.
> Instead of hanging on his every word, you want to escape from them.
> His presence wears your interest paper thin.

LOQUACIOUS

Related Traits:
> Babbling, chatty, circumlocutory, communicative, conversational, didactic, digressive, discursive, gabby, garrulous, glib, gossipy, gushy, informational, informative, instructive, long-winded, oratorical, preachy, prolix, rambling, redundant, repetitious, sermonizing, talebearing, talkative, verbose, windy, wordy.

As Seen by Others:
> Can turn "How do you do" into a small sermon.
> Would rather talk than listen.
> Nothing but a chatterbox, blabbermouth, gasbag, motormouth, windbag.
> If he says it once, he'll be sure to somehow say it again and again.
> Uses ten extra words for every one that's needed.
> Loves to chew the rag (shoot the breeze).
> Can't get to the end of a conversation without adding a big lump of instructive morality for someone to swallow.

Jumps from subject to subject as if he were dodging bullets.

Talks mostly, and endlessly, about trivial matters.

His conversation is as smooth as glass, yet as pointless as a paperwad.

Can't keep a secret.

Has more rumors on the tip of his tongue than a cat has hairs.

Listening to him talk is like being adrift on the ocean: you know land is somewhere, but you don't know where.

Feels right at home behind a podium.

Seems as though his tongue is going to run off and leave him.

Inside him is a professor fighting to get out.

LACONIC

Related Traits:

Close-mouthed, guarded, noncommunicative, pithy, quiet, reticent, secretive, sententious, silent, taciturn, terse, tight-lipped, unrevealing.

As Seen by Others:

A person of few words.

His most often-used words are "Yes," "No," "Maybe," and "I suppose."

Not many have the keys to his mouth.

If you want to know something, he's the last person to ask.

Good at pretending ignorance about something.

Handles questions as if you had put a blank sheet of paper in his hand.

Never discusses politics or religion.

Will hardly talk about his family, his job, or the people he knows.

Pares his words down to the bare minimum, using only one if one will do.

Comes right to the point, sparing everyone the preamble.

COMPLAINING

Related Traits:

Bemoaning, bitchy, griping, grousing, grumbling, lamenting, protesting, repining, resentful, whining.

As Seen by Others:

Carries personal grievances around as if they were a knapsack on his shoulder.

Always got an ax to grind.

He is a weeper and a gnasher of teeth.

Protests the wrongs he has suffered.

Protests the slights he has endured.

Protests the ills that have visited him.

Protests the opportunities of which he has been deprived.

May be heard to say, "Oh, that I had ever been born!"

UNCOMPLAINING

Related Traits:

Forbearing, long-suffering, patient, philosophical, resigned, stoical, uncritical, understanding, unresentful, unruffled.

As Seen by Others:

Blames nothing or no one for the misfortune in his life.

Keeps his annoyances or injuries all to himself.

Takes the attitude that problems in life are to be expected, dealt with, and not complained about.

Does not take the view that his misfortune is part of God's grand design to frustrate him.

Seems indifferent to great discomfort.

Refuses to openly accuse others of being responsible for whatever he endures.

He is the tree that silently suffers the woodsman's ax.

QUICK-WITTED

Related Traits:

Alert, astute, brainy, bright, clear-sighted, clever, discerning, discriminating, intellectual, intelligent, keen, knowing, perceptive, perspicacious, quick, quick-eyed, responsive, sagacious, savvy, sharp, sharp-sighted, sharp-witted, shrewd, smart, wise.

As Seen by Others:

Constantly alert with regard to what is going on.

His sharp perception allows him to make discerning comments.

Shows an above-average aptitude for learning.

Can grasp the essential nature of something almost instantly.

Has the ability to see what is important amidst those things that are less important.

Often exhibits surprising insight regarding practical matters.

Capable of making judgments based on little information.

His quickness in grasping the meaning or nature of something being said is exceptional

Able to quickly pinpoint the truth of a matter.

SLOW-WITTED

Related Traits:

Asinine, blockheaded, blockish, brainless, dopey, doltish, dull, dull-witted, dumb, empty-headed, feeble-minded, foolish, half-witted, imbecilic, lowbrow, lumpish, mindless, moronic, nonintellectual, obtuse, shallow, simple, simple-minded, slow, stolid, stupid, thick, thick-headed, thick-witted, undiscerning, unintelligent, vacant, vacuous, witless.

As Seen by Others:

You will never see his mind race ahead; it must be pulled gently along.

Too many concepts at one time confuses him.

Lacks the sharpness of mind needed to determine what is and is not important.

He very often cannot see what is clearly obvious to almost everyone else.

Ability to understand and learn is sluggish.

His mind appears to be like an unfurnished apartment.

His exceptionally low mental capacity is a result of a genetic defect.

He thinks simply and acts accordingly.

Doesn't realize it when someone makes fun of him; in fact, he's likely to laugh without knowing what he's laughing about.

BELIEVING

Related Traits:

Assured, cocksure, confident, convinced, credulous, decided, dogmatic, gullible, ideological, ingenuous, innocent, naïve, positive, satisfied, sure, trustful, trusting, undoubting, unguarded, unquestioning, unsuspicious, unwary.

As Seen by Others:

He's absolutely positive that he's right.

He and doubt are complete strangers.

His conviction not only becomes immovable but he wants others to accept it as their own as well.

If he locks onto a political or social philosophy, he will not entertain any opposition to it.

Inclined to doubt the validity of something if it disagrees with what he believes.

Tends to believe whatever someone tells him.

Can easily be persuaded that what you're telling him is the truth, or that he should do something because it's best for him.

He'll overlook signs that tell him his trust is misplaced.

Needs skepticism to stand watch for him.

QUESTIONING

Related Traits:

Cautious, challenging, diffident, disbelieving, disputatious, distrustful, doubtful, doubting, dubious, irresolute, leery, puzzled, skeptical, suspecting, suspicious, unconvinced, undecided, unimpressed, unsure, wary.

As Seen by Others:

Rarely believes the first thing he hears or sees; instead, he withholds judgment until he has chased the truth down the last alleyway.

For every answer you've got, he's got a question to follow it.

Caution often causes him to delay action.

His path to understanding and accepting something is always impeded by his reluctance to accept its validity.

Labors over conflicts and contradictions.

Tends to imagine that something is not quite right, even though there is no evidence to suggest it.

It's not the *amount* of evidence that impresses him but rather the *weight*.

Has a difficult time determining where to place his trust and, as a result, looks for still more facts to examine.

Always one of the last people to become convinced.

His motto: Show me.

PRAGMATIC

Related Traits:

Down-to-earth, efficacious, materialistic, mundane, practical, prosaic, realistic, unromantic, utilitarian.

As Seen by Others:

Doesn't have much imagination and shows no interest in the theoretical.

Takes an all-business, materialistic view.

Only attracted to those things that promise to be functional, workable, useful, and efficient.

More likely to engage himself in only those goals which are truly reachable.

Shows more interest in probabilities than possibilities.

Places more value on what has been done rather than on what has never been accomplished.

Rarely listens to an idea that floats above the commonplace and which is not firmly tied to the here and now.

Before he becomes involved in something, he wants to know how much money he is going to make or in what way it is going to soon benefit him.

Displays great interest in what serves a useful purpose and is far less concerned with how something looks.

Takes a down-to-earth, feet-on-the-ground approach to things.

IMPRACTICAL

Related Traits:

Conjectural, daydreaming, dreamy, fanciful, idealistic, moonstruck, romantic, speculative, starry-eyed, theoretical, unrealistic, visionary, whimsical.

As Seen by Others:

Usually involves himself in those things that are anchored in idealism rather than reality.

Shows a weakness for wild speculation instead of that which builds incrementally on experience.

Tends to see the whole pie and is inclined to leap for it, not being happy with taking one slice at a time.

Regularly attracted to those things that, seemingly, have no immediate worthwhile purpose or which may be too difficult to achieve.

Leans heavily toward the theoretical.

Prone to take risks, to jump without first looking.

Easily becomes enthralled with what is possible and yet is incapable of determining the steps necessary to get there.

His ideas are decidedly unusual.

CONCERNED

Related Traits:

Absorbed, alarmed, attentive, bothered, discomposed, disconcerted, disquieted, distressed, disturbed, engaged, engrossed, gripped, haunted, immersed, interested, involved, occupied, overwrought, tormented, troubled, uneasy, unsettled, upset.

As Seen by Others:

If he becomes convinced of the importance of something, it will rivet his attention and block out everything else.

Inclined to focus his mind on something to such a degree that he sometimes cannot even hear others speak to him.

Worry sits on his face like a billboard.

Seems to be bothered by something that bears no name.

Hears trouble before it is trouble.

He can be here and, at the same time, not here.

UNCONCERNED

Related Traits:

Blasé, bored, detached, dispassionate, inattentive, insensitive, nonchalant, unalarmed, unbothered, undisturbed, unengaged, uninterested, uninvolved, unperturbed, untroubled.

As Seen by Others:

No matter how bad things get, nothing seems to bother him.

He sort of accepts life as it comes.

Abstractions never get in his way and bog him down.

If he's not satisfied with the way things are, you wouldn't know it by looking at him.

Acts like he doesn't care about what's going on.

He is serenity's poster child.

RECOLLECTIVE

Related Traits:

Effusive, memoried, nostalgic, reflective, reminiscent, retrospective, sentimental.

As Seen by Others:

Prone to talk about the past as he remembers it — or chooses to remember it.

When describing the past, tends to dress it unfairly.

Able to recall precise dates, situations, and who was there.

Has a strong grasp of history or past relationships.

He can describe past events in detail, like it was yesterday.

His capacity for remembering names and faces is remarkable.

More interested in talking about the past than the present, and makes more of it than what was ever really there.

FORGETFUL

Related Traits:

Absent-minded, amnesiac, heedless, memoryless, neglectful, oblivious, unmindful, unremembering.

As Seen by Others:

His ability to recall what happened or didn't happen in the past isn't very strong.

Has a hard time remembering names, dates, birthdays, anniversaries, appointments, and so on.

Somehow, things just slip easily from his mind.

His memory has become impaired as a result of an injury.

If it held little importance for him at the time it happened, the odds are good that he won't remember it later.

His preoccupation with one thing makes him forget other things.

ANTICIPATIVE

Related Traits:

Divinatory, expectant, farseeing, farsighted, foreknowing, foreseeing, foresighted, intuitive, long-sighted, oracular, precognitive, precognizant, predictive, predictory, premonitory, presageful, prescient, prognostic, telepathic.

As Seen by Others:

Sometimes talks about having a vague feeling that something is going to happen before it actually does.

Can look at things around him and give you a general idea of what's going to happen down the road.

Has displayed the ability to look at a situation, or some facts, and make a somewhat accurate prediction about what is likely to occur.

Has been able to determine what is happening to someone at the very moment it is taking place.

Can sometimes discern a future event, though perhaps not in specific detail.

Displays a talent for seeing the future, based upon his reading of particular signs that occur.

Uses atmospheric changes, the arrangement of numbers, biblical passages, the position of the planets to determine something that will occur in the future.

UNANTICIPATIVE

Related Traits:

Inexpectant, shortsighted, unaware, unsuspecting.

As Seen by Others:

Things slip up on him, just as it does in the case of most people.

Can't even tell you what's going to happen tomorrow, much less what is going to take place far in the future.

Always caught off guard.

Surprised whenever something "unexpected" happens, though the evidence of its approach was certainly there for him to see.

Incapable of looking at the juxtaposition of events and drawing any conclusions with regard to their implications.

REPUTABLE

Related Traits:

Admirable, august, commendable, creditable, dignified, elevated, estimable, exalted, exemplary, first-rate, grand, honorable, imperial, lofty, magnanimous, majestic, meritorious, noble, outstanding, praiseworthy, principled, proper, pure, reputable, scrupulous, splendid, staunch, sterling, superlative, unblemished, unimpeachable, unsullied, upright, upstanding, venerable, worthy.

As Seen by Others:

Has acquired a good name because he is known for abiding by high-minded principles.

His traits seem unblemished.

He's done things that deserve great respect.

A purity can be detected in his actions.

He seemingly tries to do what is right.

His virtues are viewed as worth imitating.

Apparently abides by all the written and unwritten rules that define superior conduct in his society.

There is no stain on his background.

His reputation is of such sterling quality that it fills others with awe.

The praise he receives seems well justified.

DISREPUTABLE

Related Traits:

Amoral, conscienceless, contriving, corruptible, criminal, debauched, degraded, detested, discredited, discreditable, disgraceful, dissipated, good-for-nothing, ill-famed, indecent, infamous, inferior, lecherous, lewd, licentious, lickerish, notorious, odious, perfidious, petty, second-rate, self-serving, shady, shameful, slick, small-minded, sordid, tarnished, third-rate, uncommendable, undignified, undistinguished, unethical, unscrupulous, unworthy, wayward, worthless, wretched.

As Seen by Others:

Has a reputation for doing whatever it takes to promote or protect himself, even if that is at the expense of someone else.

There's a black mark on his background.

Known for bending a principle, ignoring a promise, shirking a duty.

Collectively, his traits seem furtive and hungry — a mercenary army on the loose.

Ethics do not concern him.

He's an inventor of schemes.

It is suspected that he has taken bribes; if he hasn't, he at least seems highly susceptible.

He has done things that have violated public laws.

Will go to any lengths to satisfy his lust.

Has squandered his money, and possibly that of others, to feed his vices.

Uses language like it was a bloody hatchet.

There's nothing about his past which pride could lay claim.

Has been disloyal to those who he was expected to support.

Most people agree that he has little worth.

Hidden within his friendliness is a vein of treachery.

He will not only easily stray from the high moral road but will do so without compunction.

GOOD

Related Traits:

Altruistic, benevolent, compassionate, conscientious, decent, ethical, excellent, generous, good-natured, high-minded, humane, incorruptible, irreproachable, kind, merciful, moralistic, puritanical, righteous, sympathetic, tender, transcendent, undefiled, unselfish, virtuous.

As Seen by Others:

Makes every effort to do what is right.

Attempts to prevent the suffering of all living things, human or not.

Attends to the welfare of others.

Wouldn't do anything to hurt anyone.

The unfortunate plight of others bothers him deeply.

He would, as they say, give you the shirt off his back.

If you're in trouble, he's there to help you.

Will not accept any kind of bribe, however subtle it may be.

Not tempted to succumb to selfishness, intemperance, lustfulness, conceit, revenge, dishonesty, which fouls one's soul.

Displays a gentleness toward others.

His worthiness is among the highest order.

He is religious without going to church.

EVIL

Related Traits:

Bad, baneful, barbarous, base, bestial, black-hearted, bloodthirsty, bloody, brutal, brutish, contemptible, corrupting, cruel, deadly, debased, defiling, deleterious, depraved, despicable, devilish, diabolical, dissolute, evil-minded, exploitative, ferocious, fiendish, harmful, heartless, heinous, horrible, hurtful, ignoble, ignominious, immoral, inhuman, inhumane, iniquitous, injurious, maleficent, malevolent, malicious, mean, mean-spirited, merciless, miscreant, monstrous, murderous, nefarious, noxious, outrageous, pernicious, perverted, predaceous profligate, rapacious, rotten, ruinous, ruthless, sadistic, salacious, savage, scandalous, shameless, sinful, sinister, uncivilized, unprincipled, unspeakable, unwholesome, vicious, vile, villainous, viperous, wanton, wicked.

As Seen by Others:

Attracted to the dark side of life, judging by the pleasure he takes in doing wrong.

Purposely engages in acts that will bring harm to others.

Displays instincts that are more identifiable with those that dwell in the jungle than those who live in houses.

Degrades the quality of everything in which he becomes involved, not unlike the spoors emitted by a rotten apple.

If he hurts someone, he will show no misgivings.

He'll use people for his own advantage and think nothing of it.

He is extremely poisonous to others.

He is potentially life-threatening.

Practically everything he does is contrary to what is considered to be public decency.

Collectively, his actions seemed to be aimed at making sure that someone is physically, psychologically, or socially wounded.

Initiates acts that are so abhorrent and of such magnitude that even those who are attracted to evil are dumbstruck.

He has killed and is quite willing to do so again.

Has a predatory nature, in that he will try to seize whatever suits his fancy.

Finds sexual gratification in inflicting pain on others.

Willing to harm anyone who stands in the way of his getting what he wants.

RELIGIOUS

Related Traits:

Adoring, cherubic, devoted, devotional, devout, godly, idolatrous, pietistic, reverent, reverential, saintly, venerating, virtuous, worshipful.

As Seen by Others:

Tries to structure his life in accordance with what he believes God expects of him.

There is a light within him.

Elevated by an illustrious spirit of great purity.

So that he might devote his life to prayer, has chosen permanent seclusion from others.

He is convinced that he is in possession of a spiritual truth that lies well outside human reason; it is something he has either gained through intuitive powers or as a result of contemplation.

Invests much of his waking hours in serving and adoring God.

Frequently interrupts his day with prayers.

All of his attention is focused upon the purification of his own soul.

Shows no regard for material matters and, instead, turns his attention toward the purification of his own soul.

His commitment to his religious faith is so overwhelming that he exhibits contempt for all other beliefs.

Will do anything that the leaders of his faith tell him to do.

IRRELIGIOUS

Related Traits:

Agnostic, atheistic, blasphemous, disbelieving, faithless, heathen, heretical, impious, irreverent, profane, sacrilegious, sinful, unbelieving, unchristian, undevout, ungodly, unholy, unreligious, unrighteous, unspiritual.

As Seen by Others:

Shows indifference toward religion.

He is antagonistic toward religion.

Does not believe that man is capable of determining the existence of God.

Unequivocally denies the existence God.

Speaks about God in an irreverent manner.

Always introducing opinions that serve to contradict the doctrine or tenets of a particular religion.

Has a lack of respect for anything considered sacred.

Scornful of "miracles."

Argues that people should contemplate improving the world we know something about rather than the soul, which is unknowable.

HONEST

Related Traits:

Aboveboard, artless, blunt, candid, clear-cut, direct, forthright, frank, free-speaking, guileless, indiscreet, ingenuous, open, outspoken, plain-spoken, sincere, square-shooting, straight, straightforward, transparent, truthful, unambiguous, unconcealed, undisguised, unequivocal, upright, veracious.

As Seen by Others:

Refuses to take what doesn't belong to him, no matter how trivial it may be.

What he has, he got without any tricks or sleight-of-hand.

Blunt-spoken; doesn't try to shade the truth.

Never tries to varnish his background or his capabilities.

Doesn't embellish the facts.

He will never deceive you.

You may not want to hear it, but he'll tell you.

Comes right at you; never engages in evasiveness.

He boldly says what others would like to say.

His conversation is not perforated with double meanings.

The truth is usually written on his face before he even says one word.

DISHONEST

Related Traits:

Affected, artificial, artful, calculating, conniving, crafty, crooked, cunning, deceitful, devious, disingenuous, disguised, dissembling, double-crossing, double-faced, duplicitous, evasive, false, foxy, fraudulent, guileful, holier-than-thou, hypocritical, insincere, lying, mendacious, phony, sanctimonious, scheming, shady, shifty, side-stepping, sly, stealthy, story-telling, surreptitious, thievish, treacherous, tricky, two-faced, underhanded, venal.

As Seen by Others:

Has a propensity to steal.

Has an addiction to telling lies.

With him, you hardly ever see what you think you see.

With him, everything is a charade.

His promises often wind up being nothing but words.

If it's a choice of being truthful or promoting his own interests, he'll choose the latter.

Learning his true intentions is a game for fools only.

Depending on his smile is like playing liar's poker.

All his stories end up by either making him look good or making you feel sorry for him.

Questioning him is like trying to hit a moving target.

He preaches one thing but does another.

Not above stealing someone's identity, ideas, or friends.

He's quite willing to take credit for what someone else did.

He'll sell his soul to the highest bidder.

Sees principles and allegiances as nothing more than bargaining chips.

Willing to betray a spouse or a friend, maybe even his country.

JUST

Related Traits:
Detached, equitable, even-handed, fair, fair-minded, impartial, neutral, nonpartisan, objective, reasonable, unbiased, uncommitted, indiscriminate.

As Seen by Others:
He won't favor one person or group over another.

If he's in a position where he has to dispense punishment for some misdeed, he'll make sure it matches the offense rather than exceeds it.

Has spoken out against prejudice.

It's his opinion that everyone should get the same chance at whatever prize is being pursued.

He's not influenced by the fact that someone may belong to some kind of minority.

He'll listen to both sides of an argument without taking sides.

UNJUST

Related Traits:
Biased, bigoted, discriminating, factional, inequitable, one-sided, partial, partisan, predisposed, preferential, prejudicial, sectarian, unfair, unreasonable.

As Seen by Others:
He's always taking sides.

He has shown that he is incapable of making the punishment fit the so-called crime.

His punishment is too severe for those he does not like, and too lenient for those he favors.

Tends to "categorize" human beings and mentally places his group at the top of the so-called pecking order.

Does not associate with those who are of a different race, religion, nationality, educational background, social level, political persuasion.

He is more likely to exclude people than include them.

TRUSTWORTHY

Related Traits:
Constant, dedicated, dependable, devoted, dutiful, duty-bound, faithful, loyal, reliable, stable, stalwart, staunch, steadfast, steady, true, true-blue, unfailing, unswerving, unwavering.

As Seen by Others:

If he says he'll do something, you can count on it.

Takes his responsibilities seriously.

You'll give up on yourself before he will.

While everyone else abandons you, he'll stand by you — until he finds out that his faith has been misplaced.

Insists on honoring allegiances or promises until it is no longer honorable to do so.

UNTRUSTWORTHY

Related Traits:

Disloyal, erratic, fair-weathered, faithless, fickle, inconstant, irresponsible, shaky, traitorous, treasonous, undependable, unfaithful, unreliable, unstable, wavering.

As Seen by Others:

Can't depend on him.

Always late.

Don't expect him to stand by you when you need him the most.

His moral commitment is as erratic as fish in a pond.

Tends to shirk his responsibilities if something better comes along.

He may believe what he says today, but don't expect that to be the same come tomorrow.

Likes allegiances or friendships when they're to his advantage.

REMORSEFUL

Related Traits:

Anguished, apologetic, ashamed, chagrined, compunctious, conscience-stricken, contrite, embarrassed, guilt-ridden, guilty, heavy-hearted, humiliated, mortified, penitent, regretful, repentant, rueful, self-reproachful, shamefaced, sheepish, sorry, tormented, woebegone, woeful.

As Seen by Others:

He once did (said) something that he has since always wished he hadn't.

His actions are the sacrifices that beg for atonement.

Moves through his days as if he were pulling a train.

It's hard for him to believe that he could be so hurtful.

Tries to return to someone's good graces.

Shame has hung from his heart for a very long time.

Once, he failed to do something and he wants that moment back.

UNREMORSEFUL

Related Traits:

Callous, hardened, impenitent, shameless, unapologetic, unashamed, unembarrassed, unregretful, unrepentant, untroubled.

As Seen by Others:

Everyone else believes he's done (said) something disgraceful, but he doesn't.

He's a person without a conscience.

He's at the point where nothing he does bothers him anymore.

Doesn't know the meaning of sorry.

His attitude is, what's done is done and there's no sense worrying about it.

He's so hard that he's forgotten how to care.

ACTIVE

Related Traits:

Bustling, busy, energetic, enterprising, fast-moving, frenzied, frisky, hard-working, industrious, lively, peppy, perky, productive, prolific, quick-moving, spirited, vigorous, zippy.

As Seen by Others:

He's always on the go, doing something.

Loves to work.

He does nothing slowly.

He won't postpone anything that can be handled today.

Prone to rush ahead, do things in a flash, get a hard start.

For him, sleep is an interruption.

Won't quit until the job's done.

Got more energy than two people put together.

He's always exceeded the results expected of him.

Seems to have a reservoir of energy that never runs dry.

Able to produce a great quantity of work.

Not averse to working through his lunch hour.

INACTIVE

Related Traits:

Comatose, dawdling, dilatory, drowsy, fatigued, feckless, flagging, idle, indolent, inert, languid, languorous, lazy, lethargic, lifeless, listless, loafing, malingering, ne'er-do-well, procrastinating, quiescent, remiss, shiftless, slack, slothful, slow, slow-moving, sluggish, somnolent, soporific, torpid, unenergetic, unproductive, vegetative.

As Seen by Others:

> He sort of just pokes along through life, killing time.
> Prefers to take things easy rather than do things seriously.
> Does as little as possible for as long as possible.
> Seems to be in a chronic state of weariness.
> Sometimes it's as if he can barely put one foot in front of the other.
> More likely to be found asleep than applying himself.
> Tends to put things off, half-believing he'll do them later.
> He avoids action by pretending to be sick or incapacitated.
> His slow approach to everything inconveniences others.
> Produces almost nothing useful.
> Some people call him a good-for-nothing.
> If his mind ever gets as inactive as his body, he'll be dead.

AGILE

Related Traits:

> Acrobatic, adroit, athletic, deft, dexterous, elastic, facile, flexible, graceful, light-footed, limber, lissome, lithe, lithesome, loose, loose-jointed, nimble, sprightly, spry, supple, sure-footed, willowy.

As Seen by Others:

> Has the dexterity and lightness of a dancer.
> He wields tools effortlessly, as if they were extensions of his arms.
> He's poetry in motion.
> His limbs appear to be almost rubbery.
> His muscular coordination is well above average.
> Everything he does seems to be all of one fluid motion.

AWKWARD

Related Traits:

> Blundering, bumbling, bungling, clumsy, fumbling, graceless, heavy-footed, heavy-handed, inept, inflexible, klutzy, left-handed, lumbering, maladroit, plodding, rigid, stiff, unathletic, ungainly, unhandy.

As Seen by Others:

> When he walks, his arms, legs, and torso seem to contradict one another.
> Everything about him is out of sync.
> Accident-prone.
> Liable to fall over his own feet.
> Movements lack elasticity, almost as if someone had shellacked his clothes.
> Tends to bobble and drop things.

Prone to bump into things that are stationary.

Uses tools as if each weighed fifty pounds and lacked grip handles.

If something is heard crashing, he comes quickly to mind.

Persevering

Related Traits:

Assiduous, constant, dedicated, determined, dogged, doughty, fixated, fixed, focused, indefatigable, persistent, purposeful, relentless, resolute, sedulous, steady, strong-willed, tenacious, tireless, unchanging, undeviating, unfailing, unfaltering, unflagging, unremitting, unshakable, unswerving, untiring, unwavering, unyielding.

As Seen by Others:

If he sets his sight on a specific goal, he'll keep at it until he gets there.

He's never demoralized by failure.

Danger will probably make him cautious, but it probably won't stop him.

At the core of his persistence springs an innate obstinacy.

He'll be there long after everyone else has given up.

He just keeps hammering away at you.

Tends to forget what his dedication might be doing to others around him because he is so focused.

Never allows his determination to be rechanneled in another direction.

Vacillating

Related Traits:

Aimless, capricious, changeable, desultory, erratic, faint-hearted, faltering, fickle, flexible, fluctuating, frivolous, hesitant, irresolute, irresponsible, mercurial, purposeless, uncertain, undecided, undirected, unfixed, unstable, wavering.

As Seen by Others:

He might start out with an objective, but he'll wander from the path more than once.

He is consistently plagued by doubt and gnawed by fear.

Tends to takes advice from everyone and to believe everyone is right.

His commitment swings to and fro like a pendulum on a clock.

Making him stay the course is like trying to nail fog to a wall.

He'll suddenly come up with a new plan, then abandon it.

If he was an arrow he would have two heads and be bent in the middle.

With all his hesitation, back-stepping, side-stepping, and flip-flopping, in his wake he leaves the footsteps of a staggering drunk.

DARING

Related Traits:
Adventurous, audacious, bold, brash, brave, brazen, careless, chance-taking, chivalrous, courageous, dauntless, devil-may-care, fearless, foolhardy, gritty, gutsy, hardy, hasty, heedless, heroic, impatient, impetuous, improvident, imprudent, impulsive, injudicious, intrepid, lionhearted, neglectful, plucky, quixotic, rash, reckless, risk-taking, speculative, spunky, stalwart, stout-hearted, undaunted, undismayed, unflinching, unhesitant, unthinking, valiant, valorous, venturesome, venturous.

As Seen by Others:
Tends to do things that leave people gasping.

Acts on the spur of the moment when the challenge is inviting.

He'd rather jump headlong into the unknown than cozy up to the status quo.

Purposely pursues danger, as if it were a narcotic.

Inexplicably, he will endanger himself to protect others.

Will never heed the warnings of others.

Likes using money dangerously.

Inclined to act hastily and not take into consideration what he will need in the future.

Takes the path least traveled — and it does indeed make all the difference to him, and sometimes to others as well.

In the presence of trouble, quickly makes up his mind about what to do and then does it.

Prone to ride after that unreachable star.

Dislikes talking endlessly about alternate options.

Becomes impatient with those who are patient.

CAREFUL

Related Traits:
Afraid, alert, apprehensive, cagey, cautious, chicken-hearted, circumspect, conscientious, conservative, cowardly, craven, deliberate, diligent, discreet, distrustful, faint-hearted, fearful, gritless, guarded, heedful, hesitant, judicious, leery, lily-livered, meticulous, mindful, nonspeculative, painstaking, patient, politic, poltroonish, precise, provident, prudent, pusillanimous, recreant, scared, scrupulous, skittish, spineless, thorough, timid, timorous, unadventurous, unheroic, unhurried, vigilant, wary, watchful, weak, weak-hearted, weak-kneed, yellow.

As Seen by Others:

Not likely to do anything until he has weighed all the pros and cons.

The threat of danger is uppermost in his mind, and it consistently gives him pause.

Plays it safe, stays on his guard, watches his step, proceeds on tiptoe.

Almost any advice, ominous sign, or absence of certainty will cause him to stall, followed by a rethinking of his position and objective.

Prefers the safety of his immediate environment and is suspicious of anything that lies beyond.

Always afraid of being deceived.

Avoids risks, at all costs.

To prevent being taken by surprise, keenly attentive to everything that is going on around him.

To prevent making a mistake, tends to deliberate for a very long time.

Fearing someone's displeasure, takes great pains to do a job right.

Shows excessive regard for the petty details that pull at the coattails of action.

Shows a lack of confidence when presented with a "sure thing."

Perforated by doubt.

Always looks for evidence of sound reasoning before proceeding, but he is still inclined to hesitate before acting.

Avoids any gamble, no matter how slight.

If trouble seems imminent, he is likely to bail out.

INTRUSIVE

Related Traits:

Advising, curious, examining, inquiring, inquisitive, inquisitorial, interfering, interrogative, meddlesome, meddling, nosy, obtrusive, officious, overcurious, prying, scrutinizing, snoopy.

As Seen by Others:

Wants to know what people have done, are doing, or may do, under cover of polite conversation, of course.

His ear latches on to any rumor and his curiosity makes him follow its scent.

His "innocent" questions peel away what is none of his business.

Quick to give advice, often inserting his opinion when it is not wanted.

Shows up at people's homes unexpectedly.

Butts into other people's conversations.

Insists on doing things for people, though they prefer he wouldn't and despite the fact that they tell him so.

UNINTRUSIVE

Related Traits:

Aloof, blasé, detached, incurious, indifferent, unconcerned, uninquisitive, uninterested, unquestioning.

As Seen by Others:

Does not feel it is proper to snoop into other people's affairs.

Won't go to anyone's home unless invited, and still feels uncomfortable.

Would never barge into someone's office without an appointment or without being asked.

Minds his own business rather than someone else's.

Rumors fall dead at his feet, for he sees them as invasions of privacy.

Waits until someone is finished talking before saying anything.

Keeps his opinions to himself, lest he offend anyone.

Dares not ask the question that is searing his brain.

Takes the view that what someone has done, or is planning to do, should be of no interest to him, even though he's dying to know.

PRETENTIOUS

Related Traits:

Affected, artificial, blustering, boastful, bombastic, conceited, condescending, coy, dandified, dramatic, egotistical, exaggerative, extravagant, fastidious, flamboyant, flashy, florid, gallant, garish, grandiloquent, grandiose, hammy, haughty, high-flown, high-hatted, high-sounding, highfalutin, histrionic, hoity-toity, holier-than-thou, inflated, magisterial, mannered, melodramatic, moralistic, narcissistic, ostentatious, over-modest, overbearing, overconfident, overweening, patronizing, pedantic, phony, pietistic, polished, pompous, prancing, pretentious, priggish, prim, prudish, punctilious, puritanical, sanctimonious, self-important, showy, snobbish, snooty, snotty, stagy, starchy, stilted, strait-laced, stuck-up, supercilious, swaggering, swollen, theatrical, top-lofty, uppish, uppity, vainglorious, vaunting, Victorian.

As Seen by Others:

Inclined to show off in some way.

He can act like a swelled head, put on airs, talk big.

Advertises his "qualities" to others, possibly to gain more respect than perhaps he deserves.

Feigns an affection for one or more things, but for which he truly has no affection.

Flashes his knowledge in front of someone as if that person could not begin to understand what he was talking about.

Displays little or no modesty.

Talks as though he were speaking to people from a stage or elevated platform.

He talks tough, but isn't.

Inclined to brag about his bravery.

If his nose was any higher, it would be on top of his head.

Shows off by using big words and complex phrasing, when neither are necessary.

Makes a great show of his learning and tends to debate the most trivial matters of scholarship.

Pretends like he doesn't want attention, yet at the same time you know he wants it.

Often wears clothes that are excessive for the occasion.

Clearly has a far higher regard for himself than he does for anyone else.

Leans toward overstatement; as they say, he lays it on thick, stretches a caboose into a train.

Acts as if he's shocked or disgusted regarding some infraction of taste.

His actions are so artificial that they almost seem vaudevillian.

Flaunts his new social class, by flashing the proper symbols (country club membership, a home in the "right" neighborhood, a sudden inexplicable taste for antiques, a fancy car).

Self-glorification is stately, almost ceremonial.

Makes no secret of the fact that he believes his relatives and former friends are now inferior to himself.

UNPRETENTIOUS

Related Traits:

Artless, bashful, deferential, down-to-earth, humble, inartificial, inconspicuous, informal, modest, natural, plain, plain-spoken, retiring, self-conscious, self-deprecating, self-effacing, shrinking, shy, simple, simplehearted, timid, unaffected, unassuming, unostentatious, unpolished, unpretending.

As Seen by Others:

He never acts like he's someone special.

Shuns the spotlight and makes no effort to draw attention to himself.

Always seems to be uncomfortable when he's asked to talk about himself.

The last thing he'd do is promote himself.

There's nothing phony about him.

What you see is pretty much what you get.

Has a down-to-earth way of talking and never uses big words.

To look at him and where he lives, you'd never know he was rich.

He wears sincerity like pair of comfortable old shoes.

More likely to dress down than dress up.

Hates country clubs, power lunches, pin-striped suits, and all the badges of exclusivity.

STRICT

Related Traits:

Arbitrary, austere, authoritative, autocratic, bossy, demanding, despotic, dictatorial, domineering, Draconian, drastic, exacting, firm, forbidding, hard, harsh, high-handed, imperious, inflexible, intransigent, lordly, no-nonsense, obdurate, overbearing, pitiless, punitive, repressive, severe, stern, stringent, totalitarian, tough, tyrannical, unalterable, uncompromising, unsparing, unyielding.

As Seen by Others:

Insists that the rules of behavior be obeyed, whether they are formal or informal, his or someone else's.

Prone to keep a tight rein on things that are under his control.

Will not permit any deviation.

Insists that the letter of the law be followed.

Not only imposes harsh conduct upon others but upon himself as well.

Possesses a stern morality that he thinks should be imposed upon others, too.

Makes demands on others that seem unreasonable.

His punishment for an infraction is often particularly severe.

Insists that others do what he says, and he will not tolerate any non-compliance.

Refuses to grant even the smallest concession to others.

Will not bend his rules for someone else's convenience.

Under him, far more things are forbidden than allowed.

Appears to others as a self-anointed lord.

Frequently taxes the endurance of those under his control.

LENIENT

Related Traits:

Compromising, easygoing, flexible, forbearing, forgiving, indulgent, lax, permissive, pliant, tolerant, uncritical.

As Seen by Others:

Tends to allow the rules to be bent.

Inclined to indulge the "mistakes" of others.

Does not get upset when things don't go his way.

Places more emphasis on the ends rather than the means; therefore, he usually provides others with a wide latitude, as long as it winds up achieving the desired results.

Would rather get along with others than keep them under his thumb.

Does not usually interfere with the way others discharge their duties.

Sees rules as guidelines instead of commandments.

Withholds punishment for as long as possible, and when forced to inflict it, usually tempers it considerably — sometimes to the disappointment of some onlookers.

CHEERFUL

Related Traits:

Amusing, blithe, bright, buoyant, carefree, cheery, chipper, convivial, debonair, droll, effervescent, exuberant, felicitous, gay, gladsome, gleeful, glowing, happy, happy-go-lucky, hearty, high-spirited, humorous, insouciant, jaunty, jocular, jolly, jovial, joyful, joyous, lighthearted, lightsome, merry, mirthful, pleased, radiant, sparkling, sprightly, sunny, unconcerned, untroubled, unworried, vivacious, waggish, winsome.

As Seen by Others:

Almost always in good spirits.

Seemingly does not have anything on his mind that bothers him.

Conveys the image that he is rather satisfied with the way things are going in his life.

Inclined to wish someone a "good morning" — and mean it.

A joke is forever poised to leap forward from his tongue.

His presence can be a tonic to those who need relief from their gloom.

Gives off a light that is felt rather than seen.

Seems to be only a step away from a song and a dance.

He has a smile for everyone.

Always trying to cheer up other people.

Given to teasing others in a lighthearted way, which is one way he has of showing affection.

UNCHEERFUL

Related Traits:

Anxious, apathetic, blue, careworn, cheerless, dejected, depressed, despairing, despondent, disconsolate, discouraged, distressed, doleful, dour, downcast, dreary, gloomy, glum, grave, grim, heavy-hearted, joyless, lackluster, leaden, low-spirited, melancholic, mirthless, miserable, moody, morose, mournful, pensive, sad, sedate, serious, sober, sober-faced, solemn, somber, sorrowful, spiritless, staid, sulky, troubled, unhappy, woebegone, worried.

As Seen by Others:
> Always seems to be wrestling with thoughts that strip him of every smile.
> Adept at finding gloom in the brightest of circumstances, in the warmest of moments.
> Talks about the world in irreverent terms.
> Silence surrounds him like a death shroud.
> He is winter's messenger.
> He's been defeated by misfortune and he's never gotten over it.
> He seems to expect disappointment at every turn.
> Always walks on the dreary side of life.
> Sees peril lurking within the insignificant.
> He is a piccolo played by Grief.
> It doesn't do any good to try to raise his spirits.
> Grumbles, grumbles, grumbles.
> His mind is a way station for all things grim.

ADJUSTED

Related Traits:
Attuned, compatible, complacent, contented, fulfilled, reconciled, serene, united, well-adjusted, well-balanced.

As Seen by Others:
> Like lock and key, seems to be in good harmony with things around him.
> "Fits right in."
> Never complains about the way things are going.
> Seems to have come to terms with the way things are.
> Appears to be at peace with himself.
> Likes his life just the way it is.
> He's become "one of the boys."

MALADJUSTED

Related Traits:
Alienated, aloof, detached, disaffected, discontented, disengaged, disgruntled, displeased, dissatisfied, dissident, disunited, estranged, fretful, frustrated, ill-adjusted, incompatible, malcontent, out-of-step, remote, troubled, uneasy, unfulfilled, ungratified, unhappy, unsatisfied, withdrawn.

As Seen by Others:
> He's not well-suited to his job.

He doesn't fit in well with people.

Never been the same since he got divorced (married).

With him, confusion has the upper hand.

He looks and acts like a fifth wheel.

He sometimes acts as if he is in a foreign country and is perplexed by its customs.

Wants to be part of the group, but doesn't know how.

Talks about leaving and getting a new start somewhere.

He's like a dog in a cat's den.

Never has found his center.

Acts as if he has parachuted into enemy territory.

Tries to fit in, but it's like he's trying to squeeze into a crowded closet.

Has never figured out how to march in unison.

Has lost all sense of affinity.

EXCITABLE

Related Traits:

Anxious, apprehensive, ardent, avid, disquieted, eager, earnest, ebullient, edgy, enthusiastic, exuberant, fervent, fidgety, fitful, frisky, high-spirited, high-strung, impassioned, intense, jittery, jumpy, nervous, restive, restless, skittish, temperamental, tense, turbulent, twitchy, uncomposed, unrelaxed, uptight.

As Seen by Others:

It's easy to get him worked up.

Say the wrong thing and he'll fly off the handle.

He's a bunch of loose nerve ends.

Can't sit still for two minutes.

If you could throw a bridle over his anxiety, you could go on a wild ride.

The more intense he becomes, the more his judgment becomes impaired.

Sometimes he has a tendency to act mindlessly.

He's a pacer, much like a caged tiger.

Needs only the slightest reason to make him leap into action.

Quick to become alarmed.

Has no ability to take things easily.

Working with him is like being around nitroglycerin.

UNEXCITABLE

Related Traits:

Apathetic, calm, collected, composed, cool, dispassionate, easy-going, half-hearted, imperturbable, indifferent, nonchalant, peaceful, phlegmatic, placid, relaxed, sedate, self-controlled, self-possessed, serene, smooth, stoical, tranquil, unburdened, unconcerned, undisturbed, unflappable, unmoved, unruffled, unworried.

As Seen by Others:

No matter what, he always maintains his composure.

When he's enthused about something, you never know it.

Hard to get him upset.

Rarely, if ever, does he show any anger.

He's able to enter an unfamiliar social situation without experiencing any nervousness.

Seems infected with chronic indifference.

Takes a superior attitude toward any trouble that may occur.

Unexpected disturbances do not fluster him.

Not punctuated with a passion.

His demeanor is like an ice-covered lake.

His emotions have a difficult time of bubbling to the surface.

He is a rock that cannot be reduced to pebbles.

PEACEABLE

Related Traits:

Appeasing, calm, conciliatory, easygoing, even-tempered, gentle, good-humored, good-natured, good-tempered, imperturbable, mild, moderate, mollifying, noncombative, nonviolent, pacific, placating, placid, quiet, thick-skinned, unaggressive, unbelligerent, uncontentious, undisturbed, unwarlike, well-disposed.

As Seen by Others:

Tries to get others not to rock the boat.

Not inclined to take offense at what is being said, but rolls with the punches.

Maintains an unthreatening disposition.

His temperament is not subject to any extremes.

Easy to get along with.

He'll take steps to overcome or reduce someone's hostility rather than just ignore it.

Always tries to avoid an argument, because he dislikes confrontation.

He'll bend, but he won't break.

He'll keep his opinions to himself if he thinks they'll conflict with someone else's.

Never gets upset if you tease him; in fact, he often joins in the laughter.

Has a humor that is sweetened with kindness.

Violent outbursts appall him.

Says or does nothing to make waves.

Tries to remain in the good graces of others.

He'll try to do something, or give up something, that will mollify an antagonist.

COMBATIVE

Related Traits:

Adversarial, aggressive, antagonistic, argumentative, bad-tempered, barbarous, bellicose, belligerent, bilious, brash, cantankerous, choleric, contentious, contrary, crabby, cranky, cross, crotchety, curmudgeonly, curt, disagreeable, disputatious, explosive, feisty, fierce, fiery, ferocious, grouchy, grumbling, hot-tempered, hypersensitive, ill-tempered, impudent, inimical, irascible, irritable, mercurial, militant, militaristic, peevish, petulant, polemic, pugnacious, quarrelsome, quick-tempered, rowdy, rude, scrappy, sharp, short-tempered, snappish, surly, testy, tempestuous, thin-skinned, touchy, truculent, turbulent, unpleasant, stormy, unstable, violent, volatile, warlike, waspish.

As Seen by Others:

Seems to purposely look for ways that he may pick a fight.

On nearly every subject, if he can, he'll take a view that contradicts that held by another just for the sake of contrariness.

Easily provoked, thus one has to be careful what is said around him.

Quick to start an argument.

Displays an ongoing antagonism toward things in general.

He can get worked up over the most trivial of matters.

Seems to thrive on stirring up controversy.

He's a one-man army when it comes to getting his way.

His violence and cruelty comes in spurts.

Discussing things with him is like bringing a lighted match near gasoline.

Perpetually on the attack; never on the defensive.

Likes being at the center of a disturbance.

He'd rather die than compromise.

He'll fight you to the point of exhaustion.

During a disagreement, he's not afraid of hurting your feelings or wounding your pride.

In the end, winning is more important to him than simply who is right; and if right is on his side, so much the better.

FLEXIBLE

Related Traits:

Adaptable, compliant, compromising, dissuadable, malleable, open, open-minded, permissive, persuadable, practical, realistic, reasonable, receptive, responsive, unbiased, willing.

As Seen by Others:

He's not too proud to change his mind.

If you've got a better idea, he'll go that way.

He'll give you some of what you want if you'll also grant him some concessions.

Does not insist that he is right and everyone else is wrong.

Dares to entertain the idea that he might learn something by listening instead of talking.

After hearing all sides of an argument, he is willing to adjust his thinking if necessary.

Never enters a discussion with his mind already made up.

Can easily be talked out of doing something.

INFLEXIBLE

Related Traits:

Adamant, closed-minded, convinced, dogmatic, fixed, hardheaded, headstrong, implacable, incompliant, inflexible, intractable, intransigent, mulish, obdurate, obstinate, perverse, resolute, rigid, set, stubborn, unbending, uncompromising, unpersuadable, unreasonable, unyielding.

As Seen by Others:

Holds opinions that cannot be dislodged.

Turns a deaf ear to any suggestion that a change should be made.

He finds it impossible to entertain the possibility that two people could have different viewpoints and still have truth on their side.

Only resorts to logic when it provides him with great support.

When it comes to holding fast to worn-out convictions, he is the last fence post to fall.

Tends to hold his ground even when it is no longer practical.

Getting him to entertain another notion is like trying to yank a wharf away from its moorings.

To him, compromise is a curse word.

His convictions are so strong that he doesn't feel a need to provide an explanation for them.

Spurns all appeals to his sympathies.

It is unlikely for him to see another person's point of view.

Submissive

Related Traits:

Acquiescent, amenable, bootlicking, browbeaten, conformable, complaisant, compliant, cooperative, courteous, cowering, cringing, deferential, docile, dominated, fawning, gentle, groveling, henpecked, kowtowing, law-abiding, meek, nonresistant, obedient, obliging, obsequious, passive, pliable, pliant, pusillanimous, servile, subjugated, subservient, sycophantic, timid, tractable, truckling, unassertive, unresisting, weak-kneed, yielding.

As Seen by Others:

Waits upon others as if it were his delegated mission in life.

Submits quickly to those who seem to have more authority, never questioning their wisdom.

If he fears someone's power, he'll try to ingratiate himself by using flattery and doing whatever he can to make that person's life easier.

Does not take action, but rather he is acted upon.

He leaves himself open to the whims of others.

His attention to the needs of others can be embarrassing to watch.

Acts like he doesn't have a mind of his own.

He is intimidated by, and will always give way to, those who have titles more impressive than his.

Attempts to worm himself into the confidence of others by agreeing with everything they say, even if it is contrary to what he believes.

He indulges the accesses of others far beyond what most people would tolerate.

Lacks backbone; a doormat.

He does whatever a certain individual tells him to do.

His submission is so extreme that he might as well prostrate himself.

Provides a service, yet gains nothing in return.

Unsubmissive

Related Traits:

Audacious, brazen, cheeky, churlish, contumacious, defiant, derisive, disdainful, disobedient, disrespectful, dissident, dissonant, impertinent, impudent, insolent, insubordinate, insurgent, irreverent, lawless, noncompliant, rebellious, recalcitrant, saucy, seditious, transgressive, unconsenting, ungovernable, unmanageable, unruly.

As Seen by Others:

He will resist anyone's effort to control him.

Won't do anything that he doesn't want to do.

His distrust of authority, as well as a defiance of it, is second nature to him.

If you tell him what to do, he's likely to do the opposite.

Never demand anything from him, but rather request it.

To disobey seems inherently important to him.

Refuses to do what his government tells him he must do.

Positions of authority do not impress him.

Looks at rules, customs, policies, and procedures as things to be broken.

Like the horse that twitches below someone who would try to ride him, he has a tendency to buck at the first opportunity.

METHODICAL

Related Traits:

Careful, conscientious, detail-minded, diligent, disciplined, efficient, exacting, fussy, meticulous, neat, nit-picking, organized, orderly, overprecise, painstaking, particular, procedural, scrupulous, sedulous, selective, systematic, thorough, tidy.

As Seen by Others:

Inclined to keep things in order.

Has a penchant for developing systems and methods of classification.

He has a place for everything and keeps everything in its place.

Does not allow the smallest thing or the most insignificant matter to escape categorization.

Displays an inordinate concern for what he thinks should be the proper arrangement of either physical or nonphysical things.

The misplacement of things irritates him.

Doesn't like lint on clothing, dishes in the sink, haphazardly hung towels, things out of alignment, and so on.

In the name of efficiency, habitually does the same things in the same order.

While he could make the trains run on time, he wouldn't have the slightest idea how to attract passengers.

Makes lists of things he must do.

His striving for exactness drives everyone else crazy.

Takes a line-by-line, step-by-step approach to things.

UNMETHODICAL

Related Traits:

Careless, chaotic, disorderly, disorganized, inaccurate, inconsistent, inefficient, messy, negligent, perfunctory, remiss, slack, slapdash, slatternly, sloppy, slovenly, undisciplined, unmethodical, untidy.

As Seen by Others:

Inclined to be quite careless where he puts things.

Tends to create clutter and confusion wherever he goes.

Functions in a haphazard manner and allows things to pile up.

He can easily create disorder out of order, similar to pouring dried beans onto a clear tabletop.

Tends not to place things in any particular order.

Unable to find things when he wants them.

Appears to be awash in untidiness.

He is reckless in the way he performs a series of duties.

He is the avowed enemy of ritual.

Never makes a list of things he must do, depends upon his memory instead.

Prone to do things in a nonsequential order, which later causes him problems.

Always at the center of quiet chaos.

Has a habit of filing, stacking, and closeting things in no particular rational manner, thus driving the organized person crazy.

Avoids details as if they were infectious germs.

SELF-DENYING

Related Traits:

Abstemious, abstinent, ascetic, austere, conservative, continent, economical, fasting, nonextravagant, nonindulgent, penny-pinching, prudent, saving, scrimping, self-abnegating, self-controlled, self-depriving, self-disciplined, self-neglecting, self-restraining, self-restricting, self-sacrificing, sparing, teetotaling, temperate, thrifty.

As Seen by Others:

Able to refrain from those pleasures that he would like to have and which are available to him.

He can go without and not complain about it.

Once he swears off something, he has the fortitude to stay away from it.

Will not give in to temptation.

He will deprive himself of something and, instead, give it to someone else.

He sometimes jeopardizes his well-being by neglecting what he needs.

His takes economizing to extremes.

Refrains from indulging himself with second helpings.

SELF-INDULGENT

Related Traits:

Bon vivant, dissipating, Epicurean, gluttonous, hedonistic, high-living, immoderate, improvident, intemperate, lascivious, lewd, licentious, lustful, pleasure-seeking, profligate, sybaritic, uncontrolled, undisciplined, unrestrained.

As Seen by Others:

Freely pursues his whims and desires to extract as much pleasure as he can.

Always seeking ways to gratify or amuse himself.

He does nothing in moderation.

Does not hesitate to spend money on himself, or on others, in a seemingly boundless manner.

Drinks more than he should.

Eats more than he should.

Refuses to give up what he likes, even if it is not good for him.

His weakness for something is one of his major driving forces.

Rapidly devours food to keep others from having any.

It is his opinion that pleasure, regardless of its nature, is not only good but worthy of being pursued for its own sake.

His pursuit of sensual pleasures is wildly excessive and nearly uncontrollable.

His drive for gratification makes him concentrate on his immediate wants rather than his future needs.

PROTECTIVE

Related Traits:

Conservative, guarding, guiding, illiberal, maternal, mothering, paternal, safeguarding, sheltering.

As Seen by Others:

He carefully guards those intangible things that are important to him. (Perhaps his faith, his reputation, a way of life, a method of doing things, an existing political order, an idea, a secret, etc.)

Politically, he is fearful that change can threaten treasured institutions and he prefers keeping things as they are.

Uses his influence or knowledge to help someone not make a mistake and to reach the goal they desire.

Always trying to ensure the safety of those he cherishes.

UNPROTECTIVE

Related Traits:

Liberal, nonmaternal, nonpaternal, progressive.

As Seen by Others:

Doesn't worry about keeping his reputation intact.

Not interested in maintaining the status quo.

Willing to share his ideas with anyone.

Has no desire to maintain political institutions beyond their normal life span.

Refrains from excessive protection of someone, because he is of the opinion that it deprives one of the opportunity to learn the valuable lessons that life affords.

Will not try to stop someone from receiving the punishment he or she deserves.

GENEROUS

Related Traits:

Altruistic, beneficent, benevolent, big-hearted, bounteous, bountiful, charitable, extravagant, giving, intemperate, large-hearted, lavish, liberal, magnanimous, munificent, open-handed, philanthropic, prodigal, public-spirited, thriftless, spendthrift, squandering, unselfish, unstinting.

As Seen by Others:

To help others, he donates his time.

To help others, he contributes a portion of his resources.

It is his expressed opinion that when people need assistance, the necessary steps should be taken to see that they get it.

Part of the money he donates is given to eliminate a social ill in the country.

He has given two or three times more than has been needed.

He is, as they say, an "easy touch."

UNGENEROUS

Related Traits:

Accumulative, acquisitive, avaricious, cheap, close-fisted, covetous, frugal, grabby, grasping, greedy, grudging, hard-fisted, hoarding, hoggish, mean, mercenary, miserly, moneygrubbing, monopolistic, niggardly, parsimonious, penny-pinching, penurious, petty, piggish, plunderous, predatory, rapacious, selfish, sparing, stingy, stinting, tight, tightfisted, uncharitable, wolfish.

As Seen by Others:
Doesn't like to share anything with anyone.
Always "cutting corners," thus depriving others of what they either need or deserve.
His penchant for saving is taken to the extreme.
He is not moved by pleas to show some compassion.
Scoffs at the virtue of giving.
He wants not only a sizeable percentage of something but the overwhelming majority of it, if not all.
Once he latches onto something, it is extremely difficult to wrest it away from him.
Addicted to ownership.
Hides things and pretends he doesn't have them.
If two pieces of pie were on a table, he would begrudge each bite the other person took.
He wastes nothing.

WELL-BEHAVED

Related Traits:
Cultivated, cultured, formal, genteel, gentlemanly, highbred, ladylike, nonplayful, polished, prissy, refined, restrained, stilted, unspontaneous, well-mannered.

As Seen by Others:
He acts like he came from an aristocratic family.
Seems well-educated.
Has all the mannerisms that come with good breeding.
His movements are cloaked in politeness.
Everything about him is well-orchestrated and reflective of decency.
The only thing spontaneous about him is when he sneezes.

MISCHIEVOUS

Related Traits:
Devilish, elfish, free-wheeling, frolicsome, fun-loving, impish, mischief-loving, naughty, playful, prankish, puckish, rascally, reckless, roguish, spontaneous, uninhibited, unladylike, unrefined, unrestrained, waggish.

As Seen by Others:

He loves to play harmless pranks.

One never knows what he is going to do next.

Precariously walks the line between a tease and bad taste.

Behind his smile lies plots yet unhatched.

Tweaks the nose of formality whenever he gets a chance.

Pomposity is one of his premier targets for attack.

IMAGINATIVE

Related Traits:

Artistic, bold, clever, creative, daring, dreamy, enterprising, extemporaneous, fanciful, gifted, improvisational, ingenious, innovative, inventive, mystical, nonconforming, original, resourceful, talented, unconventional, unorthodox, visionary, whimsical.

As Seen by Others:

He pulls possibilities out of the jaws of impossibility.

Because he has a strong dislike of conformity, he tends to butt heads with tradition.

He can make the most commonplace of things seem not at all common.

He develops things that make people wonder why they didn't think of that.

He's always looking for something different, a fresh way to put a new face on something quite old.

He hates beaten paths and is lured by the road not yet taken.

He strives for the fascinating, the unique.

Cannot be depended upon to walk the same rut, climb the same hill, sit on the same rock.

Finds rationality in the irrational.

Has the ability to give substance to what never was and will never be.

He is a discoverer of countries in the hemisphere of the fantastic.

UNIMAGINATIVE

Related Traits:

Barren, commonplace, conforming, conventional, down-to-earth, emulative, imitative, machinelike, mechanical, mundane, ordinary, parrotlike, pedestrian, programmatic, prosaic, run-of-the-mill, uncreative, undaring, unenterprising, unexceptional, unimaginative, uninspired, uninventive, unoriginal, unresourceful.

As Seen by Others:

Does not question conventional wisdom, but follows it.

He repeats what has become ordinary.

Does almost all the things that practically everyone else does and which he is expected to do.

He is a follower of rules, a practitioner of routine, an indefinable part of the crowd.

He is a copycat, a modifier of accepted ideas.

His work is predictable and there is nothing about it that is surprising.

There is little hope that he will ever be daring, that he will venture outside the boundaries of triteness.

Does not march to the sound of a distant drummer.

3. What Does the Character Want, Not Want, or Need?

The great American playwright Neil Simon once said that every fictional character should want something. Without analyzing this observation to the vanishing point, and assuming that he was not referring to the no-names who pass through the plot like a summer breeze, we can nevertheless conclude that in a great many cases Simon is quite right.

However, while it may certainly be advantageous to determine what the character wants, it might be almost as important to determine what he or she does *not* want, and what he or she *needs*.

Mind you, it is not written in stone somewhere that this triumvirate of possibilities should always be pondered before any character is created. However, if knowing the answers to just one of the questions would help the author define the character more sharply during the planning stage, then all three questions are worth considering.

Of course, when a writer asks one question about a character, he or she is invariably led to ask even more. There is not, however, an established sequence of questions to be asked in every instance; the questions obviously depend upon the psychological nature of the fictional character, the situation into which the author places that character within the story, and the overall nature of the story itself. Every situation is different.

But here, for example, are a just few of the questions that you may wish to consider:

When does it become clear to the character what he wants, doesn't want, or needs?

Or does it ever? Will it, for instance, remain a secret between the writer and reader, or does the character know as well? If the character does *not* know what he wants or needs, will it be one of the things that concerns him during the story? And if the character *does* know, is that knowledge available to him at the beginning of the story or later?

Does the character always want or need the same thing, or will it change?

The wants or needs of a major character often change during a story. Take the hilarious screenplay of *Tootsie*: the main character is an out-of-work actor who starts out by simply wanting a good acting job. But because his agent tells him that no one will hire him, a second "want" is added: he wants to prove that his agent is mistaken. He masquerades as a female, auditions for the part, and gets it. As new circumstances are introduced into the plot, new "wants" replace old ones, and some "don't wants" are added as well.

Does the character need the same thing that he wants?

If he doesn't, the writer is going to have to decide which one the character will get. If a character is given what he needs, the odds multiply in favor of a happy ending. But if a character is allowed to achieve what he wants — or thinks he wants — he may still be miserable because it is not compatible with what he actually needs. A character may get several things he or she wants, yet still be unhappy.

If the character wants or needs something, why does he? And if he doesn't want something, why doesn't he?

The answer to either of these questions may be important in determining the character's motive. If, for instance, Sally wants to marry Bob, is it because she loves him or because he represents a way out of her predicament? And if she *doesn't want* to be his wife, is it because she is in love with someone else or because she's afraid of something?

Does the character want something impractical?

This is a question that only the other characters in the story can answer. Suppose a girl in a Nebraska farm town wants to be a high-powered New York businesswoman, and the writer proceeds to make that wish come true. At the outset her family and friends may well believe she is being totally unrealistic. On the other hand, the writer may have other plans and elect to hit her with a strong dose of reality by keeping the dream far from her reach.

Where can the character get what he wants or needs? And who or what stands in his way?

These are plot-development questions.

The first one establishes the target. If, say, a rancher in the Southwest wants a bigger ranch to raise his cattle and he finds out it can be had in Montana for just a dollar an acre, the writer may pack the rancher and his family into their wagons and move their herd in that direction.

But it's always the second question that truly cranks up the plot. So the writer dreams up things to place in the rancher's way — obstacles such as cattle thieves, bad weather, Indian attacks, the death of a trusted cowhand, a prairie fire, and so on.

Who can help the character get what he wants or needs?

Another plot-building question, a follow-up to the preceding one. If someone like this exists in the story, he may or may not be a major character;

regardless, this individual acts as a door-opener, a conduit. Suppose a father expects his son to take over the business. But the mother may know it is the last thing the son wants, that he wants to pursue something more dear to his heart. The question is, what will the mother do to relieve her son of the responsibility his father has placed upon him?

Is there someone else who wants what the character wants?
    Still another plot-building question, obviously. If two people want the same thing, a rivalry is established in the story. Stories about power struggles, for instance, often use rivalry as part of their equation. So do love stories.

To get what he wants or needs, is it necessary for the character to give up something?
    Wants and needs often come with a price tag. For the love of a woman, a king of England had to give up his throne. Likewise, fictional characters often find themselves forced to give up something they would like to keep, so they can acquire something else they want or need. Thus the politician may achieve the high office he desired, but lose his treasured privacy in the bargain. And a husband may need to admit to his homosexuality, yet at the same time face losing the respect of his family, friends, and coworkers.

    Following this introduction are the categories. They are in alphabetical order, and most of the attending information is in the form of questions. The questions are few in number, more like starting points than anything. Indeed, the mind of a good writer will generate far more questions than this book could ever possibly offer.
    Finally, no effort has been made to be specific; that is, you won't find such clear-cut "wants" as, say, wanting to buy a car or be chosen as the prom queen. Instead, what you will see in this section are mostly broad concepts, under which the specifics your character desires can be relentlessly pursued. If you do not already know what your character wants, doesn't want, or needs, this section may draw you closer to that knowledge.
    Now, here are the categories.

ADVENTURE

    Does the character have a thirst for excitement? Does the threat of danger attract him? Does he like taking risks, doing something just for the hell of it, surprising or shocking others, or making them stand in awe? What will happen if the character is deprived of adventure or if the adventure turns deadly?
    Doesn't want: boredom, monotony, the commonplace.

AFFECTION

What kind of affection does the character want or need? Friendship? Sexual love? Public adoration? Has he previously been denied it? Did he have it and then lose it? Where does he think his chances for affection lie, and is he right? And what will happen if he doesn't get it?

Doesn't want: unfriendliness, solitude.

ATONEMENT

What wrong does the character think he has committed that leads him to want to relieve his conscience? What can he do to achieve that end? Does he wear his guilt openly, or is it hidden? And what will happen if he feels he has not gained atonement?

Doesn't want: condemnation, resentment.

BEAUTY

Does the character want to be beautiful himself? Or does he want to surround himself with beauty, *e.g.*, lovely home, attractive furniture, fine artwork, sleek automobile, a good-looking spouse, cute children, etc.? How does he define beauty or ugliness? And what will he do if beauty eludes him?

Doesn't want: plainness, ugliness.

CHANGE

Does the character want to transform? Improve? Regenerate? Convert? Reform? Rehabilitate? Revolutionize? Or substitute something? Is his desire for change rather constant — that is, is he always unhappy with the way things are and tinkers endlessly with things — or has he only become dissatisfied with one thing? Who stands to benefit from the change, and who does not? Is it a cosmetic change, or something deep and reverberating? And what will happen if the change doesn't take place as he likes?

Doesn't want: the status quo.

COMFORT

If the character wants comfort, how does he define it? Is it being free from financial worry? Is it a job that does not cause stress? Is it a marriage in which he or she is the recipient of the spouse's devotion? Is it the satisfaction that comes with knowing that he has achieved great things? Is it just an easy chair, a good book, and a drink alongside? Perhaps a conversation with old friends? And what will happen if no comfort is realized?

Doesn't want: discomfort.

COMMITMENT

From whom does the character want or need a commitment, and what will this commitment entail? Why is it so important? Is a promise that will affect a great many people, a small group, or just the character and the individual making the commitment? What will happen if he cannot get a commitment, or, if he does, the commitment becomes broken?

Doesn't want: unwillingness, hesitation, diffidence, indecision, irresolution, capriciousness, indifference, spiritlessness.

COURAGE

If courage is desired or needed, is the character afraid that he will not display it at the appropriate time (like the main character in *The Red Badge of Courage*, who was fearful that he would run when thrust into battle)? Does he desire courage to satisfy himself or someone else? Will this courage be required for an extended period of time, during which time his resolve will be tested again and again, or does he want it to visit him in a burst of undeniable glory? Does he want this courage to replace his cowardice? Is it needed to burnish an ego?

Doesn't want: cowardice, dishonor, self-hatred, timidity.

DESTRUCTION

What does the character want to destroy? A life? Several lives? A way of life? Evidence? A few rules? Customs? Inequality? Does he seek destruction because he is malevolent, or does he see himself as having a high moral purpose? What will happen if he becomes unable to be destructive? Besides himself, who wins and who loses if he is successful? Unsuccessful?

Doesn't want: preservation, restoration.

EQUALITY

If a character wants equality, does he want it for himself or for others? That is, does he envision himself as a torchbearer for broad-ranged justice, or does he just want what he believes his background and performance merit? Is his desire for equality born out of a concern for all human beings, or is it narrowly focused? And what will happen if the equality he cherishes is not forthcoming?

Doesn't want: inequality, prejudice.

EVASION

Who or what is the character trying to avoid, and why is he making the effort? Is he a fugitive from the law? Is there a certain subject he doesn't want brought up? Is there something he doesn't want others to know? Does he want to avoid someone from his past? His in-laws? The press? His boss? Is he a recluse who would like to evade people altogether, and will this pique their curiosity? And what if he encounters the very person or thing he wishes to avoid — and at a time that is quite inopportune?

Doesn't want: challenge, confrontation.

A FAMILY

Does the character want to be married? To be a part of large unit of in-laws? Perhaps experience the joy of being a parent, with all the responsibilities that entails? If so, does this mean pregnancy or adoption? Is a male or female child desired? Is a male child needed to carry on the family name? Is the child wanted because another child has died? What will happen if no child is forthcoming? What if marriage never occurs?

Doesn't want: bachelorhood, barrenness, childlessness, impotence, spinsterhood.

FORGETFULNESS

Who or what does the character wish to forget, and how old is the memory? Is it something he regrets or a moment filled with sorrow? If he has seen, heard, or experienced something that he wishes would fade with time, will that memory be so obliging or will it remain to haunt him? And what will happen when he is reminded?

Doesn't want: to remember.

FREEDOM

From whom or what does the character seek freedom? Incarceration? A social class? A marriage? A commitment? An unsatisfactory job? Guilt? The past? Or does he even know? If he does know, will he continue to endure an intolerable situation because he does not have the courage to actually pursue this freedom? To what lengths will he go to secure this freedom? Will he fight alone or seek someone's help? For a story to focus upon a character who does *not* want freedom would be unusual, although certainly not unthinkable.

Doesn't want: confinement, dependence.

GOOD HEALTH

If the character is in pursuit of good health, is it because he has been deprived of it or because he is afraid of losing it? If he is sick, does he seek a cure? If he is healthy, does he attempt to keep illness away by exercising and eating nutritiously? Is he afraid of pain? Of dying before "his time"?

Doesn't want: poor health, death, pain.

GOOD LUCK

In what situation will the character be placed where he finds the need for (and, indeed, will pray for) a little good luck? This luck need not be logical; it need only come at the right time. Thus the farmer may wish for rain; the gambler may dream of a royal flush; a player on a losing football team may pray for the other team to fumble. And what will happen if the good luck doesn't come? On the other hand, what if it does?

Doesn't want: bad luck.

HELP

What kind of help does the character want or need, and who is capable of providing it? Does he want help for himself or someone else? Is he too proud to ask for help? Is the character in trouble? Incapacitated? Lost? Confused? Is he trying to improve himself? Does he need, perhaps, someone to exert a little influence in his behalf? And what if he does not get the help he requires?

Doesn't want: rejection, indifference.

JUSTICE

What kind of justice does the character want, and does he want it for himself or someone else? Is the character driven by ethics or retaliation? If he achieves justice, will it benefit a great many people or only him? To what lengths will he go to achieve justice, and how long is he willing to wait to get it? In his search for justice, is he being impartial? Fair? Realistic? And what will he do if he fails to get the justice he desires?

Doesn't want: acquittal, injustice.

KNOWLEDGE

What is the nature of the knowledge sought by the character? And why does he want it or need it? Does he want to acquire broad information, or is he pursuing something quite specific, such as the cure for a disease, the truth about what happened on the night of the murder, or the latest tidbit of neighborhood gossip? If he acquires the knowledge, what will he do with it? And if he doesn't get it, what will he do?

Doesn't want: ignorance.

LEISURE

Does the character want leisure because he is essentially lazy, or does he wish to take a respite from what he has been doing? If he is lazy, does he have a penchant for sleep, or for watching television and sunning himself on the beach? If, however, his desire for leisure comes after a grueling period of work, does he want an extended break or just a brief interlude? Whether he is lazy or not, what will happen if the leisure he wants is not forthcoming?

Doesn't want: exertion, stress, strain.

LOYALTY

From whom does the character want loyalty? Why is it so important to him? What position does he hold that allows him to demand or expect it? And what will happen if he does not get it?

Doesn't want: disloyalty, double-dealing, faithlessness, mutiny, sedition, treachery.

MISFORTUNE

It is entirely possible that a character may actually *need* misfortune to visit him. One who is inflated with his own sense of superiority, for instance, may need his perspective changed by a situation where he not only does not get his own way but is forced to endure the same kind of indignities that others have suffered at his hands. But mostly, characters want misfortune to befall someone else — a desire almost always bred from such emotions as envy, jealousy, and anger. But what will the character do if this desired misfortune does not occur? Indeed, what will he do if it does?

Doesn't want: good luck, prosperity.

MONEY

Not wealth (*see* Power) — just enough money for a certain situation. If money becomes a priority for a character, how much money does he want and why does he want it — or need it? Is he broke? Did he lose it? Is he being bribed? Does he want to help someone out of trouble? To get what he wants or needs, what options does he have? Will he, for example, borrow it? Steal it? Beg for it? Dig into his savings? And what will happen if he can't get the money?

Doesn't want: indigence, nonpayment.

PEACE

If a character relishes peace, does he wish it would descend upon his own life, or does he want it to be broader and affect the lives of many? Who is preventing the peace from occurring, and what steps can the character take toward it? Does he seek harmony in general or in a specific sense? Does he want peace to simply satisfy his own life, or is he being altruistic? And what if peace is not forthcoming?

Doesn't want: agitation, antagonism, commotion, conflict, contention, disaccord, friction, infringement, interference, opposition, turmoil, violence.

PERFECTION

If the character seeks perfection, does he already assume that he is perfect and that others are not? Or does he restrict this high level of idealism to those things that only concern himself? Does he see imperfection everywhere but in himself, or does it depress him to know that he too must be included? Does he, perhaps, accept imperfection in all areas, except one which is vitally important to him? In striving for perfection, will he antagonize others? And what will he do if perfection eludes him?

Doesn't want: mediocrity, imperfection, blunders, negligence, thoughtlessness, carelessness, haphazardness, procrastination, oversights, recklessness.

POWER

How does the character define power? Is it being wealthy and having the means to buy what he wishes? Is it owning something and being recognized as the boss? Is it influence, in which he is able to get others, or at least one other person, to do what he wants them to do? Is it fame or reputation, which, as a result of what he has accomplished, automatically opens doors for him? Does he want people to be dependent upon him? Does he want to control their lives? Does he thirst for the favors that accompany power? And what if he does not acquire this power? On the other hand, what if he does?

Doesn't want: defiance, disobedience, helplessness, impotence, ineffectualness, refusal, resistance, weakness.

PRAISE
(*See also* Recognition)

Has the character done something quite specific for which he seeks approbation, or is he on the prowl for any kind of praise he can draw his way for practically everything he does? Is he one to wallow in flattery? Does he always seem to be saying, "Look at me"? If he receives one compliment, does he try to do something to get another? Does he want praise from one person, a few, or a great many? And what will happen if he does not receive the praise he is seeking?

Doesn't want: contempt, disapproval, disrespect, fault-finding, lampooning, rejection, reproach, ridicule, vilification.

PRESERVATION
(*See also* Prevention)

If the character wants to preserve something, is he attempting to *prevent* something as well? What does the character want to preserve? A way of life, perhaps? His reputation? Possibly something that he believes is not only important to him but to everyone? Does he feel it is something that is in danger of being lost forever? Why is it so important to him to engage in the act of preservation? And what will happen if he fails?

Doesn't want: damage, destruction, neglect.

PREVENTION
(*See also* Preservation)

If the character wants to prevent something, is he attempting to *preserve* something as well? (For example, an environmentalist may want to prevent a redwood forest from being cut down by loggers; in doing so, he is also engaged in act of preservation.) What does the character want to prevent, and why? Is it something that affects him personally, or are his efforts on behalf of either one other person or several? Does he need to enlist the assistance of at least one other person, or does he have the power to do it all by himself? And what will happen if his act of prevention fails?

Doesn't want: change.

PROPERTY

What is the nature of the property desired by the character? Is it land? A factory? An automobile? Diamonds? What tangible thing does he have his heart set upon obtaining, and what meaning does he attach to its possession? Do others attach the same meaning or importance to it? How long has he wanted it? And what will happen if he doesn't get it?

Doesn't want: forfeiture, relinquishment.

RECOGNITION

Does he desire recognition for himself? For those he represents? For someone he loves or likes? What is the nature of the recognition desired, and from whom does he want it to come? Does he want one or more people to appreciate that he, or someone else, has noteworthy skills? achieved something? performed a good deed? deserve sympathy? And what will happen if this recognition doesn't come?

Doesn't want: anonymity, disapproval, indifference, inattention.

RELIEF

What kind of relief does the character want or need? Does he want it for himself or another? Is this desire for relief a result of his (or someone else's) having suffered psychological or physical discomfort over an extended period? If he wants relief from (for instance) heat, drought, cold, pain, discrimination, or accusation, and it doesn't come, what will happen?

Doesn't want: continuance, prolongation.

RESPONSIBILITY

If the character wants or needs to be responsible for something, or someone, why does he? If he *needs* it, will his being held accountable help to change him for the better? But if he *wants* responsibility, will it show determination? Conviction? If, on the other hand, he desires that others accept responsibility for their actions, is he passing the buck or placing a moral obligation upon them?

Doesn't want: avoidance, irresponsibility, unaccountability,

SECRECY

What secret does the character want or need to keep? Is it in relation to him or someone else? Who will benefit by having the secret maintained, and who will not? Is the information important or entirely frivolous? Will keeping the secret force the character to lie? How many people know the secret? To what lengths will the character go to keep the thing concealed? What will happen if the secret is disclosed?

Doesn't want: publicity, disclosure, confession, acknowledgment.

SECURITY
(*See also* Stability)

Does the character want security, or does he *need* it? or does he both want and need it? If he wants it, does that mean he has absolutely none? How, in fact, does he define security? Is it money in the bank? An excellent job? A good medical report on his physical condition? The support of friends and family? What will happen if his security, or the security of someone he loves, is threatened?

Doesn't want: doubt, exposure, vulnerability.

SOPHISTICATION

If a character desires to be sophisticated, it means he isn't — at least by the guidelines he uses as a measurement. What are those guidelines, and in what area does he see himself as lacking? Does he wish he could talk better? Dress better? Exhibit impressive knowledge? But is his notion of sophistication a misguided idea? Whom is he trying to impress? And what will happen if he fails to reach his goal, or if others see his effort as fruitless?

Doesn't want: inelegance, vulgarity, coarseness.

STABILITY
(*See also* Security)

If a character wants or needs stability, is it because his life has been regularly yanked first one way and then the other for far too long? Does he feel that its underpinnings need shoring up? Does he have a *need* to experience a sense of permanence, which he might discover within a religion or a good marriage? Or does he simply feel comfortable with the status quo and want to keep it, thus spurning any notion of change? Do interruptions to his life send the character spinning? Does he hate ups and downs? Unpleasant surprises? Things that ruin routine? And what will happen if he cannot have stability?

Doesn't want: instability, change, discontinuity, disarrangement.

SUCCESS

How does the character define success? Does he frame it in terms of career? What he owns? What he achieves? Or possibly by the way other people value his friendship and his positive involvement in their lives? If success is a priority, will he be satisfied after reaching the plateau he once desired? And what will happen if success eludes him?

Doesn't want: adversity, demotion, failure, frustration, hardship, hindrances.

SUPERIORITY
(*See also* Power)

If a character wants to be superior, who does he wish to surpass? Will he do it through achievement, or will he simply assume himself to be better? What steps will he take to prove that he is better, or will he just arrogantly say that he is because he *wants* to be? Will his desire to be superior make him a competitor or a bigot? And what will happen if his superiority is challenged, or if he finds it does not exist?

Doesn't want: inferiority, integration, mediocrity, subordination, subservience.

TRUTHFULNESS

If a character wants the truth, is he placing a high priority on honesty as a trait, or is he pursuing it through a situation that is otherwise teeming with lies or inconsistencies? The difference is crucial. The former case would show that honesty is a virtue that he values. The latter case may involve investigation and presents numerous possibilities — among them, that he desires to prove a point, or to defeat slander, or to find what would otherwise lie hidden. Does the character seek a truth that is pure and undecorated? Does he just want to find out what happened? Does he view acknowledgments and admissions as victories along the way? Is skepticism his weapon of choice? And what will happen if the truth can't be found?

Doesn't want: delusion, dishonesty, dogmatism, fallaciousness, inaccuracy, misconceptions, misinterpretation, uncertainty, vagueness.

VICTORY
(*See also* Justice)

If the character wants to be victorious, in what way can he accomplish it? On the battlefield? In the boardroom? In an athletic game? If the desire is born out of a rivalry, will one victory be enough for the character? But if he sees victory as the sweet act of revenge, who will be the victim? And what will happen if victory is not realized?

Doesn't want: defeat, injustice.

VIRTUE

If the character wants to be virtuous himself, is it merely a wish, or does he sincerely strive to achieve that end? Or does he merely want others to view him as virtuous? What does he do in the name of virtue? Does he, for example, see himself as virtuous and thus want someone else to become so as well? Possibly a spouse? A member of his family? Also, because the path to virtue is often harsh and is traveled only by those who, metaphorically, take it upon themselves to wear hair shirts, will the seeker of virtue have a clear view of other people's shortcomings and be unable to see his own? Will this cause him to become a meddler in the lives of other people? (The extent to which this meddling takes place will be dependent upon the extent of power he holds.) And what will happen if the virtue he desires for himself or someone else is not forthcoming?

Doesn't want: misconduct, vice.

YOUTH

If the character wants to be young again, why does he? Does he associate youth with idealism? Optimism? A time free of pain, disappointment, and sadness? Does he pine for the time when he was physically vigorous, resilient, attractive? Free of wrinkles, brown blotches, and gray hair? Will his desire cause him to try to dress and act young? Pile on makeup and dye his hair? Will his craving for youth cause him to do some rather foolish things and, as a result, make him appear ridiculous in the eyes of others? And what will happen when his youth does not return? On the other hand, what will happen if he is, quite miraculously, young again?

Doesn't want: old age.

4. What Does the Character Like or Dislike?

Everyone has something he likes or doesn't like. A character may like streetcars and Van Gogh paintings, while at the same time he may dislike poodles, talking on the telephone, and anything in the color blue. These little revelations by themselves will certainly not create the basis for an interesting fictional character, but if added to his larger internal and external traits, as well as what he wants and needs — much as one might add spices to soup for the purpose of enhancing the flavor — they offer the promise of helping to add just a little extra dimension.

A character can like hot dogs, and no explanation is needed beyond that. However, in some cases it may not be enough to simply let the reader or viewer know that a character likes or dislikes something, because the audience will want to know why. For example, it will not be sufficient to let it be known that a character hates parades and simply let it go at that. How could anyone possibly hate a parade? On those occasions, of course, the writer will insert the *why*, and so we may learn that the character marched in hundreds of parades when he was in the army and, as a result, has developed an aversion to them, even if he sees them on television. This is just one example of how a dislike can reveal something significant about the character. It is up to the author to decide when to give a reason for a character's likes and dislikes.

The writer might also play upon the character's *indifference*, that barren terrain that lies between like and dislike. If, say, one character likes Thanksgiving or dislikes baseball, imagine the frustration when someone else, in a shrug of indifference, doesn't have an opinion one way or another.

Now, it would be futile to attempt to list every possible thing that fictional characters might like or not like. Instead, what follows is a listing of several major categories and some attending questions. Perhaps something you find here will inspire you to add a little dash of color to one of your characters. Perhaps that dash will in turn help to further illuminate your character's nature in your own mind.

You may not find what you are looking for here, but something may put you on the right road to discovering it.

ACCESSORIES

Perhaps the character has developed an attachment to any of the following: big front porches, screened-in patios, dusty attics, balconies with a view, big fireplaces, real wood paneling, interesting alcoves, white picket fences, flower boxes, featherbeds, round kitchen tables, walk-in closets, window seats, chandeliers, candleholders, French doors, winding staircases, or Venetian blinds. Maybe he likes or dislikes doilies, plastic-covered furniture, wall-to-wall carpeting, overhead cupboards, telephones, end tables, hassocks, roll-away beds, bunk beds, loveseats, recliners, or linoleum.

ANIMALS

Does the character like animals? If so, what kind? The usual kind, such as dogs, cats, birds, or horses? The more exotic, perhaps, like lions, tigers, snakes, lizards, monkeys, apes, bears, kangaroos, or wolves? A character who likes the water might be attracted to sea gulls, dolphins, flamingos, pelicans, seals, penguins, or whales.

A character who likes to farm might like goats, cows, steers, pigs, rabbits, mules, ducks, bees, sheep, turkeys, chickens, or roosters. One who hates farming would probably have a different view.

The city dweller might hate pigeons, mice, rats, and cockroaches. And, fictional character or not, practically everyone has a negative opinion about fleas, spiders, worms, ants, cicadas, wasps, bedbugs, chiggers, stinkbugs, and mosquitoes, but a positive one about eagles and butterflies.

ART

Does the character like art? If so, what kind? Abstractionism, surrealism, neoclassicism, impressionism, cubism, realism, romanticism, modernism? Does he prefer oil paintings, watercolors, ink drawings, sculpture, photography, engravings, or ceramics? Is he fond of an architectural style such as Greek, modern, Spanish, high Renaissance, medieval, Roman, or Gothic? Does he chuckle at movie cartoons? Political cartoons? Comic strips? Does he like computer art? Are there any of these things he doesn't like?

CELEBRATIONS, CEREMONIES AND CUSTOMS

Does the character like weddings, funerals, award ceremonies, commendations, baptisms, birthdays, anniversaries, receptions, swearing-ins, memorials, or christenings? Or does he dislike them? And how about such special days as Thanksgiving, Christmas, New Year's Eve, Independence Day, Easter,

Father's Day, Mother's Day, Saint Valentine's Day, Halloween, Saint Patrick's Day, or Veterans' Day?

Are there any customs he especially likes or dislikes, such as sending birthday cards, having Sunday dinner at his mother-in-law's house, or wearing a tie to church?

CHARACTERISTICS OF OTHERS

There is almost always something that one person will or will not like in another. It happens in marriages and in the best of friendships. A disorganized person will frustrate one who is organized. People in a hurry are annoyed by those who are cautious. And so on.

Most of the characteristics will be found in Chapter 2 (External Traits). A few typical annoyances include pretentiousness, laziness, indifference, contrariness, avoidance, jealousy, defiance, ingratitude, possessiveness, uncertainty, capriciousness, curiosity, stubbornness, dependence, dishonesty, advice-giving, dawdling, disorderliness, wastefulness, long-windedness, filthiness, unprofessionalism, fastidiousness, vulgarity, standoffishness, evasiveness, exaggeration, impulsiveness, forgetfulness, carelessness, overestimating, underestimating, prejudice, presumption, short-sightedness, gullibility, and skepticism.

Among the things that characters may tend to like are unpretentiousness, perseverance, courtesy, gratitude, restraint, honesty, orderliness, organization, cleanliness, professionalism, politeness, patriotism, informality, tactfulness, good judgment, and broad-mindedness.

CLOTHES

Some people hate to dress up; others enjoy it. One person may hate girdles but have to wear one; the same may apply to the individual who wears a necktie or high heels to work. Another may have jewelry hanging from nearly every body part; by contrast, a friend of that person may be exactly the opposite, possibly not even wanting to wear undershorts or a brassiere. What are your character's preferences or disinclinations?

ENTERTAINMENT
(*See also* Non-athletic Competition; Relaxation; Sports)

Does your character get a kick out of fireworks, parades, or kites? Enjoy a certain radio station or television program? Go to certain kinds of movies or concerts? Hang out at a certain nightclub or bar? Amuse himself by pulling off harmless pranks? Are there any of these things he doesn't like? And if so, why?

EXPLORATION

Does the character love doing research at the library? Does he like getting to the bottom of things? To him, does a forest or an old house become something magical? If he's given a clue, will he happily follow it to find another one?

FOOD AND DRINK

What is the character's favorite food? Is there anything that he positively will not eat? Does he like a big breakfast or dinner? Does he like to eat out or eat at home? Does he have a weakness for desserts, hamburgers, hot dogs, freshly baked bread, pasta, peanuts, pancakes, ice cream, chili, tabasco sauce, or hot peppers? Does he like a glass of wine, a cold beer, a special kind of soft drink, or coffee? Or perhaps a splash of Scotch, bourbon, brandy, or cognac?

HOUSEHOLD CHORES

Your character may despise sewing, ironing, washing clothes, dusting, making soup, frying chicken, balancing the checkbook, vacuuming, scouring the bathtub or sink, baking, cleaning behind the stove or refrigerator, setting mousetraps, killing roaches, gardening, canning, cleaning mirrors, making beds, changing sheets, using mothballs, peeling onions, washing windows, cleaning pots and pans, removing caked-on grease, removing spider webs, polishing the silver, setting the table, washing the dishes, or cleaning the oven. On the other hand, he may like doing one of these things.

MUSIC

Does your character like classical, jazz, rock, gospel, or country and western? Opera or musical comedy? Or barbershop quartets? Does he love the sound of a violin, guitar, banjo, trumpet, tuba, piccolo, harmonica, accordion, piano, or organ? What about drums or bagpipes; or perhaps a music box? Is there something that he can barely tolerate?

NATURE

Is there something in nature that fills the character with awe or makes him feel peaceful? Would that "something" be, for example, a range of snow-capped mountains? A great lake? A river? Is it the stillness of a desert or a cave? What about an ocean, a forest, an unexpected clearing, the jungle, or a swamp? Does he relish cold or hot weather? Is he still pleased by the sight of clouds, stars, moonlight, or a sunny day? And what's his favorite season: spring, summer, autumn, or winter?

NONATHLETIC COMPETITION
(*See also* Entertainment; Relaxation; Sports)

Does the character like to engage in a friendly game of cards? If so, does he like poker, gin rummy, bridge, canasta, pinochle? Does he drop quarters into slot machines? Wager his dollars on a game of craps or at the race track? Or does he prefer a board game, such as Scrabble, chess, checkers, backgammon, Monopoly, Chinese checkers, or Parcheesi? Possibly he prefers mah-jongg or dominos. How about horseshoes, shuffleboard, curling, or Ping-Pong? Are there any of these things he doesn't like? And if so, why?

OFFICE STUFF

If your character works in an office, perhaps he likes or dislikes one (or more) of the following: typewriters, computers, filing cabinets, in-boxes, statistics, letters, spreadsheets, budgets, meetings, reports, management directives, photocopying, paper shredding, flight reservations, conference calls, retirement parties, cost studies, supply purchasing, inter-office memos, ringing telephones, e-mail, intercoms, forms, security systems, mail, or Christmas parties. Among some of these possibilities, are there any that the character despises?

PEOPLE

Does the character dislike Caucasians, Negroes, Hispanics, Orientals, or immigrants? Has he got something against doctors, cops, organized labor, businessmen, politicians, sports stars, waiters, auto mechanics, bank clerks, repairmen, sales clerks, post office clerks, answering services, car attendants, doormen, drunks, beggars, hotel clerks, movie stars, dentists, car salesmen, mimes, the upper class, the lower-classes, snitches, cab drivers, neighbors, or meddlers? Is there anything about any of them that he likes?

PHYSICAL APPEARANCE

What if the character sees someone with whiskers, a goatee, a mustache, long hair, short hair, a toupee, a wig, pigtails, dyed hair, eyeglasses, large feet, pigeon toes, big ears, or a big nose? Is it a physical attribute that the character would not like? Does the character have a built-in prejudice against people who are short, tall, thin, overweight, bald, blonde, redheaded, gray-haired, pot bellied, wrinkled, weak-chinned, or disabled?

PLACES

Would it add anything special to the character to know that he has developed a preference for, or animosity toward, a particular kind of place where people live, such as stately mansions, apartment buildings, trailer homes, farmhouses, tract homes, shacks, military barracks, or tenements? How does he feel about city parks, libraries, museums, sport stadiums, or memorials?

If he lives in the city, surely he must like or dislike one of the following: parking garages, government buildings, traffic jams, newspaper stands, delicatessens, tall buildings, escalators, elevators, restaurants, coffee shops, big movie theaters, or subways. But if he lives in the suburbs, there are shopping malls, corner drugstores, and six-lane expressways.

Has he traveled enough to form a strong opinion about motels, hotels, airports, bus terminals, train stations, dining cars, tourist spots, rural roads, or phone booths?

And is he a true character if he does not have strong feelings about gas stations, banks, post offices, waiting rooms, public toilets, and dentists' chairs?

POLITICS

How does your character feel about politics? Has he become a cynic? Is he disgusted by smear campaigns, special-interest groups, influence peddling, wire pulling, and bombastic press conferences? Or does he in fact like all the things that go into electioneering — that is, the primaries, the nomination process, conventions, the newspaper and television editorials? Does he prefer one political party over another? If so, would you say he favors the conservative or liberal line?

RELAXATION
(*See also* Entertainment; Relaxation; Sports)

To "get away from it all," what does the character like to do to relax himself? Does he, for example, read? Work puzzles or riddles? Play computer games, pinball, pool, or solitaire? Go on camping, fishing, or hunting trips? Does he go walking, dancing, or boating? Are there any of these things he doesn't like? And if so, why?

SMELLS

What some characters find to be a pleasant fragrance, the senses of others may define it as objectionable. Your character might like or dislike any of the following smells: perfume, incense, disinfectant, hay, pipe tobacco, or cigarette smoke; the frying of bacon, sausage, onions, fish, or chicken; turkeys roasting, cakes baking, coffee brewing, peanuts roasting, popcorn popping, pies baking. What about freshly mowed grass? Honeysuckle? Fresh paint, furniture polish, or air freshener?

SPORTS
(*See also* Entertainment; Non-athletic Competition; Relaxation)

Is the character greatly attracted to some sport? If so, does he like to watch it or participate in it? Among the more obvious spectator sports are baseball, basketball, football, rugby, ice hockey, soccer, auto racing, motorcycle racing, boxing, and horse racing. Or maybe he likes to watch the Olympics.

Some of the athletic activities in which a character may participate include running, tennis, swimming, touch football, softball, handball, racquet ball, squash, golf, skiing, water polo, badminton, cricket, fencing, ice skating, field hockey, wrestling, lacrosse, polo, roller skating, sledding, volleyball, bowling, diving, hang-gliding, and discus throwing. On the other hand, are there sports activities that the character does not like?

5. What Does the Character Fear?

Any novelist, playwright, or screenwriter knows full well the powerful impact that fear can have on a character — indeed, upon an entire population. Fear is one of the devices authors use most frequently, and those who know how to use it well are able to make readers or viewers squirm, or perhaps feel protective toward at least one of the characters. Horror-story writers are particularly adept at employing fear to frighten the living daylights out of their audiences, and there is no comfort in knowing that the hero or heroine in the story is scared witless as well.

However, with no offense intended toward those who (1) write spine-tingling tales filled with dark shadows, echoing footsteps, creaking doors, and screams in the night, or (2) concoct adventure stories that leave heroes dangling from moving airplanes or running down alleyways to escape sword-wielding headhunters, this section focuses instead upon the kinds of fears with which most people can identify. The kinds of fears, for example, that silently creep up on us, begin gnawing away, and make us feel helpless. The kinds of fears that help to build plots around interesting, believable characters.

Character-centered fears may build slowly, but eventually they gain momentum and cause the character to make some kind of a decision. In determining a character-centered fear, first ask yourself this very important question: *Is the fear justified?* If it isn't, then it is probably self-inflicted. That in turn will introduce a whole new set of circumstances, but it does not make the fear any less important to the character. For example, a woman may fear that her husband doesn't love her anymore, though in fact he may adore her more than ever — but he's a salesman in debt and he must work a great deal just to pay the mortgage and keep food on the table. Obviously this situation presents numerous plot possibilities. If, on the other hand, her fears are justified, the plot will take entirely different avenues — all just as plausible.

After the writer has determined whether the fear is justified, more questions naturally follow. The following list of possible fears suggests the types of questions that each brings to the table.

ABANDONMENT

What would make the character fearful of being abandoned, and who does he think will do it? Has that person threatened to leave him before? Indeed, has the character ever been abandoned by anyone? If so, who did it? What were the circumstances? When and where did it happen?

If his fear is realized, does he know anyone who might come to his assistance? If so, who is it, and would that person actually help? Is the character afraid of being left to fend for himself in an environment that he views as hostile to his safety?

Or is his fear of abandonment not that he will be left alone physically, but rather emotionally? Has he been assured by others that they will stand by him if he decides to challenge someone's authority regarding some issue? Nevertheless, is he afraid that they would go back on their word, leaving him alone to face a serious threat?

What will happen if he is abandoned? What will happen if he is not?

CHANGE

If the threat of change frightens the character, what is its precise nature and why would it threaten him so? Or is he simply afraid that change *might* take place? If change were indeed to take place, who would gain and who would lose?

Assuming a change is imminent, does it promise to be a sweeping one or just a minor modification? Does change scare the character because he has become comfortable with the way things have been and he does not like the uncertainty that accompanies change? What aspect of the prospective change fills him with the most dread? Is he afraid, for example, that change will cause something to be irretrievably lost? Does he see change as a catapult toward disaster?

Has he always been afraid of change? Is being a holdout a part of his history? Does he cling desperately to vestiges of a time long since past?

What will happen if the change takes place over his objections? What if he is successful at preventing it?

DEATH

While it's true that almost everyone fears death, does that fear drive the character to desperately avoid death within the story? In what way does he avoid it? Has the fear of death always been front-and-center within his mind, or has it increased in prominence because of his age or because of a set of unfavorable circumstances in which he now finds himself? In the latter instance, does he perhaps fear execution, or losing his life in some other unnatural way?

Is he afraid of taking his last breath because he is convinced that the body he has will become worm food or because the darkness of "nothingness" is too frightening for words? Does the "great beyond" terrify him because he is afraid he will have to answer for what he has done in this life? Is he afraid that he has the same genetic disorder that killed one of his parents and a grandparent?

Has the fear of death rendered him a coward? Put him in a position where he is in perpetual retreat? Deprived him of peace?

DESTRUCTION

What does the character fear will be destroyed? Is it something he has revered, always tried to protect, been a part of? Is it something with a real dollar value, or does it have an intrinsic value that makes it irreplaceable (or both)? If it is destroyed, what does the character think will be lost? Who or what threatens this destruction, and who will lose if it takes place?

Has the threat of destruction been coming closer, and has the character tried to warn others? Has anything like this ever happened before? Does it portend something that the character fears even more?

What will happen if the destruction occurs?

DISHONOR

Has the character done something that he fears could bring dishonor upon himself? Who has evidence that could undo his reputation and lead to his being held up to public ridicule? Perhaps he has done nothing to be ashamed of, yet someone in the story threatens to tell a lie about him and there is a possibility of it being believed. If so, what will that fear cause the character to do?

On the other hand, is he afraid that he will be dishonored if he *does not* do something? Will this fear cause him to become involved in something that is contrary to his nature? Is he in a social climate so heated with self-righteousness that he is given no alternative but to act indignantly — and with force? Will he desperately look for a way out, while at the same time, to satisfy onlookers, appear to be heeding honor's call?

Or does he fear dishonor not for himself but for someone who is close to him, such as a dear friend or a member of his immediate family? And what will he do to protect that person's reputation?

But what if he fails to protect his honor, or that of a friend? What exactly will happen?

DISCOVERY
(*See also* Truth)

What is the character afraid will be discovered? Is it a secret, such as his true identity? A piece of valuable evidence? The missing link? His life savings buried in a box? Love letters that will expose an affair? *Who* does he fear might find what he prefers to keep hidden, and what steps will he take to try to prevent it?

Or is the fear not about what others might discover, but rather what he himself might find? If this is the case, why must he keep looking? Why not be vanquished by the fear that surrounds him and abandon the search for good? What drives him to find what he is fearful of finding?

In either case, in what way will discovery affect the character? How will it affect those who know him? And would everyone be better off if no discovery occurred?

FAILURE

Why is the character afraid to fail? What will be the consequences if he does? Is it just a matter of his self-esteem, or is it far more serious than that? For example, has he made a promise that he believes he dare not break? Or would failure mean the loss of wealth, the disintegration of fame, a great loss of respect, or perhaps the abandonment of future opportunities? What exactly is on the line if failure should come? To what lengths will he go to ensure that he does not fail? Has the character placed himself in a position where failure is unthinkable? What if failure comes anyway?

HARM

No one, except perhaps a masochist, wants to be harmed. But if your character has a greater-than-average fear of harm, does it mean that he will avoid all kinds of confrontation? Will it then be easy for others to taunt him, or for one character to make him look cowardly or foolish in front of others? Is he the type that says in all seriousness, "I don't want any trouble"? Does fear of harm make him an appeaser, or perhaps a bootlicker? Does it keep him in a perpetual defensive position?

Is the character afraid that someone will harm him by taking his money? Separate him from possessions or friends? Or is he fearful of becoming ill or disabled, and as a result become a prime target for every health craze that comes down the road? Is he always on the run from something that he thinks may hurt him?

HELL

If the character is fearful of Hell, then he apparently believes there is a place where sinners are sent after they die. What, then, is his conception of it? Is it fire and brimstone? A black bottomless pit from which no one ever returns? A trek over endless fields of wretchedness?

Does his fear of Hell cause him to go to church more than he would like? Is he likely to ask for the Lord's forgiveness for even thinking about sinful things? Does his fear prompt him always to look for signs of the Devil? Is he constantly in a wrestling match with his conscience? Does he frequently find himself in an internal sweat, wanting something that is forbidden and, at the same time, cursing himself for having the desire?

How far will his fear of damnation chase him?

AN IDEA

First of all, why would an abstraction, such as an idea, make the character fearful? If it is only an idea and not yet a reality, why not simply ignore it? Or is it an idea too threatening or significant to ignore? Does it promise to upset the status quo? Get people to talking? Does the idea contain principles or information that directly contradicts almost everything the character has been led to believe is true? Does it undermine the position he holds? Threaten his friendships or family? Contain elements that may affect the whole of his society? And what will happen if others take the new idea seriously?

Does he fear the idea because it is based upon unsound or malevolent principles? Is he afraid that if the idea is allowed to spread, it will become infectious and do great harm?

If he is fearful of the idea, what can he do to stop it? And what if he does not?

INJUSTICE

What has happened in the story that makes the character fear injustice? Or what has happened *before* the story begins that has led him to fear it? Is he familiar with the sound of its footsteps? Has he perhaps felt its sting in the past? And has that experience made him forever fearful of its return?

What is the nature of the injustice that he specifically fears? Or is it injustice by any name? Does he fear it because it threatens him, someone else, or everyone? Has injustice reared its head in the wake of accusation? Is it possible that he or someone else will not be treated fairly, become guilty by association, or be given no chance to explain? Is there someone calling for justice, when it's really injustice that person wants?

Perhaps the injustice the character fears is more in the nature of neglect. For example, is he afraid that someone will be forgotten, someone who greatly deserves reverence?

In the end, regardless of its nature, what will the character do if the injustice seems inevitable?

JEALOUSY

Whose jealousy is it that the character has come to fear? Has the character had some previous experience with this poisonous emotion, so that the possibility of a reoccurrence now fills him with dread? Does he fear the jealousy will come from one person or several? What will the character do to prevent someone from feeling jealous toward him? And if the jealousy does in fact reappear and threaten the character's well-being, what will he do to cool its passion? What options does he have at his disposal, and what has he used before?

LONELINESS

Setting aside the possibility of autophobia, which is the unnatural fear of being alone, the fear of loneliness referred to here is really quite commonplace and can take on many forms. It is that empty spot that craves companionship, that corner in the soul that needs some light. It is the thing that gives birth to singles bars and matchmakers, the thing that moans when a good friend leaves; it is that hole we all try to fill.

In what way, then, does your character fear loneliness? What bond is he afraid will be broken? Is a good friend near death? Has a spouse departed? Have the children grown up and moved away? Is he afraid there will be no one with whom to share his life, to talk about nothing in particular, to simply sit and feel the warmth that comes with liking and loving? Is there no human rock to lean upon?

Has he grown old, perhaps? Are the memories not enough?

Fearing loneliness as he does, what will the character do when it seems forthcoming or when, in fact, it arrives?

MARRIAGE

Why would the character be afraid of marriage? Is it because he has been married before and it turned out to be a dismal experience? Did he find it too confining? Too demanding of his time? Too much of one thing and not enough of another?

Or does he, perhaps, guard his independence relentlessly and fear that marriage will destroy it? Has he seen, with dismay, what has happened to his friends after they tied the knot? Did his parents argue all the time or not talk for long periods? And has that experience soured him on marriage?

Has he seen what divorces do to people, and is he afraid his marriage will end the same way? And so what will he do if his loved one wants a wedding? What steps will he take to prevent it?

OMENS

If the character fears an omen, does he have a tendency to fear them all? Or is there just one that fills him with dread? In either case, does this fear mean that he is superstitious? Is he always looking for signs of the future?

Does the character try to tell others about what he sees? If so, what do they say when they hear his concerns? Are the omens he fears of ancient vintage? Just where, in fact, has he learned them, and why does he tend to accept them unequivocally?

If an omen occurs within the story, how will it be delivered? Will someone speak it, such as the soothsayer did in *Julius Caesar* ("Beware the Ides of March"), or will it be observed within the hand of nature (the possibilities of which are numerous)?

POVERTY

If the character fears poverty, is it because he once experienced it and never wants to live through it again? Does this fear cause him to be stingy with the wealth he has obtained? Does it make him want more than he could ever possibly use?

But does the character live modestly among others and have no great material possessions? If so, is the poverty he fears more terrible than any he has so far experienced? Is he, for example, the poor dirt farmer who watches his farm being sold at auction? Is he the person who, without any insurance and perhaps no job, watches the flood waters draw closer to his house?

What recourse does the character have if his fears draw closer to reality?

PUNISHMENT

What has the character done, and to whom has he done it, that he has come to fear some degree of punishment? Has he committed a crime? Engaged in a mortal sin? Broken a promise, perhaps? Is he afraid he will somehow be punished for his display of cowardice, or his weakness of the flesh, or the lies he blatantly told? Whose wrath makes him writhe: that of God, or someone human? And what does he think will be the extent of the retaliation? Does he fear tit-for-tat or something much worse?

Does he fear punishment that is physical in nature, or is more psychological, perhaps ostracism? Does he fear losing what he can never regain?

Will someone in the story come to his defense? On the other hand, who will not?

REJECTION

From which direction has the character come to fear rejection, and why does he place so much importance on the opinion of that person or group? Does he lack self-confidence, and would disapproval shatter his already badly broken ego? Has he suffered rejection in the past, thus establishing in his mind the likelihood that it will happen again? Was he, for example, rejected by his mother, father, or someone else he loved? A group he wanted to join? An employer? Has he ever been fired or expelled? Has he or his family been refused admittance to a certain neighborhood? And why — because of his skin color? His religion? His background?

Or is the character's fear of rejection focused in another direction? For instance, is he afraid that if he issues orders they won't be followed? That if he tells someone to do something, he will hear laughter or snickers?

What will he do to prevent rejection? And what will he do if it happens anyway?

RESTORATION

What does the character fear will be restored? For him, what will the restoration bring to an end or threaten? Perhaps he is afraid his parents, who have been separated, are reconciling, and he doesn't want what he experienced before. Or maybe he fears that his country is reestablishing a system of government that didn't work the first time and he is sure will not work again. Or could it be that his spouse is reverting to the kinds of habits that threatened the family last time?

What pain may accompany the restoration if it comes? What can the character do to prevent it from taking place? What is he unable to do?

SEPARATION

From whom is the character fearful of being separated? (Note: The key words are "fearful of being," not "doesn't want to be"). And why would the separation make him afraid? What does he stand to lose by not being with that person? Does he desperately need someone's presence nearby?

Or from *what* is the character fearful of being separated? A job that he dearly loves? A way of life with which he feels quite comfortable? Is he afraid of leaving something he has found, because he is convinced it will not be there when he returns?

What are his options to prevent such a separation?

SUCCESS

We are all so attuned to reaching whatever lies just beyond our out-stretched hands that it may be hard to imagine a character who fears success. Such a fear is nevertheless quite possible. For example, someone who has grown accustomed to living a rather uneventful life, and who in fact rather enjoys his lackluster daily routine, may suddenly become quite fearful if for some reason he is faced with unusual success. It could upset his status quo, and the liabilities that attend his success could truly frighten him.

Imagine, if you will, a downtrodden character who wins the lottery. Hav-ing survived his own rush of excitement, he begins to see that his life will never be the same again. His in-laws want money; his neighbors beg for loans; his kids want new cars; strangers with confusing investment schemes are knocking on his door and calling him on the phone; and his wife has seem-ingly gone half crazy and is too busy to put food on the table for him. The only thing that has remained constant is his dog, which he pets as he vacantly stares into the unknown. His fear of monetary success is real.

Or how about this? The character has a good idea — the likes of which he will never come close to having again — and he is suddenly promoted by his employer. Might he become fearful that everyone will find out he's not nearly as smart, or as imaginative, or as clever, or as farsighted as they think he is? His unexpected career success might immobilize him.

THEFT

What is the character afraid will be stolen from him? Is it something that can be easily seen, or is it hidden? Is it worth a lot of money, or its value exclu-sively sentimental? And who does he suspect might try to steal it from him? Has anyone ever tried to steal it before? If so, why did the attempt fail?

What can the character do to ensure its safekeeping? Could he put it in the hands of someone he trusts? Is there a place where he can hide it?

What will happen if the theft takes place?

TRUTH
(*See also* Discovery)

Why would the character be fearful of the truth? What is it that he doesn't want to know? Is it something he suspects, but does not want to accept? Would that truth dismantle everything he has always believed? Why does he prefer the fiction over the fact? Does the truth threaten to lead him to a place where he does not want to go? Will it, in the end, upset his world? Alter his affections? Make him walk into a light that he has tried to avoid?

How will a new revelation affect those whom he knows? Would their knowing make things quite difficult? Does he fear the results that the truth would bring?

What will he do to evade the truth? And what will happen if he cannot?

VIOLENCE

The person who fears violence should not be confused with one who fears harm. The fear in this case results from the character's observation of a developing trend, one in which the tentacles of violence appear long before the whole monster becomes apparent, and that view will make him shudder with concern — not for himself but for others.

For example, such a person might have lived in Nazi Germany and seen the cruelty emerging. Such a person would certainly be shaken by present-day incidents of terrorism.

The fictional character who is fearful of violence will see things on a broader scale. The question is, what will he do to help the intended victims? What will he do to stop the offender?

A Word About Phobias

Phobias are irrational fears. Sometimes they are inexplicable. A writer who instills a character with a phobia generally has three choices: (1) use it to merely heighten the dramatic impact of an upcoming scene and add spice to the plot; (2) carefully and gently weave it into the character's overall psychology throughout the story and make it one of the key factors that increasingly causes him to avoid what he sees as potentially hazardous situations; (3) both of the foregoing.

Take the first option. Early in the movie *Raiders of the Lost Ark*, the audience learns that the hero has an inordinate fear of snakes. Planting this phobia in the mind of the audience is important, because later in the story the character suddenly finds himself hanging precariously over a pit that is teeming with all kinds of snakes. At the sight of the snakes, viewers audibly gasp, and their empathy for the main character is decidedly swift. Mind you, snakes are scary anyway, but the character's phobia intensifies the scene. Receiving the information about the character's phobia early in the story made the scene much more exciting to watch.

The second option raises the stakes considerably. When a character is provided with a phobia that affects his everyday behavior, it requires a deft touch and considerable patience on the part of the writer. It is not sufficient to lightly implant the notion of a phobia in the mind of the reading or viewing audience and hope it will be remembered when the time comes. The writer must keep nailing the concept home — but carefully. The skillful writer will usually do this by establishing the character's mental aversion very early in the story and then putting obstacles in his path that will help bring that phobia front and center, not just once but several times.

Sometimes it is important to relate the incident that originally instilled the phobia. Indeed, the reader or viewer may not take the phobia seriously if that phobia's starting point is not clear (the character can talk about it; it doesn't always have to be shown). The foundation of that phobia could prove crucially important not only to character development but also to plot development.

Imagine that you are writing a story in which one of your main characters has claustrophobia. It began with an experience in childhood, and that fear of closed-in spaces has only gotten worse over the years. He must live in a place with lots of windows; he cannot bear small rooms (he is terrified of closets and basements); and he has gotten to the point where he can hardly ride in an automobile. How does this behavior affect his family? His friends? What steps does he take each day to prevent confronting his fears? In the hands of an insightful and sensitive writer, this claustrophobic character can wring great sympathy from a reader or viewer. Moreover, the character need not necessarily find closure by conquering the fear or doing something in spite of it, *e.g.*, nervously going into a cave to save his daughter, who is trapped. To prevent collapsing the story into melodrama, the writer may prefer to have that character continuing to struggle with claustrophobia after "The End" is written.

If the writer chooses the third option, however, then a pay-off scene will be required, in which the character is forced to come face to face with the phobia in a big way — that is, in a manner that will cause the reader to gasp right along with the character. This will have a greater impact than if the writer simply chose the first option, primarily because the writer will have laid plenty of groundwork during the story. But the author who wants a scene that plays big at the end of the story will first have to paint the character with meticulous brushstrokes, with each stroke leading up to a convincing and affecting portrait in the moment of do-or-die.

Here are some phobias that offer some potential:

animals (zoophobia)	dark (nyctophobia)
anything new (neophobia)	dead bodies (necrophobia)
being touched (haptephobia)	death (thanatophobia)
blood (hemophobia)	depth (bathophobia)
burial alive (taphephobia)	dogs (cynophobia)
cats (ailurophobia)	falling asleep (hypnophobia)
closed spaces (claustrophobia)	food (sitiophobia)
contamination (mysophobia)	high places (acrophobia)
crossing streets (dromophobia)	light (photophobia)
crowds (demophobia)	lightning (astraphobia)

men (androphobia)
mice (musophobia)
open spaces (agoraphobia)
pain (algophobia)
poison (toxiphobia)
sea (thalassophobia)
sex (genophobia)

snakes (ophidiophobia)
strangers (xenophobia)
syphilis (syphilophobia)
thunder (brontophobia)
water (hydrophobia)
women (gynophobia)

6. What Does the Character Believe?

It's not necessary for a writer to be concerned about what a fictional character believes if that belief is not going to add anything important either to the development of the story or to a better understanding of the character himself. Suppose, for example, that a character believes vegetables are healthier than meat. That information is not going to do much more than possibly set up a good joke for another character. Apart from that possibility, it is scarcely worth mentioning, because the author has more important things to do with the plot. If, however, this same character believes that Caucasian gentiles are a superior race, the impact of this belief could be very important. As a result of such a belief, the character may belong to a neo–Nazi group and could be making plans to kill a local Jewish shopkeeper. Serious stuff, in terms of storytelling and character development.

Every writer knows that creating a story populated by interesting characters is a discovery process. The purpose of this chapter (indeed, of all the chapters in this book) is to help you discover as much as you can in the shortest possible time. This chapter will not tell you when and how to insert a character's belief, nor what kind of belief should be used. Rather, it simply points the way to areas that are available for your exploration. If you find something that you think fits your character and could possibly help to provide a dimension that you may have otherwise neglected, then this chapter will have been worth your review.

Let's begin by stating the obvious: a writer may provide one of his characters with either a temporary belief or a core belief — or both, for that matter.

A *temporary belief* exists only until it is proven wrong. That doesn't mean the belief cannot be firmly encased within the mind of a character: indeed, anything that is just half believed wouldn't even qualify as a temporary belief. It just means that nothing has come along in the story to shoot the belief down. For instance, Tom can believe Dick murdered Harry, but if he later finds out that John was the killer — poof! Goodbye, belief.

The death of a temporary belief can often be detected when one character says to another, "I find it hard to believe that she could do such a thing." But she did. Scratch one belief.

All temporary beliefs have the potential for creating action. If, for example, a character decides to settle a dispute between two people because he *believes* he has influence over one of them, he may find out not only that he was wrong but that they have also turned their anger upon him. The ensuing comedy could be delicious, as the peacemaker tries to hide from them and the plot takes a different turn altogether.

A *core belief* is something that a character acquires over an extended period of time, and it is always the result of education, either formal or informal. Core beliefs accumulate over a person's lifetime, and in the end they form a makeshift philosophy. Pieced together, they become as unique as a set of fingerprints, for no one else will think about everything in exactly the same way as that particular person. It will be a hodgepodge of such influences as church instruction, the belief of one's mother and father, the things one reads, some public attitudes, and first-hand experience. Moreover, it usually takes a great deal more than a single piece of evidence to make anyone let go of a core belief; indeed, any attempt to dislodge such a belief constitutes a great psychological threat, and a person will usually defend a core belief with considerable vigor.

Whether a belief resides in a person's core or is destined to be only temporary, the reasons can be narrowed down to six:

1. *The character has experienced something.*
2. *The character has seen something.*
3. *The character has heard something.*
4. *The character has read something.*
5. *The character has been taught something.*
6. *The character has intuitively felt something.*

When the writer decides that a character's belief is somehow essential to the story he or she is trying to tell, the nature of the belief may require the writer to make at least one of several different decisions. For example: Is it necessary to explore the roots of the character's belief? Is it the result of a conversion? Is the belief incorrect? If the character finds out he is wrong, will his belief change? In what way do the character's beliefs control him? Does he share his beliefs with others, or does he keep them to himself? Is there anyone in the story who is appalled by what the character believes? Does the character try to convert anyone else to his way of thinking? Finally — and this is very important — is the character truly in possession of this conviction, or is he only serving as a mouthpiece for you, the author?

Now, let's look at some possibilities.

FORMAL PHILOSOPHIES

What follows is a brief explanation of some specific philosophies. In trying to fashion a rather loose philosophy for a character you have in mind, you may find something here that fits his nature. You could even use a combination of two or more.

Agnostic

Holds the opinion that nothing in life, including God and the origin of life itself, can be known by man.

Atheist

Convinced that God does not exist. Lacks any true faith. Sometimes called an infidel.

Deist

Believes that God exists, but completely rejects the idea that the Christian scriptures (Bible) are God's revelation.

Dualist

Believes that the universe is neither idealistic nor materialistic, but rather is comprised of mind and matter. A *theological* dualist sees life as a struggle between the forces of good and evil. An *ethical* dualist, however, thinks it is proper to alter one's conduct to satisfy the social group one is in.

Empiricist

Thinks that all knowledge is gained through the senses.

Hedonist

Believes in self-indulgence; permits himself to excessively engage in all pleasures available to him.

Humanist

Believes that man's cultural and practical interests and developments are more important than those that are material or scientific.

Materialist

Places more value on man's earthly interests.

Mystic

Convinced that he is especially in union with God and that he has been given spiritual knowledge, gained through either intuition or meditation. In this capacity he may initiate, or be a rapt witness to, certain occult rites.

Naturalist

Holds the belief that all things occur because of natural causes and that they can be scientifically explained.

Nominalist

Thinks that abstract ideas have no reality and are names only.

Pantheist

Believes that everything that exists, including that which we cannot see — such as the boundless journey of our minds — is, in fact, God.

Positivist

Rejects pure speculation. Believes that only well-known facts, including that which can be perceived, represent the only worthwhile knowledge.

Pragmatist

Accepts the reality of intangible ideas and thoughts, and yet measures their worth by their practicality only.

Rationalist

Convinced that elusive truth and knowledge can be gained only through reason, not experience.

Realist

Spurns ideals and accepts only what he knows to be facts; yet he believes that abstract concepts, *e.g.*, love and hate, have an existence that is more real than physical matter.

Supernaturalist

Convinced that a higher power transcends natural law, that events are divinely inspired.

Theist

Feels sure that God is perfect; that He is the creator and ruler of the universe.

Utilitarian

Believes that the greatest good for most of the people should be the goal, and he leans heavily toward material needs rather than spiritual. In his eyes, usefulness is the great leveler.

Vitalist

Holds that intuition is greater than intellect, and esteems man's inherent creative power. Believes that the beginning of life was not organic or material.

INFORMAL PHILOSOPHIES

Everyone has an informal philosophy of some sort. It is always nameless and is comprised of convictions that cover a broad range of subjects. An informal philosophy is always in the process of being recreated, with some parts being dropped and new ones added. What follows are several of the categories from which informal philosophies are born. Bear in mind, however, that there is some overlapping — that is, some beliefs will appear in more than one category but possibly under a different name.

Basic Concepts

Based solely upon what the character has observed during his own lifetime, and therefore placing all textbook definitions aside, in what way does the character view courage, cowardice, wisdom, unkindness, nobility, morality, corruption, success, achievement, friendship, justice, injustice, selfishness, beauty, forgiveness, ingratitude, respect, freedom, virtue, vice, wrongdoing, education, love, marriage, a promise, blame, fairness, friendship, change?

Does he have any convictions about the field of business, big or small? For example, does he think the free enterprise system works for everyone or just a minority? Does he believe the businessman must be constantly monitored, lest he take unnecessary advantage of the common man?

Does he believe a parent owes a child anything? If so, what is it? Love? Attention? Lodging? Food on the table? Schooling? Clothes? And where does the obligation end, or does he think it ever does?

What are his convictions regarding work? That no job is too small to do well? That if he doesn't do it, no one else will? That a person is measured by the quality of the job he or she does? That the common man does all the work and the big shots don't do any? Or, like Eliza Doolittle's father in *My Fair Lady*, does he believe that "with a little bit of luck" the work will be done by someone else?

With respect to the past, does the character believe that one must learn from it? That one can never go home again? That what's done is done, and nothing comes from regret? That the present is far more important?

Regarding the future, does the character believe that one should prepare for it, or is he of the opinion that what will be, will be?

Duty to Oneself

Does the character believe his only responsibility is to look out for himself? That it's a dog-eat-dog world and no one is going to look out for Number One if he doesn't do it? Does he believe that the welfare of others should not be his concern? Is he of the opinion that, to get what he wants, all other things might be sacrificed? Is he convinced that the pursuit of self-gratification should stand at the center of one's thinking?

Duty to Others

Does the character believe he is morally obligated to help, protect, and care for others when it is within his power to do so? Does he believe in doing unto others as he would have them do unto him? Does he believe he must value friendships? Keep promises? Be forgiving? Display good manners? Respect opinions different from his own? Be fair in his dealings with others? Tell the truth? Does he think it is incumbent upon him to be an educator when necessary? To provide charity when it is needed? To engage in compromise?

Eternal Questions

What are the character's beliefs regarding God and Satan? How does he feel about creation and evolution? Heaven and Hell? Man's free will or predestination? Reincarnation, ghosts, and angels? Prophecy? Evil spirits? Omens?

What does he believe constitutes a good person — that is, what does the character believe is virtuous? (For example, Plato named justice, temperance, prudence, and fortitude as the four cardinal virtues. To this group the Christian moralists added three more: faith, hope, and charity. Are these the traits your character believes represent moral excellence?)

Does the character believe that the worth of individuals should be measured by what they display in terms of fairness, honesty, sexual purity, kindness, trustworthiness, sense of obligation?

But how about wickedness? Does the character believe that the seven deadly sins, as described in medieval literature, are avarice, sloth, wrath, lust, envy, pride, and gluttony? Does he believe that human vice includes dishonesty? Corruption? Abandonment? Malevolence? What does he believe constitutes an evil person?

Feelings About the Government

What beliefs does he hold regarding the role of government in the lives of people? Without necessarily being a member of a political party, does he align himself with the principles of one of them? Does he believe what is espoused by the conservatives? The liberals? The radicals? Or those who try to stay in the middle of the road?

What does he believe to be good about his government, and what does he think are its bad features? If he believes changes should be made, what are they?

Does the character believe in a democracy, a monarchy, a dictatorship, a socialist state, a communist state?

Does he think people should be taxed? Does he think his political system ignores the needs of one class and promotes, as well as protects, the interests of another? Is he of the opinion that a little rebellion now and then is a good thing?

PROVERBS

Just about everyone, at one time or another, will utter a cliché that will in turn summarize how he feels about a certain situation. These statements usually serve as a verbal shorthand and provide a quick insight with regard to something that an individual believes. Some examples:

> **Practicality:** Handsome is as handsome does.
> **Sexual Equality:** What's good for the goose is good for the gander.
> **Perseverance:** If at first you don't succeed, try, try again.
> **Leniency:** Spare the rod, spoil the child.
> **Compromise:** To get along, you've got to go along.

Do you know of a proverb that one of your characters might use that would summarize how he feels about something?

EXTREMISM

A person who leaps head first into extremism — *i.e.,* the total acceptance and fervid promotion of all tenets pertaining to a particular philosophy — is almost always a person who spurns all reason and sees things in black and white only. Consequently, his beliefs are "good" in his eyes and anything contradictory is of course "bad." In his mind, there are no gray areas and therefore there is no room for discussion. More often than not, he becomes an unqualified mouthpiece for the philosophy he supports, spewing slogans in all directions like a volcano belching ash.

The three most common extremists are the disciple, the dogmatist, and the fanatic, and writers have frequently used them as characters in their stories, within which they usually appear as either tragic or comic figures. The line that divides these three is extremely fine, and some traits that can be found in one can also be found in another.

Disciple

The disciple accepts, without question, all aspects of a particular doctrine or the teachings of someone who espouses that doctrine, or both. He frequently promotes not only the tenets of the doctrine but the virtues of its leader as well. He is melded into the group and becomes subservient to it. As such, his personality becomes significantly modified. He takes pride in the sacrifices he has made, the hardships he has endured, and the time he has devoted on behalf of the "cause."

Dogmatist

The dogmatist and disciple are much alike, except that the dogmatist is more prone to slide into anger whenever his beliefs are challenged. For the most part, the dogmatist is likely to be quite stubborn and inflexible. He does not like to admit he is wrong. He will speak long and loud about what he sees as the merits of his philosophy, but he will have no patience whatsoever with any statements that counter his claims. To him, dissent is intolerable. The dogmatist is, metaphorically, a table-pounder. If any subject comes up that challenges his beliefs, he will fight to have the last word; otherwise, he may well be silent and look for instances where he can feed and greatly nourish his convictions.

Fanatic

The fanatic is a character whose self-conviction is no longer enough; he must pound everyone else into his way of thinking as well. He is a lightning bolt of lopsided thought. Rather than compromise, it is kill or be killed. So dark and stifling is his extremism that simple reason — poor thing — has no room to breathe. His frenzy of enthusiasm for or against something perverts his behavior and twists it completely out of the norm. This is a character who supports measures that place him at the forefront of danger. Here is the anarchist, the zealot, and the wild-eyed radical who is willing to sacrifice himself and others in the name of the cause.

7. What Are the Character's Strengths, Weaknesses, and Habits?

The strengths or weaknesses that cause plots to thicken are almost always members of a character's internal family of traits (a rather extensive list of which appears in Chapter 1). In *Othello*, for example, Shakespeare uses the persuasive skill of one character (Iago) to play upon the gullibility of another (Othello), who easily becomes convinced of his wife's infidelity.

Some strengths or weaknesses, however, are secondary, and if they have any plot-generating ability at all it is severely limited. Case in point: In the motion picture *Rainman*, one of the main characters (brilliantly portrayed by Dustin Hoffman) is autistic, but he has the remarkable ability of instantly calculating large numbers in his head. His brother takes advantage of that skill to make himself some quick money at the gambling table. Afterwards, this particular strength fades quickly in importance, and a much greater emphasis is placed upon the evolving relationship between the two brothers.

The purpose of this chapter is to draw your attention to those *secondary* strengths, weaknesses, and habits your character may have — the kind that add only an extra interesting facet and little more.

Now, in most cases, whether it is of principal or secondary importance, a character's strength will be seen as a positive trait and his weakness as a negative one. On the other hand, it may depend upon who's doing the looking, for strengths and weaknesses can surely be an arbitrary matter. One character may view another's strength as a weakness and his weakness as a strength. It all depends on how the author tells the tale, and upon which character he bestows the ability to understand the difference.

In either case, it will do the writer little good to assign a particular strength or weakness to a character if it is not somehow going to be tested during the story. For example, it would be pointless to let the reader or viewer know that a certain character has a photographic memory if he or she is never going to be placed in a situation where that strength can be displayed.

Besides strengths and weaknesses, this chapter will also briefly examine some habits — another device for adding true-to-life detail or dimension to your characters.

STRENGTHS AND WEAKNESSES

There are two kinds of strengths and weaknesses: inherited and acquired. The difference is important.

Bestowed at conception, an *inherited strength* is viewed as a blessing and is often called a talent. Its presence is inexplicable, and it can develop into an extraordinary skill.

By contrast, an *inherited weakness* is usually seen as a curse that is blamed upon the recipient's ancestors. It is usually called a failing, and often inspires mean remarks like, "You can't turn a sow's ear into a silk purse." Usually, someone with very little ability in a certain area will not show much interest in it. Obviously, there are exceptions: there are bad actors in the movies and in the theater, for example, and press reviews attacking their ability seem unable to diminish their enthusiasm.

An *acquired strength* gives credence to that old saying, "Practice makes perfect." One is not born an expert marksman, for example; it takes a lot of shooting (and missing) to become one.

An *acquired weakness*, on the other hand, is an inability to pass up what the body or mind has become accustomed to. At some point in life a person may be irresistibly lured toward the direction of something that should be left untouched, and forever after he may suffer the same temptation. To resist the temptation, even just once, is to enjoy a small moment of heroism. Ex-smokers know the feeling.

Does one of your characters have a particular strength or weakness that may help to distinguish him from others in the story?

In terms of strength, for example, does the character have a strong memory? Exceptional will power? An aptitude for mechanics or mathematics? Does he have a strong sense of direction? Outstanding eyesight? The ability to recuperate quickly? A keen attention to detail? Does he have a superb physical agility or stamina?

Regarding his weaknesses, is he afflicted with asthma, poor eyesight or hearing, bad coordination, a low sex drive? Is he forgetful? Is it hard for him to pay attention? Does he have below-average organizational skills, or perhaps rotten taste in clothes? Is he unable to stay away from cigarettes, candy, beer, whiskey, or desserts? Is he a coffee junkie?

It is not practical, or even possible, to list all the strengths and weaknesses that one might encounter among human beings. The important thing is to start thinking in that direction. As you develop your fictional character, surely you will be able to develop the strengths and weaknesses that are more pertinent.

But it might help to think of a character's strengths and weaknesses as falling into one of three categories: physical, mental, or social. The *physical* could include anything that involves using the body in some way, with hand quickness, singing, nimbleness, extraordinary eyesight, and stylishness being among some of the possibilities. *Mental* strengths or weaknesses could involve numbers, intuitiveness, the arrangement of concepts, navigation, memory, solving puzzles, keeping track of things, and so on. The *social* aspect always involves interacting with other people; some of us are good at it and some of us are not. A character who has a strength or weakness in this area could be either gifted or woefully inadequate when it comes to keeping peace in the family, telling jokes and stories, motivating others, lovemaking, developing friendships, mixing well with strangers, and so on.

HABITS

Essentially, there are two kinds of habits in which human beings will engage: voluntary and involuntary.

Voluntary habits are those routines we follow on a regular basis, and they need not necessarily be accompanied by sound reasoning. *They are the kinds of actions that, for some reason, we do not like to see interrupted; when they are, conflict often results.* If, say, there is one washing machine in a small apartment building and a certain tenant has a habit of washing her clothes on Monday, imagine the argument that might ensue if a new tenant wanted to wash her clothes on Monday as well. In that light, a character's particular habit can be used to say something important about his or her nature, as well as perhaps add a new dimension to the plot.

An *involuntary* habit usually occurs with no help from one's conscious mind. It represents a form of behavior that, while not necessarily persistent, will occur often enough to be viewed as a habit by others who observe it. *For storytelling purposes, more often than not it is the kind of habit that gets on other people's nerves.* A character who unconsciously picks his nose while reading a book, or blinks his eyes a lot, or invariably clears his throat while speaking, or nervously taps his fingers, or hums off tune in the shower could eventually test someone's patience.

Whether voluntary or involuntary, a character's habit may not be seen as either a strength or weakness. Rather, it will be a peculiarity that could possibly have some potential for plot-building or comedy, or both.

8. What Is the Character's Background?

What is there about the character's background that is important for the reader or viewer to know? What purpose will be served by presenting it? Put another way, would anything be lost, or would the nature of the character be rendered less clear, if nothing at all was written about some of the things that have happened in the character's life prior to the beginning of the story?

Or look at it from your side: What could possibly exist in the character's background that would help you, the writer, to better understand him or her, and which in turn would possibly allow you to convey that character to your audience more effectively?

If it is in fact important for the reader or viewer to learn something about the character's background, how should that information be presented? Should it appear in the form of one or more flashbacks? Should it be revealed through a casual first- or third-person narrative? For the sake of suspense, would it be better to merely hint of the past and not get into specifics? Should insight into a character's background be limited to only a throw-away line, or should it consume one or more chapters? Only you know what's best for your characters and your story. Only you know what kind of imprint the past has left on a character's psychology.

If you wish to delve into a character's past, either for the benefit of your audience or because you have a need to know as much as possible about someone before committing him or her to paper, what follows are some background categories that you may wish to review. Among the questions presented within a particular category, there may be something that could lead you to a truth you might have otherwise overlooked — or to further questions that will eventually point you in the right direction.

ACHIEVEMENTS

What, if any, achievements can the character point to in his life? For example, has he, under adverse conditions, raised a child of whom he is extremely proud? Has he built a business from scratch? Paid off all his debts? Delivered on a promise? Saved someone's life? Become successful when no one thought he would? Did he, to his credit, take the high moral ground on a particular issue while others chose the opposite approach? Did he attain what some thought was impossible?

If he was successful at doing something, how many others know about it? Is it something that he keeps to himself? How long did it take him to realize the achievement?

ADVENTURE

Has anything happened in the character's life that he categorizes as an adventure? What is its nature, and what attributes does it have that tend to set it apart from all other experiences that the character has had? Did it happen when the character was a child or an adult? Has there been more than one adventure?

Who else was involved in the adventure? Did it happen unexpectedly? If not, how did it exceed the character's expectations?

Is the adventure the kind of thing the character still likes to talk about? Does he still find it hard to believe that it actually happened? Does he wonder how he ever got through it? Is it something he wishes he could do again?

CHILDHOOD

On the day the character was born, did anything particularly newsworthy happen, such as a tornado, fire, or important political event? Did the character have a good childhood or one that he would rather forget? In what kind of neighborhood was he raised? Was he seen as a "hell raiser" or a "good kid"? Who were his best friends, or did he have any? Among other kids in the neighborhood, was he a leader or a follower? What did he like to do more than anything else? What did he dislike the most? Was he afraid of anyone or anything? Did he have a recurring dream?

What was his biggest disappointment? When he was a child, did anything especially memorable happen — good or bad — that he has never been able to forget? If so, how has it affected his adulthood? What did he always say he wanted to be when he "grew up"? Did he have a hero?

Did he have more disagreements with one brother or sister than with the others? Was he ever seriously injured? Was he liked by the neighbors? Did he have a pet that he still remembers fondly? Did he have a secret hiding place?

EDUCATION

What happened while he was going to school or college that, in turn, had a profound effect on him? Was the character an outstanding, good, fair, or poor student? Did he study hard or hardly enough? Did he learn quickly, or did things come hard for him? Did he finish high school or college — and if he did not, why not? What subject gave him the most trouble? Which subject gave him the least trouble?

Was he popular in school, or did others barely notice him? Was there a particular teacher or professor he liked or disliked, and why? Did he ever get into any trouble while going to school or college? If so, what was it and who else was involved? Did he attend social or athletic functions such as dances and football games? Did he belong to a fraternity or sorority?

Did he grow up in one town and go to one school, or did he have to attend several different schools? If he attended college, did he live away from home? If so, where was it and what were some of his experiences?

Did they give him a nickname in school? If so, was it one of affection or derision? (*See* Chapter 11 for more about nicknames.)

FAILURES

Has the character failed at anything? Has he, for instance, failed to live up to others' expectations? Neglected to fulfill a promise he made? Reneged on an obligation? Let down a friend? Permitted a wonderful opportunity to pass him by? Has the failure instilled within him a measure of guilt, regret, loss, disappointment, bitterness, or resignation? Moreover, does the character see it as a failure, or is that how the other characters in the story see it? While a failure to do something usually produces a negative result, is it possible that his failure to do something produced a positive result?

FAMILY

Is there anything important that should be known about the character's parents? His brothers or sisters? His aunts, uncles, cousins, grandparents, or ancestors? Is there something about one of them that the character cannot forget, or which he respects or disrespects? Because of what has happened in the past, does he feel emotionally closer to one relative than to any of the others?

How have the values, attitudes, struggles, social status, education, or lifestyle of his immediate or extended family affected him? Were his relatives strict? Lenient? Thrifty? Overindulgent? Always working? Frequent church-goers? Friendly with the neighbors? Law-breakers or law-abiders? Politically active or inactive?

Why does he feel close to them, or detached? Is he ashamed or proud of them? Was there a death in the family that was particularly troubling to him?

LOVE AND MARRIAGE

Who was the character's first great love, and at what point in the character's life did it take place? Was it a childhood crush, or did it occur during adulthood? Did the character marry that person? If not, why not? Did he ever love someone that he now wishes he had married?

If the character was or is married, is it necessary to know the circumstances leading up to the character's marriage? For example, was it arranged by the character's parents? Was it a "shotgun" wedding, following an unwanted pregnancy? Was the match one of convenience, or was it the culmination of what was viewed as pure love?

Did the marriage produce any children? If so, did the birth of a son or daughter have a profound impact on the character's life? As a parent, is he strict, lenient, affectionate, or distant? Had he not produced children, how might his life have been different?

Has the character or the character's spouse ever had an extramarital affair? If so, what is known about the affair? Have there been any repercussions? Is guilt a part of the equation?

Has the character been divorced? If so, why didn't the marriage work out? Was one of the parties more at fault than the other, or is that just how the character sees it?

MILITARY

Has the character ever been in the military? If so, was he drafted or did he enlist? Was he a part of the Air Force, Navy, Army, Marines? What rank did he achieve? Where was he stationed? In what way did his military experience change him? Was he patriotic or just doing his job?

Has he ever been in a war? Was he ever wounded? Did he see any of his buddies get killed? If he has been in armed conflict, in what way has that had an impact upon his life? Did something happen that he never talks about, and is it something that he unsuccessfully tries to put out of his mind?

Is there someone he remembers with affection or disdain? Did he hate the discipline or did it fail to bother him? Did his experience alter his opinion about the role of the military in a civilized society?

MISFORTUNE

In what way has trouble been a factor in the character's background? Has he witnessed the death of someone he cared about? Has either he or a member of his family experienced a serious illness, lost a limb, or suffered in some way? Has his life been threatened in any way, and did the experience have an effect on his thinking?

Has he had a first-hand, life-altering encounter with poverty, war, drought, prejudice, deception, danger, failure, injustice, revenge, imprisonment, secrecy, greed, ignorance, defeat, carelessness, ingratitude, sorcery?

Has the character ever lost a job? Has he been the victim of a fire, flood, earthquake, tornado, or some other disaster? Did someone steal something from him? Did he lose something of great value belonging to either him or someone else? Has he ever been the victim of any sort of crime?

Did the misfortune change the way he looked at life in general, or did it turn the knob on something quite specific? Is it something he could have prevented, or was it beyond his control?

MONEY

Looking over the character's background, would you say that money, for the most part, has successfully eluded him, or has it somehow always found a way into his pocket?

Was the character born into a family that had little money, and has he since maintained the family tradition? Has he always scratched for a living? Has he always been the person who is full of big dreams and little prospects? Like the kid in front of the candy store, has he always been on the outside, looking in? When he gets a little money, does something invariably come along and take it away? Is he a borrower? If so, does he have a history of not paying back what he owes? Is he someone who usually makes bad investments?

Does his background reflect someone who has established a pattern for saving his money? Has he bought insurance policies or made astute investments in the stock market? Or has he been regularly "bailed out" by his family? Has he never appreciated the value of a buck?

PLACES

Has geography had an impact upon the character's life? How has he been shaped by the places where he has lived, and the cities, villages, or countries he has visited? What kinds of experiences did he have in any of those places that he now views with either affection or distaste? Is there one place he simply cannot forget? If so, why?

Regarding one of the houses or apartments where he lived, does he still remember it with affection or dislike? Has he been awed by the mountains, the ocean, the big city, the desert, the tropics, the jungle? What memorable travels has he experienced by bus, boat, train, car, plane, motorcycle, wagon, or donkey cart?

What influence has the character's home town had upon his life? How has it stamped him? Has it sent him into the world as one prepared or unprepared?

POLITICS

In what way has politics had an influence on the character's life? Was he, for example, born into a family who held fast to the principles of a certain political party, and has he since come to see himself as a believer in that party as well? Has he ever changed his political allegiance? If so, why?

Looking at the terrain of the character's life, does it seem shaped by right-wing or left-wing thinking, or by a centrist philosophy? Has he usually gone along with the crowd, or is he a renegade?

Did a certain political event — e.g., a particular election, a scandal, an investigation, an assassination — affect his life? Has he ever become personally involved in supporting a winning or losing candidate, and how did the experience shape him? Has any candidate deeply disappointed him? Did the fact that his favorite political candidate lost an election embitter him?

Did he ever consider running for political office himself? Has he failed to vote in any election because he has no interest in the democratic process or because he does not understand the importance of his small contribution?

REPUTATION

Reputation is a valid background category, though it exists solely in the minds of the other characters and thus may have no basis whatsoever in truth. If, as they say, a character's reputation precedes him, it is the writer's prerogative to determine how much of it is valid.

What has the character done, or allegedly done, that may cause others to form an opinion of him before he even enters the story? Has the truth about his background been greatly distorted? If so, is the character himself aware of that distortion? How does the character's reputation threaten or embolden others? If the character is fully aware of his reputation, does he use it to his advantage, even though he knows some or all of it is not true?

TURNING POINT

Has something happened in the character's past that proved to be a major turning point in his life? If so, what was it? How old was he? Who else was involved? Where did it happen? How did it happen? How did it turn him in a different direction? In the end, in what way did it change him?

Mind you, whatever this turning point might be, it must have great significance. If the character has the insight to be able to identify it, his thinking *after* it happened must be considerably different from his thinking *before* it happened, even though a considerable amount of time may pass before he can truly assess its impact. And if the *direction* of his life has not been substantially altered because of it, there should at least be a dramatic shift in his *emotional* outlook.

For example, was his life changed because he once experienced a great injustice? Has he been the victim of rejection, ridicule, selfishness, envy, neglect, or failure? Was something either taken from him or given to him, which in turn had a major impact on the way he saw things in the world? Did he see something that he has never been able to forget? Did he either lose something or leave something behind, the absence of which has been devastating? Was he the beneficiary of a timeless love that ended, unexpectedly, in tragedy? Did he submit when he should have disobeyed, or permit something that he should have forbidden?

While most turning points in the background of a character may have been imperceptible when they first occurred, only through the binoculars of hindsight — or through the information the author surreptitiously passes on to the reader or viewer — does it become clear that a life has been redirected, for better or for worse.

WORK

What kinds of jobs has the character had, or has he held just one for many years? Has his employment been in the same general discipline, or in a variety of fields? Did he like any of his past jobs? Hate any of them? Have his past jobs placed little demand on his true capabilities, or has at least one of them required more than he is able to give? Has he ever been fired? Laid off? Been part of a labor strike? Has there been a job that he wanted badly, but didn't get?

Has he always dreamed of having his own business someday? If the character has been self-employed in the past, what kind of business did he run? Did he like it or dislike it? Was it successful or unsuccessful? Did something happen to cause him to lose it? Did he start the business from scratch? Inherit it? Invest in a partnership? How many people did he employ, if any? Who were his competitors? What was his worst experience? What his best?

Has the character always enjoyed working (perhaps even been called a workaholic), or has he always lived for weekends, vacations, and holidays? Does he just do what is expected of him and no more, or does he get involved in extra things while on the job?

Did he ever have a boss whom he greatly respected or disrespected? Did he ever have a conflict with a co-worker or an employee? If so, what was it about and what were the repercussions?

What has he learned from his jobs that can be seen as valuable? In his mind, of what has he been deprived during his years of employment?

(For more on jobs, *see* Chapter 12.)

9. What Is the Character's Self-Assessment?

While busily instilling internal and external traits, fears, desires, strengths, weaknesses, likes, and dislikes into a character, perhaps the author may want to step back for a moment and let the character have a say. Doing so may provide some extra insight.

Suppose a character proclaims, "I'm the *sole* decision-maker in this company. All I do is give it to the legal department for their review." Such a claim suggests that the character may be indulging in a bit of self-deception, for if he was truly the only decision-maker he wouldn't let any legal experts crimp his style. Embedded in that statement might also be such traits as caution, reliance, and pomposity—any of which the writer may use to full advantage as he develops his character.

Sometimes you can present and destroy a character's self-assessment in a single sentence. Example:

> Jack Smart prided himself on his ability to make quick, independent decisions—each of which came layered with countless coffee-drenched committee meetings attended by those who, like miners, labored in the lower echelon of management with only their computer screens providing them light.

Characters often weigh the sum of their own parts at some point, and the conclusions they draw become their self-assessments. And if the characters don't *say* it, they will often *think* it. For example:

> "Look, I'm the breadwinner in this family, and don't you forget it!" Joe reminded them.
>
> I've been a hermit while drowning in a sea of people, thought Herman.
>
> "Oh God, I'm such a loser," Franklin moaned.
>
> "I'm your door-opener. I hold the keys to your future success," said Billy Joe softly.
>
> "I'm a lucky guy. Always have been," smiled Fred.

Now, while it may not be necessary for the character to actually utter or think his self-assessment during the story, it may indeed help the writer to know what his character *would* say if the occasion demanded it. The manner in which a character might quickly define himself could have a great bearing on what he does, or how he thinks, as the plot unfolds. Such miniature self-assessments may be right on target, or they could suggest, as I have mentioned before, that the character is engaging in self-delusion. In the latter case, the writer is obligated to discreetly inform his or her audience of the truth.

A self-assessment that is way off the mark can be the basis for comedy or tragedy, or for both. For example, let's say part of a male character's self-assessment is that he is a great lover. Now, the author can set up some wonderful comic scenes in which a rude, grossly overweight, beer-swigging Casanova is always left empty-handed, cursing the insensitivity of women who have fled for their lives. But in a tragic turn, his true-blue wife of over 30 years may die of cancer near the end of the story, leaving this "great lover" as helpless as a beached whale.

Besides self-deception, a character's self-assessment may reflect, for example, self-admiration, self-loathing, self-importance, self-congratulation, self-reliance, self-accusation, self-pity, or perhaps self-righteousness.

The categories that follow may permit one or more of your characters to provide a self-assessment. Many categories contain actual quotes; some have sample assessments that have been devised for that category. There are, of course, no limitations on how many may be selected.

ACTION

What might the character say about himself that would tell us about his need to engage in physical or mental activity, or his aversion to it? Regarding action, a character's self-assessment may reflect his commitment to doing things rather than talking about them, or perhaps his general passiveness and possibly his willingness to talk things to death. The character might paraphrase a statement made by Eleanor Roosevelt: "I must do things I think I cannot do."

ADVERSITY

Before a character will be able to make a statement about adversity in his life, he will have to have experienced hard times. In 1977, Don Grant was quoted in the *New York Times*: "I'm like an old tin can in an alley. Anyone who walks by can't resist kicking it." Or maybe your character shows fortitude, and would say something like, "I've never run from trouble." A self-assessment might show how the character has handled either long, well-entrenched misfortune or the sudden appearance of short-term trouble. When adversity has appeared, has the character been a problem-solver? Has he panicked? Become a worrywart? Or has he waited until the misery has passed?

BEAUTY

The character who provides a self-assessment regarding physical beauty will more than likely fall into one of three camps: (1) beauty is present; (2) beauty has vanished, but the memory hasn't; (3) beauty has never been present. If the character has never had physical beauty, does the self-assessment reflect displeasure, resignation, humor? Or perhaps speculation about what it would be like to be beautiful? In the latter instance, a character might say, "Just once, I'd like to know what it feels like to be in a room and know that men are stealing glances at me." On the other hand, maybe the character's definition of beauty goes beyond the exterior. Dwight D. Eisenhower made the following assessment in a 1943 letter to his wife: "Decency — generosity ... assistance in trouble ... these are the things that [I find] of greater value...."

CHANGE

A character's comments on his reaction to change may tell us a great deal about him. If he reveals that he does not adapt well to change, an author may want to put changes in his path and, in the process, stir things up a bit — test the character's spirit and flexibility in full view of all the rest of us. Another character may well acknowledge that taking advantage of change in his earlier days helped to make him very wealthy, and yet he may admit that the more successful he has become, the more conservative he has turned out to be. Still another character might say, "The only time I get an itch to change something is when things aren't going well." A self-assessing statement may mirror the character's fear of those shocks that naturally inhabit new systems, new trends, and the abandonment of old principles.

CHILDREN

If the character dislikes children, will he admit it? If the character has children, how does he assess himself as a parent? The character who provides a self-assessment that uses his own children as the topic may speak of his success or failure in parenting, or the wisdom of using or not using discipline, or the pleasures or tortures of educating them (which may include the first day of school and the last), or the favoring of one child over another, or the continuous effort expended to look good in their eyes.

COURAGE

The character who makes an assessment of his own courage need not have displayed courage to any degree. In fact, he could say, "I've spent the greater part of my adult life being fearful of saying something that others would feel is inappropriate and afraid of doing something that may be seen as being contrary to the actions of the crowd." Lyndon Johnson said, "I'd rather give my life than be afraid to give it"; but if he was never in a position where he had to prove it, was he wrapping himself in a kind of self-romanticism?

If a character is embarrassed by his own obvious display of courage, self-assessment will be of little use; the writer will have to depend on someone else to do the talking.

DUTY

For a character to say anything meaningful about the obligations he feels, his moral code will doubtlessly have to be more pronounced than someone who simply says, "I've never missed a day's work in my life," because that same character may spend his nights in a bar, drinking beer with the boys, while his wife and kids are at home alone. Unless the character is indulging himself in self-delusion, a statement about duty will only take on meaning when the audience hears something like, "I can't say 'no' to my friends." Or: "We didn't go to war because we wanted to, but because our country needed us." The character may express a duty to himself, if not to others. Whether he has fulfilled an obligation or simply acknowledges that he has such an obligation and expresses his commitment, it is the stuff of which duty is made.

EDUCATION

If a character says something about his education, will he stress the importance of the knowledge he gained in the classroom, or outside of it? For example, if he is a businessman whose education has been gained through the school of "hard knocks," will he still regret not getting a college diploma even though he has made a lot of money without it? How might the character define an ignorant or an educated person? What importance has the art of listening played in his life? The character, who might be a teacher, an industrialist, a scientist, or a journalist, might say, "What I've always tried to do is get people to think." Or the entrepreneur who has long since left the classroom could say, "I have learned not to shoot down an idea during its maiden flight."

EXPECTATIONS

Our skills and our intelligence often cause other people to expect us to meet certain standards, simply because they know we are capable. Likewise, some of us recognize our own abilities and place goals at some distance from ourselves, with full intention of reaching them. In the high-jump it would be called "raising the bar." In truth, a great many of us either do not meet the standards expected of us, or we fall short of reaching our own objectives. In that situation, a fictional character's self-assessment may range from embarrassment to accusing others for his failure. If, on the other hand, he achieved something that surpassed everyone's expectations, that character might say, somewhat gleefully, "I did it, and proved all those S.O.B.s wrong." But if so far he hasn't been successful, the self-doubting character could say, "Maybe I set my goals too high."

FAILURE

Unless the character has failed at least once in his life, a self-evaluating comment on the subject seems unlikely, though certainly not out of the realm of possibility. The self-deluding character who looks only at his successes might say, "I've never failed at anything." For that person who learned from his mistakes: "Each of my failures served as the bedrock of my later success." But a comment from a self-pitying character might be, "Everything I touch turns to dust." What does it say about the fictional character who admits that he has failed? Or the one who denies it? If he will not accept the blame for his flops, upon whose head will he place it?

FAME

A character who has never wanted fame may say so. A character who wanted fame and didn't get it may blame himself. But the character who has had fame may complain that it has made him unhappy in some way, for example: "I can't go anywhere or do anything without some photographer sticking a camera in my face." In a 1979 *TV Guide* interview, Howard Cosell complained, "I have been called a company pimp, a prostitute, and a man with no trace of decency or morality. I have been vilified by people I have never seen." Or take the character who once had fame, but doesn't any longer: "The road to the top was hard and exhilarating; the road down has been quick and humiliating." A self-assessment may take on meaning for a fictional character if fame, for example, magnifies his vanity, disturbs his privacy, undermines his freedom, intensifies his loneliness, increases his hostility, amplifies his greed, or has jilted him for another.

FREEDOM

The character who delivers a self-assessment about his own personal freedom need not frame it in terms of a constitutional right. The character could simply be a henpecked husband or an abused wife, either of whom may desire freedom and yet be frightened by the unknown: "Every time I think about leaving, I don't know where to go." The cloistered monk could experience an invigorating freedom within a very small room ("The silence transports me"). Someone who has been denied freedom all his life might say, "Just once, I'd like to know what true freedom really feels like." If a character should evaluate his life in terms of the freedom he enjoys or doesn't have, no matter what field of endeavor he might be in, among the things he might address could be the freedom to speak ("I watch what I say because it could get back to the boss"), or the freedom to think differently ("I joined the Republican party because that's what my family expected").

FRIENDSHIP

When someone says, "Oh, I've made tons and tons of friends in my life," we put it in the box marked Exaggeration. Wisdom eventually allows us to differentiate between friends and acquaintances, and thus we tend to place a lot more trust in the individual who says, "I have one good friend. I think." In his book *The Fabulous Democrats*, David Cohn quoted President Warren G. Harding's self-assessment about his relationship with his friends: "I have no trouble with my enemies. But my goddamn friends ... they are the ones that keep me walking the floor nights." A character who assesses his friendships may deceive himself, or display as much caution as a poker player trying to draw to an inside straight, or be vitriolic. Whatever he says, it will tell us something about him and the people with whom he associates.

HAPPINESS

A self-assessment on the subject of happiness is tricky. The biggest problem is that happiness can be so transitory and deceptive. Give someone too much of a good thing and he becomes bored and unhappy. If happiness was a mountain range, many of us would probably feel that we spend a good part of the time in the valley. A fictional character who is asked to make a pronouncement about his own personal happiness may first question what is meant by the word "happiness." Then, weighing the good times against the bad — not to mention all those in-between times — the character may wind up saying, "Well, I'm not *unhappy*, if that's what you mean." Just like the rest of us, fictional characters — except for those times when love has screwed their heads on silly or when good fortune springs out of the dark and kisses them on the cheek — will usually be at a crossroads, hoping that if they turn left, right, or go straight ahead that things will be better than what they have experienced so far. Only the truly miserable are likely to give a solid, definitive answer.

HEALTH

The character who says, "All my days have been a succession of aches, pains, sneezes, coughs, acid indigestion, and blurred vision," gives us better self-assessment than the character who merely says, "Lately I get tired just bringing the fork to my mouth." A character's appraisal of his own health would be especially advantageous to the writer who wants to make that character's physical condition an integral part of the plot. With luck, that writer would wind up with something as deliciously comic as the hypochondriac in the last play Molière ever wrote, *The Imaginary Invalid*. But how a character feels about the state of his health or what he says about the trends it has taken in his own family could dictate how he conducts his life. For example: "Heart disease runs in my family on my mother's side. And if the pattern holds, I'll never see 40."

HOME

What does "home" mean to the character? Is it a town, a neighborhood, a street, a house — or the people who either live or once lived in that house? Said Senator George McGovern of his hometown: "I still love to go back to Mitchell and wander up and down those streets. It just kind of reassures me again that there is a place that I know thoroughly, where the roots are deep" (*Life*, 1972). Has the character ever had a place that he could call home? Has he always felt like a stranger regardless of where he has lived and how long he was there? If a character owns a 15-room mansion, what part of it, if any, is really home? When a character provides a self-assessment about home, does his idealism, regret, or confusion about it get in the way? Or does it conjure images of coziness, or wearing what he likes, or the comfort that comes with intense familiarity?

INDIVIDUALISM

A character may believe himself an individualist when he is actually anything but. For example, if a character thinks that wearing a black motorcycle jacket, a ponytail, and an earring makes him a nonconformist, he is doubtlessly laboring under a delusion, for there are hundreds of thousands who are dressed just the same way. The true individualist will not speak of joining something, but instead will be the first to form a radical group and will show no hesitation about upsetting tradition. The character who informs us, in his unique self-esteeming way, that he has always steered his own ship, that he is the last of a dying breed, and that he does whatever he wants, whenever he wants, may be bragging too much to be a real individualist. The individualist will be that person who refuses to imitate; who will not conform to standards he views as contrary to his nature; and who has striven to do those things which interest him despite the possible absence of crowd approval.

MARRIAGE

The character who is or has been married could say something quite meaningful that would help sharpen the image we have of him, especially when the marriage has a great bearing on the story. From the character whose marriage has ended in divorce: "I tried to get more out of the marriage than there was in it" (paraphrased from *The Roycraft Dictionary and Book of Epigrams*, 1923). Among some of the things that a character may touch upon during a self-assessment of his role as a spouse might be these: the struggle to understand the other; the clarification of boundaries; the assignment of responsibilities; in-laws; the loss of independence; the alignment of forces; the wrestling with compromise; and the discovery that love has phases. Or: "I married beneath me" (Nancy Astor, *Womanlist*, 1981).

MORALITY

The character may tell us how decent he feels his conduct has been and to what lengths he has been driven by conscience — for example, to what degree he has stood on principle and how virtuous he believes he is (or isn't). In a 1974 *Time* interview, Jeb Stuart Magruder said, "Somewhere between my ambition and my ideals, I lost my ethical compass." Perhaps the fictional character may give us an evaluation of his charitability, loyalty, and honesty, *e.g.*, "Dishonesty and I have always been mortal enemies." If the character's self-assessment indicates a relentless drive toward integrity, will he also be able to show that he has compassion for those who are weaker? Maybe he will tell us that he is beleaguered by some element of guilt; or perhaps he (mistakenly) believes that the respectability he has earned wipes clean a slate upon which many sins have been written. Confusion about morality is always a possibility, *e.g.*, "I've been known to get right and wrong a little mixed up sometimes." So is its total neglect: "I owe the public nothing" (J.P. Morgan, *The Robber Barons*, 1934) and "I've always figured, do unto others before they do unto you."

OPPORTUNITY AND LUCK

If at least once in the character's life events converged to create a favorable set of circumstances, can he or can he not claim that he took advantage of the situation? ("I missed the opportunity of a lifetime. Had I invested, I'd be a rich man today.") Or was it a moment of bright-faced luck skipping unexpectedly into the picture? ("I shudder to think what would have happened to me if that Nazi soldier had not pulled me out of that line.") When an opportunity appears, it is always the character's decision whether to seize it; either way, the result can make a big difference in his future. Luck, whether good or bad, can likewise alter the course of one's life, but the character does not seize it; instead, he is seized by it. With opportunity, timing can be crucial; thus, in his self-assessment, it is possible that the character may admit to acting too early or too late. With luck, however, because it strikes so seldom and so randomly, the character is more likely to complain about its absence: "Hell, if I didn't have bad luck, I wouldn't have any luck at all," or "I was born at the wrong place at the wrong time."

PERSEVERANCE

If a character discloses that he has a persevering nature, will his self-assessment also tell us something about his self-direction, self-reliance, or self-denial? ("If I start a job, I put everything on hold until I finish it," or "When I hear the word no, I keep at it until I hear the word yes.") Will he provide a contrasting view by telling us that, in the causes dear to him, he maintains a fierce pace while others fall by the wayside? And what will his perseverance tell us about his tolerance for leisure? The character who sees perseverance as one of his major attributes may, at the same time, express his disdain for defeat, or his faith in himself, or his adoption of discipline, or his stubbornness, or all of these. But the character who lacks perseverance is qualified to make a self-assessment as well: "I don't hang around where I'm not wanted."

POSSESSIONS

What a character says about what he owns could prove enormously revealing, for it is often the so-called trophies we collect — particularly those which have been gained through our hard work, skills, and stratagems — that allow us to air our pride. The rancher who benefited from a free land grab, who has chased away Indians and bribed government agents, and who may have surpassed the expectations of his father, could sweep his arm in the direction of the horizon and say, in a grand, self-congratulatory way, "It's all mine, as far as the eye can see. Every acre, hole, cow pile, and toad frog." Overall, it usually doesn't matter what a character possesses — property, material goods, money, pets, some sort of keepsake — but rather his positive or negative comment regarding ownership. For example, the character who says, "I've tried keeping up with the Joneses, only to find out that they were trying to keep up with me," may reveal that the race to own was more important than what was actually owned. Statements like "I still have my mother's diary, and I wouldn't take anything for it" reflect sentimentality, while "This table has been in my family for 100 years" resonates with tradition. Mother Mary Madelva, in *My*

First Seventy Years (1959), spurned possessions when she wrote, "I like to go to Marshall Fields in Chicago just to see how many things there are in the world that I do not want." A character who has toiled his whole life and wound up with very little to show for it will have an entirely different viewpoint because of the lack of possessions in his life.

PREJUDICE

Where prejudice is involved, the nature of a self-assessment will depend largely upon whether the character has been on the receiving or delivery end of the prejudice, and whether the prejudice can be classified as positive or negative. Positive prejudice is expressed as favoritism, *e.g.*, "Mama always liked my sister best," and, "I hire women cashiers, because I think they're faster, they don't complain, and they're prettier." Negative prejudice is automatic disapproval toward an individual or group: "No matter what my stepfather did to please me, I made his life miserable," and, "We're all God's children, except for you-know-who." W.C. Fields said, "I am free of all prejudice. I hate everyone equally." When a character's self-assessment includes prejudice as part of its fabric, it is possible that the reader or viewer may discern the absence of reason or compassion, or both. Rare, of course, would be the character who sees his true image and would say, "I have seen the bigot, and he is me."

REPUTATION

A character can only speculate about his worth as seen through the eyes of others. If he believes he has a good reputation, he is likely to talk about it openly: "People know they can count on me." But the character who engages in such speculation is certainly a prime target for self-delusion, because there may be at least one other person in the story who, upon hearing that self-assessment, would not provide a supportive vote.

If the character's reputation is not sterling, he might feel he is being judged unfairly and will complain, "People have got the wrong idea about me." Rare would be the character who, during a self-assessment, would admit that the bad reputation which has long dogged him is well deserved. Even rarer would be the character willing to share that information with others in the story.

ROMANCE

Has romance, or the lack of it, had a telling effect on the character's life? When the character assesses himself as a lover, will we hear the strains of regret, appreciation, affection, expectation, fond memory, bewilderment — to name just a few of the enormous possibilities? Perhaps the statement about the love or loves a character has experienced will contain irony, *e.g.*, "I never liked the men I loved, and never loved the men I liked" (Fanny Brice, *The Fabulous Fanny*, 1953); or possibly give us a glimpse into his self-education, *e.g.*, "I have learned that love is the hunter and cannot be hunted."

SECURITY

What might the character say about himself that would reflect either his long-held need to feel secure or his general disregard for his own well-being? His comment about the dangers of taking risks, the absence or presence of caution in his life, and how he defines his so-called comfort zone could well sharpen his image in the mind of the reader or viewer. For example, if the character opted for a secure job early in his life instead of pursuing something more risky that had the potential of a big pay-off, his self-assessment might be revealed in a statement to his grandson: "Don't make the same mistake that I did. Don't stay on the ground with that humdrum crowd and allow that rollercoaster to leave without you. Jump on it and ride it for all it's worth." It is a statement that rings with regret. But to the housewife whose husband has left her and who's always found it hard to make ends meet, security may be all-important, and she could say, "All my life I've felt that I've been standing on a sandy knoll while the water was washing away the bottom part." Has the character shown he is willing to take risks, or has the thought of possible consequences always pulled him back?

SUCCESS

Only the character who has experienced success is qualified to assess what role it has played in his life, even if what he once had is now elusive. A "failure" who still works feverishly to better himself is really in no position to assess his life in terms of achieving success, other than the fact that it has continually bypassed him. An important prelude to this self-assessment is the character's definition of success; without a definition he is incapable of determining whether he has ever enjoyed it. If he thinks in terms of monetary success and he's made a lot of money, he might well see himself as being successful. If he thinks that success is holding a position of influence or fame, and he has in fact been in that position, again he will declare that he has succeeded. But when the character strays from the obvious, moving into areas in which perhaps his achievements are measured, or his spiritual values come into question, or his social contributions are weighed, his self-assessment becomes increasingly harder to gauge. The character who finds himself in this position may be perennially in doubt about his success, because there always seems to be more things to achieve and more contributions to make. The achievements of Mother Theresa, for example, are legendary, but perhaps she never felt that she had succeeded in all she hoped to do.

As for the "successful" character, does he recognize his blunders as well? In retrospect, does he place more value on the climb or the celebration that accompanies success? Is success all that he thought it would be? More? Less? And is he happy that his "success" has made others happy as well? Example: "I've been at this job for 30 years. Daddy's real proud of me."

SUPERIORITY

Except for the egomaniac, those who cast themselves in a superior role will often either give their self-assessment a nice backhanded slant, *e.g.*, "The capacity to admire others is not my most fully developed trait" (Henry Kissinger, *The White House Years*, 1979), or state it with salesmanship and humor, *e.g.*, "I'm the greatest!" (Muhammad Ali, before and after his boxing matches), in which case few become offended. But the character who dares admit to feeling superior can be so self-delusional ("My greatest strength is that I have no weaknesses"—John McEnroe, *New York Times*, 1979), or so self-admiring ("If I had a little humility, I would be perfect"—Ted Turner, *New York Times*, 1977), that another character — or the reader or viewer — may wish for a handy pin with which to poke a few holes in the ego.

WORK

In terms of self-assessment, among the things a character is likely to talk about are his work ethics; the quality of that which he produces; his acceptance, or rejection, of either drudgery or repetition; performing under pressure; intrusions; stealing time from his family; a search for dignity; the captivity or freedom of self-employment; maneuvering his way up through the hierarchy; the bureaucracy; the humiliation or education that came with being fired. What kind of job the character has may make no difference whatsoever. The character who states, "I have never been able to say, with any degree of confidence, 'This job is done,'" would probably be a perfectionist regardless of what kind of work he did. And the character who would say, "I go on working for the same reason that a hen goes on laying eggs" (H.L. Mencken, in Will Durant's *On the Meaning of Life*, 1932), could mean that he is either committed to production or that nature prevents him from doing anything else. Finally, if a character declares that his approach to work is, "First, I try to get someone else to do it," his laziness would not disappear if he changed jobs.

YOUTH

Unless the character is presently in his childhood, he will be able to look back and make some sort of appraisal of himself in his early years. The nature of a person's behavior during those formative years will not necessarily be the same social posture that he maintains as an adult; thus, the shy little girl who hardly ever spoke to anyone in the eighth grade may become the movie star-let who shocks everyone with her outrageous actions and interviews. As a character, she might say, "When I was in school, I mostly stood on the side-lines and watched everyone else have a good time." It's not that the author has his or her creation out of sync; probably the character simply reached a point in her life when she got tired of watching and decided to participate.

A self-assessment about his youth provides the character with an oppor-tunity to say something about his parents, his siblings, his teachers. He can tell us what he lost, gained, ignored, missed, or wasted. Other possible top-ics include the old neighborhood, the endless optimism of childhood, and prudence vs. adventure. Some quotes: "I was the kind of kid who didn't like to admit she'd lost her faith for fear of hurting God's feelings" (Chris Chase, *How to Be a Movie Star, or a Terrible Beauty Is Born*, 1968); "It all seems rosy and romantic to us who were young then, because we will never feel quite so intensely about our surroundings any more" (F. Scott Fitzgerald, "*The Crack-up*," 1945); "The first thing you'll probably want to know is ... what my lousy childhood was like ... and all that David Copperfield kind of crap, but I don't feel like going into it, if you want to know the truth" (J.D. Salinger, *The Catcher in the Rye*, 1951).

10. What Is the Character's "Type"?

When some writers hear the term "character type," they immediately think of stereotype and all the bad connotations that word carries with it. But a character type can be an important starting point for a genuinely well-developed character. A great many writers begin to develop a fictional character while having only a certain type in mind.

An author, for example, may choose to develop a Scrooge-type character for a story; however, while that character may well turn out to be a mean-spirited penny-pincher, he can still be very different from Dickens's Scrooge. One can also create a straightforward and fun-loving Huck Finn type without setting the story on a Mississippi raft. A Captain Bligh–type character might be the chief executive officer of a corporate conglomerate rather than a captain of a ship, with nuances that would give the character a completely separate identity; and the authors of *Mutiny on the Bounty*, Nordhoff and Hall, wouldn't even recognize the connection.

Obviously, a character type becomes a stereotype only when the writer does not have the imagination to build upon the primary layer and provide his character with complexity. A character type, it must be said, serves only as a beginning; it should not be used as an end in itself. It is only meant to provide a broad view. Something far greater lies within the details, trusting the ability of the writer to bring it out.

Here, then, are some so-called types, many of which will be instantly recognizable. They are presented in alphabetical order and briefly explained. As you review the list of possibilities, please remember that a fictional character need not be wholly one type or the other; he or she can be a combination of several.

THE ACCOMMODATOR
(*See also* the Bootlicker; the Pacifist; the Poltroon)

An inveterate "yes man," even though he may hold a position of power. Bends, gives way, pampers rather than objects. More likely to comply with a request than refuse one. Permits a breach of his authority rather than punish the abuser. Tries to satisfy someone's wishes when he would rather not. Intimate with surrender. Doesn't like to interfere with the wishes of others, even though he is inconvenienced. Gives a nod and a wink when he knows he shouldn't. Does not want to make waves. A spoiler of those who wish to be spoiled. Gives a free hand, plenty of latitude. Often seen leaning over backwards for that person who barges in, or wants something done his or her way, or is insensitive to his needs.

May also be called: appeaser.

Adjectives: acquiescent, agreeable, appeasing, compliant, docile, easygoing, forbearant, gracious, indulgent, lax, lenient, long-suffering, meek, noninterfering, obliging, passive, permissive, placating, submissive, tolerant, unresisting.

THE ACCUSER

Because something was done or not done, attempts to lay blame on a particular person or a group. The motive of the accuser may take on one of many different colors. For example, he may try to shift the blame away from himself and thereby avoid any responsibility. He may, in an act of indignation, accuse another of immoral behavior, or of a lack of professionalism, or of acting illegally, or one of many other things. On the other hand, the accusation may be borne out of spite rather than indignation. In any of the aforementioned situations, impugning the reputation of the innocent is certainly a possibility. Feeds off scapegoats, carving up their innocence with his tongue and finger-pointing.

May also be called: seeker of justice, witch-hunter.

Adjectives: accusing, denunciatory, destructive, discriminatory, exaggerative, imaginative, incriminatory, misinformed, mistaken, recriminatory, retaliatory.

THE ADDICT

Must have something and is convinced that he cannot do without it. (One who has become hooked on drugs, cigarettes, or alcohol would know the feeling well.) The compulsion sits enthroned in his mind consistently, and all of his other actions dance around it and pay homage; it is his personal predetermination. Deprived of what he has come to depend upon, an alarm goes off in his bones and every joint becomes a battle station. He is a slave of his own blood, a prisoner in his own mind. He is chained to a desire that he would rather not have. His treadmill has no "off" button.

Adjectives: compulsive.

THE ADVENTURER
(*See also* the Braveheart)

Takes risks. Willing to hazard his well-being, wealth, or reputation to either prove something to himself or to others. His proverb: Nothing ventured, nothing gained. Lets the breaks fall where they may. Attracted to possibilities rather than probabilities. Always seeing how far he can stretch his luck. Never plays it safe, but rather purposely seeks out danger. Bucks the odds. Looks at the unknown and bets that he can beat it. The first to thrust his nose into dark places, cross uncharted waters, to walk the tightrope without a net. Bored by the status quo. Responds quickly to dares, for it is bait that goads him into action.

May also be called: daredevil, fire-eater, gambler, madcap, risk-taker, speculator, trailblazer.

Adjectives: adventurous, audacious, bold, brave, daring, dauntless, fearless, heroic, impetuous, impulsive, intrepid, mettlesome, plucky, spunky, stouthearted, unafraid, undaunted, unfrightened, unshrinking, untimid, valiant, valorous, or venturesome.

THE ADVERSARY

With or without good reason, an unalterable foe of at least one other character, and rare would be the writer who would not know that most stories will have one. Indeed, many of the character types listed in this section have the ability to become an Adversary. An Adversary's antagonism toward another may be instinctive, occur as a result of what another character did or did not do, or it may happen as a result of one of several other reasons. The adversary, whether human or not, and as every writer knows, helps to establish the conflict in the story.

May also be called: antagonist, enemy, foe.

Adjectives: acrimonious, antagonistic, grudgeful, hostile, inimical, malicious, rancorous, resentful, spiteful, threatening, unfriendly.

THE AMATEUR

Has very little, if any, experience. Still wet behind the ears. Can't yet be trusted with the important stuff. Doesn't know what's up or what's what. Got a lot of learning to do. Green as grass. Tends to put the cart before the horse and can't see an inch beyond his nose. Left alone, he's likely to gum up the works, make a mess of things, put the saddle on the wrong horse. Couldn't maneuver a fish downstream. Desperately needs some on-the-job training. Must be carefully supervised.

May also be called: greenhorn, rookie, rube, yokel.

Adjectives: book-learned, inept, inexperienced, maladroit, raw, unacquainted, unprepared, unqualified, unskillful, untried.

THE AUTHORITARIAN
(*See also* the Intimidator; the Warrior)

Principally engaged in the exercise of power; comfortable in the use of it and knows what he wants to accomplish with it. May control one person or many. Able to keep others in line. Here is the domineering spouse, the gang leader, the field commander, the labor boss, the chairman of the board, the dictator, or anyone in fact whose word is law. For the authoritarian, instilling fear is not an objective but simply one of several by-products resulting from the position he holds. Has veto power.

To get things done his way, must always have the upper hand. Knows how to exert influence and pull the necessary strings. His word carries weight, and "no" is his favorite. Able to eject, expel, discharge, banish, exile, outlaw, exterminate, or purge. Permits little or no wiggle room. Inflicts punishment. Likes to keep others under his heel, beneath his thumb. Takes pleasure in leading people by the nose or wrapping them around his finger. Prone to seize control, and what he says goes.

If he sets himself up as an expert, he browbeats others with the knowledge he believes is at his command. Professes insight. Wields credentials. Displays documentation. Resents challenges.

May also be called: autocrat, boss, dictator, headmaster, oppressor, puppet master, slave driver, taskmaster, tyrant.

Adjectives: arbitrary, bossy, commanding, demanding, despotic, dictatorial, domineering, exacting, forbidding, forceful, imperious, inflexible, insistent, kinglike, magisterial, monarchial, omnipotent, oppressive, overbearing, powerful, prohibitive, royalistic, ruling, stern, strict, stringent, tough, tyrannical, unpermissive.

THE AVENGER

Seeks revenge for a wrong he believes he, or someone he knows, has suffered at the hands of another. Attempts to repay the perpetrator in a tit-for-tat manner, or he wants the punishment to be even more severe than the original injustice he, or someone close to him, experienced. Plans his retaliation carefully, or he attacks mindlessly. Dedicated to giving someone his comeuppance, his just deserts, or exactly what's coming to him. Has an overwhelming desire to get back at, to settle an old score. For him, the wound never heals. Able to carry a grudge for a long time without it ever losing its intensity. On a far lesser level, may try to punish someone by pouting and giving him or her the silent treatment.

May also be called: vindicator.

Adjectives: embittered, grudgeful, plotting, punitive, rancorous, retaliatory, retributive, revengeful, vengeful, vindictive.

THE AVOIDER

There is something that he always tries to avoid, something that he wishes to keep his distance.

May be skilled at looking for loopholes, sidestepping, beating retreats, and dodging the so-called bullet. If so, he will show considerable on-the-spot creativity as he deftly circumvents a particular situation while acting as if he is not. He will offer alternatives that allow him to squeak past, and he will have excuses that drip with plausibility. Will know all the avenues of escape and will regularly develop new ones. An expert when it comes to backing out and seeking sanctuary.

Or his avoidance may be characterized as having the strength of mind not to indulge himself in something that unquestionably has a lure, such as alcohol, sweets, rich food, drugs, gambling, etc. Does not give into temptation. May attempt to instill guilt in those who have less self-control.

Adjectives: abstemious, abstinent, ascetic, celibate, elusive, evasive, fasting, puritanical, self-controlled, self-denying, slippery, temperate.

THE BEGRUDGER

Eaten alive with envy. In the words of Onasander, he is afflicted with the "pain of mind that successful men cause their neighbors." Sucks the thumb of resentment. Gnashes his teeth at the sight of a competitor's prosperity or achievement. Speaks disparagingly of that person who has what he wishes he had.

Adjectives: begrudging, covetous, envious, resentful.

THE BELIEVER

A captive of conviction. Does not permit contradictions. Attaches great weight to someone's utterances or to a particular source of information. Sees mountains of probabilities within a pinhead of evidence. Keeps the faith. Without reservations, accepts something as being true. Self-inflicted with blind enthusiasm. Has "seen the light." For him, it's an open-and-shut case. Feels no need to verify, to question, to double check. Has found the answer for which he has always been looking. Convinced that his country is the best and that it is always right.

May also be called: cat's paw, convert, devotee, disciple, dogmatist, dupe, fanatic, follower, fool, patriot, trusting soul, zealot.

Adjectives: ardent, chauvinistic, cocksure, confident, convinced, devoted, devout, dogmatic, fanatical, nationalistic, overconfident, patriotic, pontificating, positive, reverent, superstitious, sure, trustful, undiscriminating, undoubting, unquestioning, worshipful, zealous.

THE BOOTLICKER
(*See also* the Accommodator)

Spends his life administering to the needs and wants of others. Another's wish is his command. His motto: At your service, sir. Deprives himself so that he will not disappoint others. Tied to another's apron strings. Remains at someone's beck and call. Does what he is told. A doormat, for all intents and purposes. The puppet at the end of the string. Psychologically, he is persistently kow-towing. His freedom can only take place in those precious moments away from his responsibilities, and even then it is suspect. Persistently attempts to ingratiate himself. Utters false compliments and tends to overpraise. Receives his financial support from the very person whom he flatters.

May also be called: apple-polisher, back-scratcher, backslapper, bondman, cajoler, deadbeat, fair-weather flatterer, fawner, flunky, footman, freeloader, gofer, hanger-on, lackey, leech, parasite, serf, servant, slave, soft-soaper, sponger, sycophant, truckler, vassal.

Adjectives: acquiescent, capitulative, compliant, deferential, docile, enslaved, fawning, flattering, groveling, ingratiating, mealy-mouthed, meek, ministering, obedient, obeisant, obsequious, passive, pliant, servile, serving, slavish, subdued, subjugated, submissive, subservient, sweet-tongued, sycophantic, toadying, truckling, unctuous.

THE BORE

Says nothing whatsoever of interest. All vestiges of amusement and drama are missing from his verbal reflections and opinions. Those "listeners" who have no way out of their predicament are glued to their chairs by a politeness they wish they had the courage to expunge. He comes close to having the power to render others comatose. Repeats himself. Speaks in a monotone. He approaches tedium's dead center. Turns one minute into ten. In a social gathering he is the proverbial dripping faucet that no one can turn off. It is said that he can bore one stiff or bore one to tears.

Adjectives: boring, dreary, dry, dull, flat, insipid, irksome, monotonous, prosaic, stodgy, stuffy, tedious, tiresome, unentertaining, uninteresting, wearisome.

THE BRAVEHEART
(*See also* the Adventurer)

Unlike the Adventurer, he does not purposely court danger, yet he will not try to avoid it if it should block his path. He will throw down the so-called gauntlet if challenged; he will draw the proverbial sword and rush forward to do battle, if that's what it takes to win the day. His stance is one of defense, not aggression. Responds fiercely to such adversity as threats, accusations, indifference, narrow-mindedness, neglect, deception, malevolence, and selfishness. He does "without witness everything that one is capable of doing before all the world" (La Rochefoucauld). Pushes aside fear of retaliation and does what he thinks is right. Listens to only one voice: that small one that guides his soul. Faced with trouble, he performs in that manner which others secretly wish they could have.

May also be called: gallant, hero, heroine, stalwart.

Adjectives: audacious, brash, brave, brazen, courageous, daring, dauntless, doughty, foolhardy, game, gritty, heroic, incautious, intrepid, knightly, lionhearted, mettlesome, nerveless, plucky, rash, resolute, spunky, stouthearted, undaunted, unfearful, unflinching, untimid, valiant, valorous.

THE BUNGLER

A symphony of uncoördination. Has two left hands. All thumbs. Seemingly trips over his own two feet. Should never be put in charge of anything where he has to move something from here to there. Tends to make a mess of things, turn steak into hash, bring the house down upon his ears. Could screw up a glass of water. Things break when he's around. Glue could slip through his fingers.

May also be called: clodhopper.

Adjectives: accident-prone, awkward, butterfingered, clumsy, heavy-handed, left-handed, oafish, ungainly, ungraceful, unhandy.

THE BUSYBODY

Desires to know who did what, where, and when it was done, and also why. A merchant of gossip who trades what others are doing and saying, or have supposed to have done or said. Feeds off private lives. All eyes and ears. Loves dishing the dirt, rolling out a scandal that will create a cascade of whispers. Not interested in the good, only the bad. Does not ask for proof, but something juicy. A human megaphone that advertises the dalliances and miscues of others.

May also be called: gossip, rumormonger, scandalmonger, talebearer, tattletale.

Adjectives: curious, inquisitive, interrogative, nosy, snoopy.

THE CHATTERBOX

Words pour from his mouth as if they were rain and he was a gutter downspout. Talks endlessly about nothing in particular. Jumps from subject to subject like a surfer in rough water, even interrupting himself with new thoughts that, to him, demand expression. Doesn't listen very well, if he does at all. Only by mistake does he utter something truly important. Seemingly does not pause to think. Everything apparently comes flying off the top of his head, or from a deep well of memories. Roller-skates through his mind and ticker-tapes what he finds there.

May also be called: babbler, chatterer, gabber, gasbag, gossip, jaw-box, magpie, prattler, talker, windbag.

Adjectives: chatty, gabby, garrulous, gassy, glib, loquacious, talkative, windy.

THE CONCEALER

A keeper of secrets that are of his own making. A self-designated trustee of information or experiences that may or may not have importance. Does not wish to share what he knows about someone or something, and he will, as they say, take it to his grave. Doesn't breathe a word. Plays dumb when asked about something that he wants to remain covered up and relishes the perpetration of mystery. Guards the skeletons in the closet and the sights that were not supposed to be seen. Does not trade his inside information. Places a lid on something he knows and is never tempted to reveal it, possibly because of the harm it might do and possibly because he believes it is no one's business. Fearful that others will misconstrue the facts.

Adjectives: close-mouthed, concealing, evasive, secretive, unrevealing.

THE CONFORMIST

Walks the same path worn smooth by the great majority. Follows the rules. Keeps in step with the prevailing fashion, dutifully maintaining the cadence laid down. Unable to improvise. A chorus member rather than a soloist. Inclined to wear the same kind of clothes, live where he is expected to live, speak the words he believes to be acceptable, pursue the same dreams that all the others chase, and have his values verified by them. Leads a rather commonplace life. A slave to monotony; inclined to endure, without complaint, the trite and tedious. Very little is expected of him, and he obliges by not doing anything unusual that will set him apart from the great mass of people. Spends most of his time trying to make ends meet and attempts to suck some moments of pleasure from the years that rush by. Dreams of having a pension and living comfortably in old age. He will love, but not greatly; and when he dies, the record of his existence will trail off into oblivion as family members continue to recall less, photographs yellow and disappear, and visits to his grave are discontinued.

May also be called: humdrummer, second-rater, traditionalist.

Adjectives: conventional, dreary, imitative, ordinary, orthodox, unexciting, unimaginative, unoriginal.

THE CRITIC
(*See also* the Grouch)

Would find fault with the tilt of an angel's wing. Persistently dissatisfied with the performance of others. Invariably sees such things as incompetence, laziness, and waste wherever he looks. Never at a loss in his attempt to find something of which he can disapprove. Nothing ever quite pleases him. Knows where all the "soft spots" are in other people. Giving compliments is foreign to his nature. Talks disparagingly about people behind their back. Casts aspersions as if he were fishing with a large net. Maliciously circulates criticisms that have no basis in fact. Even when things go well, he can still find something to bitch about. Sets himself up as the judge of everyone else. Leaps to conclusions. Places a high value on those things that are truly trivial. Has a vocabulary filled with poison darts.

May also be called: backbiter, disparager, faultfinder, henpecker, muckraker, mudslinger, nag, slanderer.

Adjectives: backbiting, belittling, caustic, censorious, critical, defamatory, denunciatory, disapprobatory, hypercritical, insulting, maligning, nagging, obnoxious, offensive, quarrelsome, recriminatory, reproachful, sarcastic, scolding, slandering, uncomplimentary.

THE DAWDLER

Takes him forever to get something done. Plods along, dillydallies, and does not pull his fair share of the load. Shirks his responsibilities for as long as he can, preferring to do things at his own convenience. Takes long breaks and has plenty of time to gab with co-workers. Frequently late.

May also be called: foot-dragger, goldbricker, goof off, laggard, malingerer, nap-taker, slowpoke, sluggard.

Adjectives: dawdling, fatigued, lazybones, lethargic, lingering, listless, loitering, lumpish, slow-footed, slow-moving, slow-paced, somnambulant, turtlelike, unproductive, weary-footed.

THE DECEIVER
(*See also* the Hypocrite; the Pretender)

He is not what he appears. Psychologically, he is a sleight-of-hand artist, a Venus flytrap, a pirate who flies a false flag. Adept at obscuring the truth, framing bold lies, setting traps, identifying dupes, being something other than what he is. His skill at "pulling the wool over someone's eyes" is only surpassed by his sheer enjoyment of it. Purposely deceives another to gain something monetarily. Has no compunction about creating elaborate ruses to gain the confidence of others and, in the end, get something from them. Has more tricks than a caterpillar has legs. Adept at plotting and maneuvering. Lives by his wits.

May also be called: Artful Dodger, bamboozler, carpetbagger, charlatan, cheat, chiseler, con man, faker, flimflammer, four-flusher, fraud, gypster, horse trader, hypocrite, impostor, liar, perjurer, Philadelphia lawyer, phony, prevaricator, quack, schemer, sharper, slyboots, snake in the grass, swindler, trickster, two-timer, a wolf in sheep's clothing.

Adjectives: artificial, clever, cunning, delusive, dishonest, double-crossing, double-dealing, exaggerative, false-hearted, foxy, fraudulent, guileful, hypocritical, insidious, insincere, Machiavellian, manipulative, mealy-mouthed, pretentious, scheming, shifty, sly, smooth-tongued, treacherous, tricky, truthless, two-faced, unctuous, underhanded, ungenuine, untruthful, wily.

THE DIPLOMAT
(See also the Peacekeeper)

Exceptionally tactful in all social situations. Speaks and acts in such a way that no one is likely to become offended. Does not want to be seen favoring one side over the other, and yet, when he is through, each side is likely to think that he stands with them. His smoothness is disarming, his attempts at good naturedness seemingly sincere. If he wants to make a point or relate a piece of bad news, he will go to great lengths to cushion the blow of that information. Consistently tries to stay in harmony with the situation.

May also be called: fence-straddler, politician.

Adjectives: buttery, civil, complimentary, courteous, discreet, facilitating, flattering, glib, gracious, greasy, honey-mouthed, judicious, polished, polite, slick, slippery, smooth, smooth-tongued, suave, tactful, uncritical, well-mannered.

THE DISREGARDER
(See also the Yawner)

The accent is on indifference. His attitude: So what? Displays a complete lack of interest in either a particular series of events or someone's behavior pattern. Looks at something as being unworthy of his attention. When presented with some facts, replies that he has more important things to worry about. Has no desire to know what someone has done or not done, or what has happened or not happened, and would like the subject to be dropped. Acts as if he were blind to what is going on. Regarding a particular subject, tends to brush it aside, turn a deaf ear, think no more of it.

Adjectives: blasé, disregardful, distracted, heedless, inattentive, indifferent, lackadaisical, negligent, neutral, nonchalant, oblivious, unconcerned, unenthusiastic, unmindful, unobservant, unprepared, unwatchful.

THE DISSIPATER

Lacks self-control. Forever at the mercy of whatever his body craves, *e.g.,* liquor, food, sex, drugs, etc. Lacks the will to contain his desires. Goes on binges. Falls from grace.

May also be called: backslider, barfly, boozehound, boozer, drug addict, drunkard, free liver, glutton, hedonist, lush, rounder, sensualist, sot, tippler.

Adjectives: alcoholic, besotted, debauched, gluttonous, intemperate, licentious, overindulgent, piggish, self-indulgent, sensual, unrestrained.

THE DREAMER

Without being ambitious or optimistic, yearns for something while not knowing how to achieve it and while harboring no hope that it will ever happen. Trapped on the island of Idle Fancies in that he may dream of being wealthy without any skills of making money, or of being famous without knowing what he could do to make most people realize that he is alive. Dreams of faraway places, wild adventures, and sizzling romance. Delicious thoughts of glory, intrigue, and danger transport him from his commonplace world to a place where his presence is valued, his decision-making sharp and momentous.

May also be called: castle-builder, daydreamer, moonraker, pipedreamer, Walter Mitty, woolgatherer.

THE DUPE

Has a trusting nature and is always the prime target of the deceiver. Accepts most things he hears as being true. Swallows something hook, line, and sinker. Easily swindled, taken advantage of. Does not use his head to question something that is too good to be true. Persistently unaware of evil.

May also be called: babe in the woods, believer, easy mark, greenhorn, innocent, pushover, sap, Simple Simon.

Adjectives: deceivable, deludable, exploitable, foolable, green, guileless, gullible, ingenuous, naïve, unassuming, unsophisticated, unsuspecting.

THE ECCENTRIC

Displays behavior that is decidedly different from the norm, that which others may call perverse, odd, out-of-the ordinary, or just plain weird. Causes people to raise their eyebrows, to talk in hushed tones about him, and to say, "Well! If that doesn't beat all!" Or he may raise giggles or cause smiling heads to shake good naturedly. Some may think his mind has slipped a gear, that his thoughts are running in reverse of clear reason. Others will humor him and take in stride, perhaps, that he tries to catch mosquitoes with chopsticks.

May also be called: caution, crackpot, curiosity, flake, nonconformist, oddball, oddity, queer duck, screwball.

Adjectives: abnormal, bizarre, buggy, crotchety, erratic, flaky, peculiar, queer, uncommon, unconformable, unconventional, unnatural, unorthodox, unusual, wacky.

THE ECONOMIZER
(*See also* the Keeper)

Tries to stretch his money as far as it will go, but he will nevertheless come to someone's aid — if he can. Always looking for bargains. Collects string, buttons, and various odds and ends, so as not to have to buy them later. Puts his money in the bank, religiously. Performs wonders with leftovers. Does not waste what he has today, for fear that he will need it tomorrow, and the waste he sees happening consistently in the world depresses him. If he attends an event, he buys the "cheap seats."

Adjectives: economical, frugal, penny-pinching, saving, self-depriving, self-sacrificing, sparing, stinting, thrifty.

THE EGOTIST

Admires the "virtues" he sees in himself. Sitting in vanity's corner, he is likely to put on airs, to brag, and to be so self-admiring sometimes as to make a cat laugh. He is, as they say, stuck on himself and the only modesty he knows is what he might see in other people. Because he is so wrapped up in what he perceives as his own superior talents, accomplishments, beauty, or social status, it is unlikely that he will pay much attention to anything that does not come out of his own mouth. Likes to see heads turn his way when he enters a room. Believes he has accomplished far more than he really has. In his own mind, no one can measure up to himself. Has time for no one but himself.

May also be called: blowhard, boaster, braggart, dandy, egocentric, exhibitionist, fop, grandstander, know-it-all, peacock, prig, snob, swaggerer, swellhead, show-off.

Adjectives: affected, boastful, bombastic, cocky, conceited, dandified, flashy, grandiose, haughty, high and mighty, high-hatted, high-nosed, high-toned, hoity-toity, inflated, insolent, ostentatious, pompous, pretentious, prideful, puffed up, self-applauding, self-centered, self-congratulatory, self-devoted, self-esteeming, self-inflated, self-praising, self-satisfied, showy, snooty, strutful, stuck-up, swaggering, swell-headed, theatrical, top-lofty, uppish, vain, vainglorious.

THE EXPLORER

Seeks knowledge. Beset with an innate curiosity. Always probing, investigating. Must get to the bottom of something. Pokes about. Tracks things down. Wishes to deepen his understanding through the avenue of books. Pursues discovery through trial and error. Intrigued by other places, customs, cultures. Travels down well-worn paths hewed out by old arguments and looks for detours, dead-ends, and escape routes. Chases the finer points of truth through labyrinths. Has more questions than answers.

May also be called: analyzer, eavesdropper, examiner, inspector, investigator, researcher, scholar, seeker, student, traveler.

Adjectives: cross-examining, exploratory, inquiring, inquisitive, interrogative, intrusive, meddlesome, nosy, officious, probing, prying, questioning, snoopy.

THE EXTROVERT
(*See also* the Reveler)

At ease among others and seeks their company. Likes rubbing elbows with the crowd. Quickly adapts to almost any social situation. A creator of superficial friendships, a cultivator of countless acquaintances. Uses words like "buddy" and "honey." A smile merchant whose welcome mat is always out. Finds pleasure in idle conversation and parties; indeed, he is the bee who buzzes from group to group at any festive occasion. If you are new, he is among the first to welcome you. Drops in unexpectedly, just to say "hi" and pass the time of day. Inhospitality perplexes and disturbs him. Likes to embrace and touch others, and to talk about old times. A better talker than he is a listener.

May also be called: backslapper, belle of the ball, gadfly, mixer, socializer.

Adjectives: affable, agreeable, amiable, amicable, approachable, chummy, communicative, companionable, congenial, convivial, cordial, entertaining, fraternizing, friendly, gregarious, harmonious, hospitable, jolly, neighborly, sociable, unreserved, vivacious.

THE FLIRT

Skilled at using an inherent charm to attract the opposite sex. But on the part of those not taken by that charm and who see it as a sham, the flirt may be accused of casting goo-goo eyes, whispering sweet nothings, or laying siege to someone's affections. Plays cat-and-mouse games that are sexual in nature. Toys with those who become captivated; seduces through tender endearments, soft embraces, or even copulation. Always seems to have a come-hither look. Consistently engaged in the act of courtship, without wanting to be burdened with the obligations that come with it. Likes to conquer the affections of another, but does not want to nurture them. A butterfly that flits from flower to flower. Loves being chased while, at the same time, it seems to the casual onlooker that he is the one doing the chasing. Knows how to snuggle at just the right moment, how to seem helpless and in need of protection, how to turn a head when needed.

May also be called: coquette, gold digger, ladies' man, masher, philanderer, skirt chaser, vamp.

Adjectives: coquettish, flirtatious.

THE GIVER

Unselfishly generous. Will sacrifice at least a portion of what he owns, or will donate his time, to help someone else. Has a need to share with others. Tries to make others take what they do not want, with advice often being one of them. A patient listener. His acts of giving frequently go unnoticed, for they are done without the knowledge of the recipient. Provides someone with what that person needs before the latter even asks for it. Takes great pains to make others comfortable. Can hardly pass a beggar on the street without giving something. At his most generous level, may be heard to say, "What's mine is yours"—and mean it. Can be counted on to chip in, supply, aid, or subsidize. Gives freely and cheerfully. Spares no expense. Willing to forgive for past wrongs suffered.

May also be called: almsgiver, befriender, benefactor, contributor, donor, Good Samaritan, helper, lender, philanthropist, subsidizer.

Adjectives: benevolent, big-hearted, charitable, considerate, forgiving, generous, gracious, kindhearted, liberal, magnanimous, munificent, openhanded, philanthropic, sacrificial, unselfish, well-intentioned, well meaning.

THE GO-GETTER
(*See also* the Hound; the Hustler)

Trademark is ambition. Wants to gain something, *e.g.*, fame, wealth, justice, honor, popularity, respect, a higher social status, etc. Without being greedy, believes he can attain more than he has. Does nothing halfhearted. Has targets in his mind, however vague. If there is a "pecking order," he knows its structure and how to use it to his advantage. Burns the so-called midnight oil. If he takes a fancy to something, he makes plans on how to get it.

May also be called: aspirant, dynamo, eager beaver, hustler, workaholic.

Adjectives: aggressive, ambitious, aspiring, assiduous, desirous, determined, diligent, eager, energetic, enterprising, enthusiastic, high-reaching, industrious, inspired, motivated, purposeful, up-and-coming, upward-looking, yearnful, or wishful.

THE GRIEVER

Yearns for the presence of someone, *e.g.*, a spouse, child, parent, family member, or friend, who has died. Remembers the good times they had together or the special bond that had been built between them. The absence is so painful that he can no longer visit the places where they used to go together. Something always happens every day that makes him think lovingly of that person. Memories bring smiles and tears. Visits the gravesite.

May also be called: lamenter, mourner.

Adjectives: funereal, grieving, lamenting, mournful, plaintive, regretful, sad, sorrowful, tearful.

THE GROUCH
(*See also* the Critic)

A thorn in the side of everyone else. Paint his attitude black, his reasons gray. A stranger to courtesy. A sour face that beckons no smile. A volcano that never erupts but constantly rumbles. A chronic complainer who is never happy with anything. Differs significantly from the Critic in that his faultfinding is usually not comprised of lightning bolts directed at specific targets; instead, he can be heard mumbling to himself like distant thunder. A huffer and puffer who, on the surface, seems to like no one and for no particular reason. Griping about things seems as natural to him as breathing. Crusty on the outside, soft on the inside.

May also be called: bellyacher, crab, grouser, grumbler, sourpuss.

Adjectives: cantankerous, complaining, crabby, cranky, curt, grouchy, gruff, grumbling, grumpy, ill-humored, ill-natured, inhospitable, insufferable, irritating, misanthropic, obnoxious, offensive, scowling, sour-tempered, testy, thin-skinned, touchy, unfriendly, ungracious, unsociable, vexatious.

THE HARDHEAD

After deciding that something is true or not true, holds his ground and won't yield an inch. Weathers the storm. Convictions are deeply rooted and not movable. Compromise is out of the question. Remains firmly committed long after everyone else has gone to the other side. Will not listen to any reasoning that introduces the possibility that he may be wrong.

May also be called: bulldog, die-hard, pighead.

Adjectives: bullheaded, determined, entrenched, firm, fixed, headstrong, immovable, indefatigable, indocile, indomitable, inflexible, intractable, obstinate, pigheaded, recalcitrant, resistant, resolute, rigid, stiff, strong-minded, strong-willed, stubborn, tenacious, tough, unbending, unbreakable, unchangeable, uncompromising, unpliable, unrelenting, unsubmissive, unyielding.

THE HOTHEAD

Loses his temper easily. May hurl invectives, throw things, or threaten bodily harm — if in fact he does not come to blows with someone. Something that is seemingly inconsequential can set him off, make him go on a tear, send him into an orbit of fumes, flares, and beet-red flushes. A walking powder keg. Others are careful what they say around him. Can't take a joke, if it's at his own expense. Patience is virtually nonexistent within him. "Sudden and quick in quarrel" (Shakespeare).

May also be called: fire-eater, holy terror, spitfire.

Adjectives: contentious, excitable, explosive, hot-tempered, impatient, irascible, quarrelsome, quick-tempered, scrappy, short-tempered, rampageous, turbulent, volcanic.

THE HOUND
(*See also* the Go-Getter; the Hustler)

Committed to the chase. Whatever it is that he seeks, leaves no stone unturned in his effort to find it. Keeps at it, despite setbacks. Takes a never-say-die attitude. Hates to admit defeat. Stays after something from the beginning to what may become the bitter end. No obstacle is too high; no clue is too small; no journey is too long. Does not hesitate. His purpose may be so fixed that it may become a detriment to other parts of his life.

Adjectives: assiduous, constant, diligent, dogged, indefatigable, persevering, plodding, resolute, tenacious, tireless, unhesitating, unrelenting, unremitting, unswerving, untiring.

THE HUSTLER
(*See also* the Go-Getter; the Hound)

Full of energy and a hard worker, though not necessarily ambitious. Tries hard and makes a special effort to do something right. Always in a hurry, on the move. Goes all out. Darts ahead. Takes the attitude that he must be doing something most of the time. Once committed to something, devotes a great deal of time toward it. Does nothing halfway. Walks fast. He is the one who makes things hum, who keeps the pot boiling, and who doesn't let the grass grow under his feet. Will practically break his neck to get something somewhere and on time. May be heard to say, "Let's get a move on!" or "Shake a leg!" Likely to skip lunch to get a job done. Doesn't know how to relax. Can go longer than most without sleep and will burn the midnight oil. Pitches in without being asked.

May also be called: dynamo, eager beaver, go-getter, hard worker, hustler, man of action, workaholic.

Adjectives: aggressive, assiduous, bustling, diligent, energetic, enterprising, hurried, industrious, peppy, productive, speedy, spirited, vivacious, workaholic.

THE HYPOCHONDRIAC

Consistently depressed about the state of his health and tends to imagine he has every disease he reads or hears about. Manufactures symptoms where none exist. Feels he is not far from death's door. Takes his blood pressure too often, makes too much out of a sneeze, and takes medicine and vitamins as if they were candy. The common cold can nearly kill him, psychologically. His name appears often on the doctor's calendar. Wears his family and friends out with his anxiety. Always on the prowl for remedies. A perfect dupe for the quack.

May also be called: complainer, imaginary invalid, neurotic.

Adjectives: anxious, apprehensive, fretful, tormented.

THE HYPOCRITE
(*See also* the Deceiver)

Engages in deception, for he secretly takes part in the very behavior he openly condemns. Convinces others that his actions are decent, when in fact they are indecent. Quick to accuse, but self-excuses. Embraces pretense. A contradiction. A wolf in sheep's clothing. An angel with badly tarnished wings.

May also be called: charlatan, fake, four-flusher, impostor, phony, quack.

Adjectives: affected, artificial, counterfeit, deceitful, double-dealing, goody-goody, hypocritical, insincere, mealy-mouthed, oily, overnice, over-refined, sanctimonious, smooth-tongued, superficial, two-faced.

THE IDEALIST

Believes the impossible can happen — given the right opportunity and if others are shown what is within their grasp. Convinced that people — if educated, or given options, or appealed to in the right way — will in turn act for the good of the general welfare. Has a higher regard for mankind's mentality than the latter has proven is deserving. Breathless in his passion for the way things could be, rather than the way they are and have always been. Embraces obscure principles as if they were commandments from Heaven itself. The prince of all panaceas.

May also be called: castle-builder, dreamer.

Adjectives: dreamy-eyed, impractical, romantic, starry-eyed, unpractical, unrealistic.

THE IMMORALIST

No interest in improving his spiritual nature, but is instead lured toward those things that appeal to his base instincts. Bereft of conscience, he takes delight in corrupting the morals of others. Shows no misgivings for having done something that somehow harms someone, as he has attempted to please himself. Sees nothing wrong with deception if it gets him what he wants. Spurns those actions that lift the soul above the snarls, and then sighs for more. Unable to understand what possible difference it could make to strive for even the lowest level of goodness. Attaches little or no importance to loyalty or reputation. Shocks others by engaging in behavior that is considered scandalous by the majority. Shuns those principles requiring the sacrifice of a deeply embedded carnal desire. His need to be instantly gratified is overpowering. Sometimes he unintentionally allows his desire for self-satisfaction to slip into an act of cruelty. Has an ongoing love affair with injustice, in all its forms. Scoffs at the notion that one should be considerate of others, that having a sense of duty provides one with a passport to respect.

May also be called: black sheep, crook, desperado, hoodlum, lost soul, profligate, reprobate, sinner, skunk.

Adjectives: adulterous, amoral, base, contemptible, corrupt, debauched, decadent, degenerate, despicable, dishonest, disreputable, double-dealing, ignoble, immoral, iniquitous, loose, lost, obscene, perfidious, scandalous, self-indulgent, sinful, treacherous, unchaste, unclean, unconscientious, underhanded, unprincipled, unscrupulous, unvirtuous, vile, wanton, wayward, wicked, wretched.

THE INTELLECTUAL

Reasons things out before acting. Wants to know the who, what, where, why, and how of things. Examines both sides, looking for weaknesses and strengths. Argues both sides in his mind. Wants answers, and is forever in pursuit of elusive truth. Likes solving things. Attracted to riddles. Always comparing, weighing one thing against another. Theorizes, hypothesizes, and speculates. Has a desire to know something inside out. Some may see him as a walking encyclopedia. Inclined to meditate and reflect. Able to concentrate on a matter for long periods. Mentally peels away the layers of a subject rather than accept what, at first glance, seems obvious. Examines and re-examines. Tireless in his mental search, even if he has to feel his way.

May also be called: analyzer, examiner, logician, seeker, thinker.

Adjectives: analytical, astute, contemplative, deliberative, discerning, examinational, exploratory, inspectional, interrogatory, investigative, judicious, logical, perceptive, philosophical, questioning, reasoning, scholarly, well-educated, well-informed, well-read.

THE INTIMIDATOR
(*See also* the Authoritarian; the Warrior)

Unlike the Authoritarian or the Warrior, the power he exerts over others rests solely upon their fear of him. Here, for example, one will find the toughest kid in school, the terrorist, the mean-spirited tax collector, the wife-beater, the tyrannical boss or parent. Takes his stand openly or resorts to hit-run-and-hide tactics. Avoided by those who are afraid that he will attack their soft spots, or rub their patience raw, or use his position to their disadvantage. Behind his smile lies the distinct possibility of great harm. Takes pleasure in tormenting others in some way. Does not know the meaning of pity. Maltreats those who try valiantly to remain loyal to him.

May also be called: abuser, anarchist, browbeater, bully, goon, harasser, heckler, hoodlum, hooligan, merciless, militarist, persecutor, pitiless, ruffian, terrorist, tormentor, ugly customer, warmonger.

Adjectives: aggressive, bellicose, belligerent, chauvinistic, combative, contentious, cutthroat, distressing, exasperating, galling, hurtful, intimidating, irritating, jingoistic, militaristic, provoking, pugnacious, tormenting, warlike.

THE INTROVERT

Keeps to himself, choosing to go unnoticed as if he were an undusted bottle on a forgotten shelf. Not at all unfriendly, but his self-imposed timidity makes him uncomfortable with the social niceties, *e.g.*, the ready handshake, the warm greetings, the idle chit-chat. Afraid of making a fool of himself. Hides within his self-imposed shell. Self-consciously squirms under the gaze of others. Blushes easily. Inclined to compare himself to others and, in the process, underestimate his abilities and contributions. If he does feel pride, he holds it tightly to himself rather than flourishes it. Envies the extrovert's ease among others. Has no outward affectations to draw attention.

Adjectives: humble, inaccessible, meek, modest, mousy, reserved, restrained, reticent, retiring, self-conscious, self-depreciative, self-effacing, shrinking, shy, timid, unassuming, uncommunicative, ungregarious, unpretentious, withdrawn.

THE JUMPER

Inclined to act on the spur of the moment. Spends almost no time in thinking things through and evaluating what may be the potential consequences of his swift action. The proverbial bolt out of the blue. Overall, does most things in an ill-considered manner. Does not deliberate, play it safe, or pay much attention to advice. His life seems to be one long improvisation. May seek direction after he learns he has made a mistake, but scant may be the hope that he will even listen then.

Adjectives: careless, hasty, heedless, impetuous, impulsive, undeliberate, unthinking.

THE KEEPER
(*See also* the Economizer)

Does not want to share with anyone, no matter how small the possession may be. Personal proverb: It is more divine to hold on to something than to give it away. Views his possessions and his time as things quite precious; thus, he withholds them from others. Getting money from him may be akin to extracting an infected tooth from a rattlesnake. Ownership is extremely important, and he likes to "corner the market" and be recognized for having more of something than anyone else. Does not appreciate that he has far more than he could ever possibly use. Resents mooching of any stripe. To keep more of what he has, would deprive even himself of some of the smallest pleasures. Because it is his, he cannot even let go of that which no longer serves a real purpose. Can never be heard to say, "What's mine is yours." Rare is that which slips through his fingers. His relinquishment for the good of another would be extraordinary, for once something is within his grasp it almost always remains locked there.

May also be called: acquisitor, collector, curmudgeon, miser, money-grubber, monopolizer, pinchfist, possessor, skinflint, tightwad.

Adjectives: acquisitive, cheap, clinging, closefisted, grasping, grudging, hoggish, illiberal, miserly, moneygrubbing, monopolistic, niggardly, parsimonious, penny-pinching, penurious, piggish, possessive, retentive, scrimping, selfish, stingy, tenacious, tight, ungenerous.

THE KNOW-NOTHING

Lacks knowledge, either by his own doing or because of a mental deficiency. Wouldn't recognize beans if the bag was open. Anything beyond the simplest direction confuses him. Cannot read or write. Unable to discern the many shades of gray that lie between the black and white of a subject. Can be easily led astray by those he likes. An empty vessel.

May also be called: dunce.

Adjectives: bonehead, dense, doltish, dopey, dull-witted, dumb, empty-headed, featherbrained, foolish, ignorant, illiterate, muddleheaded, oafish, slow-witted, stupid, thick, unaware, uneducated, unenlightened, uninformed, unintelligent, unlearned, unreasoning, vacuous.

THE LACONIAN

Says as little as possible, regardless of the subject. Uses words as if each one cost five dollars, sticking to "yes" or "no" when either will suffice. Despises small talk and all forms of gossip, and his friends are likely to feel likewise. Won't talk idly about the weather. Often viewed by talkers as being standoffish.

Secrets are often safe with him, if not essential to him. Because he says so little, may be mistaken for being a good listener.

May also be called: man of few words.

Adjectives: close-mouthed, distant, inaccessible, laconic, private, reserved, restrained, secluded, silent, taciturn, terse, tight-lipped, uncommunicative, untalkative.

THE LAGGARD

Has no ambition. Tends to fall behind because he takes things easy, one day at a time; does not know the meaning of "buckling down," of putting his "nose to the grindstone," of "applying himself"; sees nothing worth getting excited about. Low-energy level. Gets ideas as easily as clouds slip past the moon but he puts things off. Sleepwalks through life.

May also be called: bench warmer, dillydallier, good-for-nothing, idler, ne'er-do-well, putterer.

Adjectives: aimless, idle, inactive, indolent, languorous, leisurely, negligent, nonaggressive, purposeless, remiss, shiftless, slothful, sluggish, unambitious, unenterprising.

THE LONER

More likely to be seen alone than with another person. His solitude creates a mystery that causes others to speculate about him. Probably doesn't have a close friend. Fiercely independent. One gets the feeling that he could be stranded somewhere and still survive without any trouble. Does not depend on anyone. If he was in a bar, you would find him at a corner table that was farthest away from the crowd. There is fierceness about him. Has a rough-hewn determination that lacks any well-defined goal. Smiling doesn't come easily to him, but he is not unfriendly. Accompanied by a stillness. Freedom is terribly important to him. The furthest thing removed from a gadfly. If he is married, the unwritten contract of give-and-take won't be an easy one for him to honor.

Adjectives: aloof, distant, independent, private, reclusive, self-governing, self-reliant, standoffish, suspicious, uncompanionable.

THE LOSER

Has fallen well short of his potential. Has fizzled out, missed the mark, bitten the dust, fallen on hard times, been a victim of circumstances. Has not lived up to his advance billing. Had everything within his reach, but lost it. Blew his big chance. Made a wrong turn in life; zigged when he should have zagged. The conquered rather than the conqueror. Has never been able to buy a break. Held back for some reason, and now it's too late. Went out into the world unprepared and has taken more than his fair share of lumps. Laid an egg. Might as well fold up his tent and go home. Crapped out. Has no prospects of ever rising above his present life's station. If his debts were fleas, he would be itching all over. Lives hand-to-mouth.

May also be called: also-ran, big flop, boob, down-and-outer, failure, flunky, have-not, pauper, poor man, poor white trash, thud, washout.

Adjectives: bankrupt, bested, borrower, conquered, debtor, defeated, destitute, down-and-out, down-at-the-heels, financially embarrassed, indigent, jinxed, licked, needy, obstructed, pauperized, penniless, poverty-stricken, stone-broke, strapped, unaccomplished, unlucky, unmoneyed, unprosperous, unsuccessful, vanquished, whipped.

THE LUMINARY
(*See also* the Winner)

Seen by others as being important, or distinguished, or exceptional. Rated highly. Said to be the biggest frog in the pond, a person to be reckoned with, one whose reputation precedes him. Holds a position of some authority in society. Has done something that has brought him fame and respect. "The observed of all observers" (Shakespeare). Causes a flurry of excitement and interest.

May also be called: big shot, big wheel, bigwig, dignitary, magnate, mogul, notable, tycoon.

Adjectives: distinguished, eminent, famous, illustrious, important, notable, prominent, reputable, well-thought-of.

THE MALCONTENT
(*See also* the Repenter)

Wrestles with uncertainty. Has become disillusioned, discouraged, or brokenhearted. Feels victimized by something he cannot name. Believes he should be somewhere other than where he is, but the direction may well be hidden from him. Displeasure rises like a flood tide and fills the caverns of his composure. Questions about what he should do and not do keep him off balance. Walks about looking for answers. Humor has left him and he fidgets beneath the hands of some misfortune on his back. Has lost something that cannot be retrieved. A shadow hangs over his soul. Wishes things were otherwise. Looks about for a handhold in which to pull up. Cannot put Humpty-Dumpty back together again. Fights grief blindfolded. Wishes things were like they used to be. Got a bad case of the mopes.

Adjectives: anxious, apprehensive, bothered, brooding, careworn, cheerless, dejected, depressed, despondent, disconsolate, discontented, discouraged, disenchanted, disgruntled, disillusioned, dispirited, disquieted, dissatisfied, doleful, dreary, forlorn, gloomy, glum, grave, heartsick, heavy-hearted, long-faced, melancholic, miserable, moody, moping, restless, solemn, tense, tormented, tortured, troubled, uncheerful, uneasy, unhappy, unsatisfied, vexed, wistful, woeful, worried, wretched.

THE MARTYR

An egotist who needs to have others indebted to him. Tries to bury guilt and gratitude in the minds of others as a result of what he believes he has done for them, *e.g.*, "Look what I've done for you" or "I don't know what you'd do without me." Constantly seeks appreciation while affecting modesty for his deeds. Often knows what psychological buttons to push. Convinced that others cannot do without him. Must gain leverage by proving his indispensability. Overestimates his contributions, which are carefully catalogued in his mind. The classic martyr is the parent who won't let the child forget what has been done on his or her behalf.

May also be called: company man.

Adjectives: manipulative, praise-seeking, self-sacrificing.

THE MENTOR

Dispenses wisdom to another. Wants others to benefit from the lessons he has learned, the errors he has made, the things he has discovered. Provides words of caution. Not afraid to scold his "student" when the latter acts in an imprudent manner or forgets to follow the lessons taught.

May also be called: advisor, counselor, instructor, teacher.

Adjectives: admonitory, advisory, enlightening, informative, instructive.

THE MISFIT

Not in harmony with his or her environment. Unable to adapt to his surroundings. Quietly frustrated with most things around him, but lacking any notion on where to find contentment. Without knowing exactly why, feels uncomfortable with what he is doing, who his acquaintances are, and who everyone thinks he is. He is a chord in search of a symphony, a wolf in the suppressive desert, a bird whose wings are clipped, a rocket on a hardware store shelf.

Adjectives: ill-matched, inharmonious, unsuited.

THE MORALIST
(*See also* the Paragon)

Feels a strong obligation to duty, fairness, honesty, and benevolence.

Strives to do what is right. Cornerstone of his nature is marked by a sense of honor, which he takes every precaution not to blemish. Possesses an innocence that is seemingly unspoiled by the world's many deceptions. Has the strength to ignore that temptation which would grant him pleasure but which would leave someone else less well off. Hears, loud and clear, that small voice of conscience. Guided by principles that forbid him to take advantage of anyone. If he pledges his word, you can count on it.

May also be called: altruist, do-gooder, first-rater, paragon, straight-shooter, topnotcher.

Adjectives: artless, conscientious, correct, decent, dutiful, duty-bound, good, guileless, high-principled, honorable, proper, reputable, upstanding, virtuous, wholesome.

THE NEGLECTER

Careless about the way he conducts his affairs and performs his responsibilities. Tends to throw things together in a haphazard manner. Leaves things undone, lets things slide, loses track of what is important. Always putting things off until tomorrow. Does things piecemeal, dragging them out far beyond the time when they should have been done. Throws things in a pile, fudges the numbers in a hurry, and files it away in no particular order. Skips over the hard part. Leaves a lot of loose threads hanging.

May also be called: procrastinator.

Adjectives: careless, disregardful, forgetful, heedless, hit-or-miss, inattentive, negligent, reckless, slipshod, slovenly, unexacting, unmeticulous.

THE NOBODY

Has done nothing that would draw attention to himself; thus, no one notices him. He is blanketed with unimportance, relegated to being a face in the crowd. His name is easily forgotten, and his job is something that is impossible to remember. Fades into the woodwork. A name in a telephone book. A nonentity in clothes and shoes.

May also be called: John or Jane Doe, man in the street, small fry.

Adjectives: common, commonplace, insignificant, ordinary, small-time, unexceptional, unimportant, unnoteworthy.

THE NONCONFORMIST

Has an aversion to conformity; frequently shocks those who embrace the ordinary; always at odds with the status quo; breaks with tradition, questions accepted truths; leans in the opposite direction of which the majority demand that he go; contemptuous of blind obedience and dogma; attracted to that which lies off the beaten path; perennially out of step by his design.

Adjectives: audacious, daring, defiant, eccentric, oddballish, unconformable unconventional, undisciplined, unorthodox, unyielding.

THE OPTIMIST

A repository for hope, that which Emily Dickinson describes as "the thing with feathers that perches in the soul." Convinced that things will either get better or that they happen for the best. Buoyed by bright expectations. Infused with an inextinguishable inner cheerfulness. Immune to failure. Can spot a tiny drop of promise in a sea of dread. A living antidote for defeat. Looks at the world through rose-colored glasses. Makes the best of a bad situation. Counts his chickens before they are hatched.

May also be called: Pollyanna.

Adjectives: anticipative, blithe, buoyant, cheerful, confident, encouraged, enthusiastic, expectant, forward-looking, hopeful, optimistic, sanguine.

THE ORGANIZER

Likes to keep things in order. Has a place for everything and wants to keep everything in its place. Prefers establishing a systematic approach to things and determining priorities. Dislikes irregularities, unevenness, spasmodic or intermittent occurrences, fluctuation, haphazardness. Hates loose ends. Strives for tidiness. Wants things to fall neatly into place. Categorizes, tabulates, and files things by rank, alphabetical order, and general classification. Tinkers with methods, with the hope of streamlining them. Daily habits help lend structure to his life. Makes preparations for the unexpected.

May also be called: neat freak, fussbudget, picture-straightener.

Adjectives: businesslike, efficient, exacting, fussy, methodical, orderly, systematic, precise, punctilious, structured, thorough, tidy.

THE OUTCAST

Stands rejected by those who feel he no longer holds any worth for them, for he has either done something or been accused of something that has offended them. Denied entry into a group that may once have gladly accepted him. Brushed aside as no longer important. Bears the silence of others' disapproval. Has become guilty of something that no one gives a name. Loses favoritism as a result of his associations. The focal point of great dislike. Repelled by those who are sickened or embarrassed by his physical deformity.

May also be called: castaway, pariah, untouchable.

Adjectives: abandoned, blackballed, disapproved, discarded, disdained, disowned, forsaken, rejected, renounced, scorned, spurned, unappreciated, uninvited, unloved, unvalued, unwanted, unwelcome.

THE PACIFIST
(*See also* the Accommodator; the Bootlicker; the Poltroon)

Takes special care not to offend anyone in any way. Willing to make concessions. Inclined to accept the terms dictated by an aggressor rather than make a "big deal" out of something. Will go considerably more than half way to get along with others. Tries to disarm belligerence toward him with a smile, a nervous giggle. Confrontation upsets him. If someone gets mad at him, he is the first one to try to patch things up. Says, "I'm sorry" quite a bit. The Prince of Neutrality in that he steers a middle course and will not take sides. Does not want to be controversial. For him, he feels it's a lot better to go along so that he can get along.

Adjectives: cautious, nonaggressive, noncombative, nonconfrontational, nonpartisan, pacific, peaceable, unbelligerent, uncontentious, unhostile, unpugnacious.

THE PARAGON
(*See also* the Moralist)

The Moralist at his highest level of excellence. His virtues sparkle. Finds value in the effort that others devote toward improving themselves, but pays no mind to the level he himself has attained. Anger slips away from him like water. Does not desire what others have. Refuses to harshly judge others for what they did or should have done. Views the future with optimism. Unsparing in his effort to help others. Does all those things that are characteristic of saints, but not because he wishes to be recognized as one.

May also be called: one in a million.

Adjectives: angelic, excellent, first-rate, flawless, good, highly-polished, irreproachable, magnificent, moral, pure, saintly, sinless, splendid, spotless, superexcellent, superior, uncorrupt, unsoiled, unsullied, virtuous.

THE PEACEKEEPER
(*See also* the Diplomat)

Looks for things that bring people together rather than what sets them apart. Attempts to avert conflict between them. Seeks areas where they might find compatibility rather than confrontation. Tries to mediate, patch things up, settle differences, heal wounds, disarm aggression. Seeks concessions from both sides. Preserves the middle ground. Believes that people should try to get along. Builds bridges between people and attempts to dismantle the barriers they have erected. Sees war as nonsensical and destructive, whether it is broad-based or simply between two people.

May also be called: arbiter, conciliator, go-between, intermediary, mediator, middleman, moderator, negotiator, noncombatant, pacifist, referee, spokesman, umpire.

Adjectives: diplomatic, fair-minded, impartial, intercessionary, mediatory, neutral, nonpartisan, peaceable.

THE PERFECTIONIST

Meticulous about almost everything that is important to him — it must be "just so." May have some traits that are peculiar to the organizer, but is essentially quite different in that he continuously strives for excellence — sometimes in the case of others as well. Will not do anything halfway. Shortcomings found in his own efforts cause self-incrimination, followed by more work to achieve improvement; errors on the part of others bring him dismay and a renewed effort to help them achieve perfection. Prone to read the fine print in a contract and to follow step-by-step written instructions. Hard to please. Overly concerned about trivial matters. Insists that all forms of etiquette be precisely followed.

May also be called: fuddy-duddy, fussbudget, stickler.

Adjectives: conscientious, disciplined, exacting, fastidious, finicky, hypercritical, meticulous, painstaking, particular, persnickety, picky, punctilious, rigid, scrupulous, selective.

THE PESSIMIST

Holds the view that everything in life has been designed to make man's life perfectly miserable and that anything promising is merely a mask over some yet-to-be-seen torment. Sees unnamed impediments around every corner. Distrusts anything that would motivate most people to feel good. Estranged from hope. Feels that universal forces have conspired to make him unlucky and therefore miserable, no matter what he does and how hard he tries. Fully expects the worst to happen; when it does, he not only feels justified but has something else with which to replace it. Hears the approaching footsteps of danger, but is deaf to those sounding the approach of good times. Carries the blues on his back like a knapsack. Defeated before he even begins.

May also be called: crepehanger, defeatist, killjoy, skeleton at the feast, sorrow-seeker, spoilsport, wet blanket, worrywart.

Adjectives: brooding, cheerless, cynical, despairing, despondent, disconsolate, doleful, downhearted, funereal, gloomy, glum, inconsolable, joyless, low-spirited, melancholy, miserable, moody, mournful, somber, sorrowful, uncheerful, woeful.

THE PLAIN DEALER

Speaks honestly and expects the same in return. Says what he thinks, not what he believes someone wants to hear. An "open book." Never puts on airs.

May choose to say nothing if the truth threatens to harm someone unnecessarily. Doesn't act one way around one person and then behave another way when he is with someone else. Never embellishes a fact. Does not get involved in transporting conjecture.

Adjectives: candid, direct, ethical, forthright, guileless, honorable, matter-of-fact, open-and-aboveboard, principled, reputable, sincere, square-dealing, straightforward, straight-shooting, undeceptive, unpretentious, truthful, veracious.

THE POLTROON
(See also the Accommodator; the Bootlicker; the Pacifist)

Tries to stay out of harm's way. Intimidated by anything that could potentially threaten him. Always on guard. Unlikely to do something without having total confidence that the outcome will be favorable. Only bets on sure things. Inclined to worry and be full of questions that begin with "What if," *e.g.*, What if I make a mistake? What if I lose my job? What if they get mad? Tends to become immobilized by doubt. Easily daunted, he remains a perfect candidate for others to browbeat, bully, harass, terrorize, or demoralize, for they will sense his timidity and wish to exploit it. Has an on-going affair with Anxiety. Does not accept dares. Others accuse him of being afraid of his own shadow, of backing out when the going gets rough, of turning tail at the slightest provocation, of abandoning what's right in the face of might. Knows a place where he can feel sheltered.

May also be called: alarmist, big baby, chicken, coward, fraidycat, jellyfish, knee-knocker, milksop, safeguarder, scaredy-cat, weakling, white feather.

Adjectives: afraid, apprehensive, chickenhearted, cowardly, cowering, craven, fainthearted, fearful, gritless, hesitant, lily-livered, panicky, pusillanimous, qualmish, reluctant, self-protective, skittish, slinky, terrified, timorous, unadventurous, uncourageous, undaring, unheroic, unvaliant, unvalorous, weak-kneed, white-livered, yellow.

THE POSSESSOR

Anoints himself as the landlord of someone's affections, and is always on the alert that that person will cast some or all of it toward someone other than himself. Feels a sense of ownership, which in reality does not exist. Does not want to share someone's love and attention, but wants it all. Could become revengeful if he thinks he is being slighted. His fear of being replaced causes him to erroneously read the actions of those whom he wants to hold close. Tries to limit the freedom of those whom he watches over.

Adjectives: confining, doubtful, fearful, guarding, jealous, monopolistic, possessive, protective, restrictive, selfish, stifling, suppressive, suspicious, ungenerous, watchful.

THE PREACHER

Speaks at length on almost any subject with which he is conversant. One person may constitute his audience. Delivers long, rambling opinions. Pounds things to create exclamation marks. Has the so-called gift of gab, as words percolate out of him in one grand profusion. May blast the ear, utter thunderous proclamations, stir emotions from among a collection of blank faces. Hurls words at the heart of his listeners, which may arouse them, frighten them, or set their minds to singing. At his best he can inflate a dwindling passion; at his worst, his words will be met with a desire for him to shut up.

May also be called: lecturer, phrasemonger, speechmaker, windbag.

Adjectives: discursive, dramatic, eloquent, flowery, forceful, high-sounding, long-winded, lyrical, majestic, melodramatic, passionate, sensational, silver-tongued, theatrical.

THE PRETENDER
(*See also* the Deceiver; the Hypocrite)

The pretender deceives himself rather than someone else, and his motives are usually glaringly obvious. Does not have the credentials to be what he would like others to think he is, but that does not stop him from acting the part of the group with which he wishes to be associated. Has possibly convinced himself that if he appears to be what he wishes he was over a long enough period, that it will somehow become true. Thus, if he does all the fashionable things necessary to keep up with the Joneses, he will one day catch up with them. If he pretends to be a sophisticate, with all the responsibilities that entails, surely some of the necessities will one day rub off on him. Or if he pretends to be highly moralistic, or knowledgeable, or successful, or whatever else he wishes others to see him as, perhaps the day will come when he will indeed be fully compatible with the thing he is imitating.

May also be called: bluenose, fake, fine lady, fop, four-flusher, fraud, goody-two-shoes, impostor, man about town, mannerist, masquerader, phony, prig, puritan.

Adjectives: affected, artificial, counterfeit, dandified, dressy, flashy, foppish, gaudy, goody-goody, highfalutin, high-toned, grandstanding, mannered, ostentatious, over-refined, pompous, pretentious, prudish, puritanical, Quakerish, showy, stagy, strait-laced, swaggering, theatrical.

THE PRISONER

Psychologically rather than physically behind bars. Has a desire, for example, to escape from what he perceives as a suffocating restriction, one which may involve his family, a marriage, a romantic relationship, a job or career, a social environment, an economic level, his own past, some form of monotony, etc. Could be a prisoner of his own lies. Similar to a dog that is tied outside, stretches whatever rope he is given until it is taut and no more slack is possible.

THE PROGNOSTICATOR

Possesses an inexplicable sixth sense that provides some special insight into the future, which may or may not be in great detail — or he either thinks or pretends he does. (If the latter is true, *see* the Deceiver.) Instinctively feels that something will happen somewhere or to someone in particular. Subject to occasional visions. Perceives trends before their conception. Reads omens that appear in the natural world. Looks for omens in nature. Interprets historical parallels. Reads tea leaves, crystal balls, human palms, the juxtaposition of the stars. Warns others of bad days coming. Talks of Judgment Day and the Day of Reckoning. Predicts special things that will take place in the lives of others.

May also be called: astrologist, diviner, forecaster, fortune-teller, oracle, palmist, predictor, prophesier, prophet, psychic, seer, soothsayer.

Adjectives: divinatory, farsighted, foreknowing, foreseeing, intuitive, messenger, precognizant, predictive, presageful, prognostic, prophetic, second-sighted.

THE PROMOTER

Always engaged in the practice of selling himself to others. But since almost everyone becomes a promoter at one time or another — for example, a job interview is a promotion and so is a simple argument between two people who try to "sell" their conflicting viewpoints to each other — what separates the actual Promoter from those who do their promotions sporadically is that his desire to "sell" is the cornerstone of his nature, if not essential to his survival. In the latter instance, his reputation, his livelihood — indeed, his very life — may well hinge on his ability to persuade someone to do or not do something. His powers of persuasion and dissuasion are above average. His ability to encourage, tantalize, and seduce are essential tools in his arsenal. Makes offers, overtures, and requests. Haggles, drives a hard bargain, negotiates, sweetens the pot. Pursues the close of the deal. Forcefully presents his case.

May also be called: booster, hawker, huckster, lawyer, peddler, petitioner, pitchman, preacher, salesman, solicitor, stump speaker, wheeler-dealer.

Adjectives: dissuasive, enticing, persuasive, promotive, provocative, seductive, self-promoting.

THE PROTECTOR

Chooses to be protective of someone or something, *e.g.*, the watchful parent, the best friend, etc. Has a need to ensure someone's safety, or from being taken advantage of, or being humiliated in any way. But the guardianship may be directed toward keeping someone's memory alive in the minds of others — that is, making sure that they honor what the deceased represented. As a protector of something that is nonhuman — for example, an environmentalist who wants to protect nature's gifts or the person who wants to preserve some government institutions — he may be filled with civic pride.

May also be called: defender, guardian, safekeeper.

Adjectives: sheltering, shielding.

THE PSYCHO

Has an inability to reason effectively. Hallucinates frequently. When he broods or displays elation it is usually excessive. Exhibits two or more distinct personalities. Has delusions of grandeur or persecution. His fears and his passions are always in the extreme, *e.g.*, may consistently worry about his health while also being terrified of medicine. In the grip of a compulsion, such as stealing, telling lies, or having sex. Avoids realities by imagining nothing but pleasantries. Lives in a fantasy world. Has a need to burn things or set off explosives.

Adjectives: demented, deranged, insane, unbalanced.

THE QUIBBLER

Often seems to speak with two tongues in that he is inclined to leave his listeners confused about what he means to say on a particular subject. A creator of double meanings. Presents two possible interpretations within the same breath. A riddle-maker. A generator of doubt. A masker of full-blown truths. A creator of the obscure. Mixes his pros and cons in such a way that someone else is unable to determine if he is for or against something. Never seems to come to the point. At all costs, avoids making a declarative statement.

Adjectives: ambiguous, enigmatic, evasive, hair-splitting, indefinite, indistinct, perplexing.

THE RASCAL

Attracted to mischief, though without intent to harm anyone. Enjoys a harmless prank, something to give everyone a big laugh. In school, he is forever the class cutup. Addicted to practical jokes. Lacks verbal wit, so his teasing is rather trite. Always looking to see what kind of innocuous trouble he can find to amuse himself.

May also be called: caution, cutup, imp, knave, mischief-maker, prankster, rogue, scalawag, scamp, tease.

Adjectives: mischievous, naughty, playful, rascally.

THE REALIST

Riveted to the here and now, to what's practical rather than what's remotely possible. Wedded to the physical world around him. Unimaginative in that he does not produce quaint pictures in his mind nor chase shooting stars of his own creation into the far-flung blackness of thought. Only interested in what he can see, hear, or touch. Judges the merit of things based upon their immediate usefulness to society. Capable of making the dreamer's ideas usable. Not interested in the romance of the thing, but whether or not it will work and if someone can use it. Remembers things as they really were and refuses to attach any more importance or significance than is deserving.

May also be called: pragmatist.

Adjectives: down-to-earth, matter-of-fact, practical-minded, unimaginative, unromantic, unsentimental.

THE REBEL

Naturally inclined to oppose, to run counter to, to contradict, to resist. Has the nerve to say "no" to those who expect an unqualified "yes sir." Displays a penchant for protests, confrontation, and mutiny. Warms quickly to the thought of dissent, disagreement, and protest.

May also be called: insurrectionist, insurgent, mutineer.

Adjectives: anarchical, antagonistic, belligerent, contentious, contrary, discordant, disobedient, disregardful, hostile, incompliant, insubordinate, insurrectionary, pugnacious, rebellious, recalcitrant, revolutionary, seditionary, undutiful, unsubmissive.

THE REFORMER

Wants to transform, reshape, amend, convert, rehabilitate, or overthrow what already exists. Desires to do what is right rather than expedient. Subordinates himself to a principle, *e.g.*, democracy or gun control. Believes that truth is on his side and appeals to the conscience of others. Intolerant of injustice or exceptions to the rule. A world-improver.

May also be called: moral leader, perfectionist, preacher, radical, rebel.

Adjectives: crusading, ethical, high-minded, high-principled, insurrectionary, judgmental, obsessed, revolutionary, self-disciplined, self-righteous.

THE REPENTER
(*See also* the Malcontent)

Has either said something about someone or has done something that has adversely affected that person, and it now weighs heavily on his conscience. Feels a need to somehow compensate for his infraction, to do something to offset the pain of his guilt. Ponders how he might counterbalance his own insensitivity. Agonizes over how he might salve the wounds he caused while not losing face in the process. Has a desire to make amends, to somehow square accounts. Needs to feel atonement, no matter what the personal cost may be.

Adjectives: apologetic, conscience-stricken, contrite, grieved, guilty, heart-stricken, heavy-hearted, miserable, penitent, plagued, regretful, repentant, rueful, self-accusing, self-condemning, self-reproachful, sorrow-laden, tormented, uncomfortable, wretched.

THE REVELER
(*See also* the Extrovert)

Principally interested in entertaining himself. His motto: Eat, drink, and be merry, for tomorrow we may die. Loves a good game, parties, a night on the town, and clowning around. Relishes going places where he can have some fun, kick up his heels, and raise a little hell. Addicted to music, the louder the better. For him, life is a banquet and he wants his seat at the table. He will dance and sing long into the night, even if he can do neither very well. Lives for the weekends. Has a storehouse of jokes and amusing experiences that he can use to enliven a situation, to jump-start a gathering. Enjoys making love and all the advantages that come with engaging in romance, but doesn't want his good times spoiled with talk about commitment.

Adjectives: amorous, carousing, comical, frolicsome, party-goer, playful, rompish, sportive, waggish.

THE RUBE

Has no understanding of the fine arts, though to impress others a dishonest claim of appreciation is certainly possible on his part. Lacking such an appreciation, however, does not preclude his ability to be quite intelligent. At the same time, the perception may well be that he is vulgar and without the sensibilities to associate with those of a more sophisticated nature. A victim of the environment to which he is born rather than the one he has chosen. Sees the highbrow as a phony or a stuffed-shirt. Vocabulary is imbedded with a certain coarseness. His manners are noticeably rough. Gazes in astonishment at things he has never seen before, but which may nevertheless be commonplace. Overall knowledge is at best superficial. Out of his so-called element, he appears hopelessly awkward and ill at ease. A member of the middle or lower class. A haystack on a city street.

May also be called: boor, bumpkin, clodhopper, hayseed, hick, know-nothing, provincial, ruffian, rustic, vulgarian, yokel.

Adjectives: coarse, common, crass, crude, hickish, illiterate, ill-mannered, indecent, loutish, lowbrow, rough, uncivilized, uncouth, uncultured, ungenteel, unkempt, unlearned, unpolished, unrefined.

THE RUT WALKER

Establishes a wide array of routines, each of which is performed almost daily, in virtually the same order, and at times that do not vary greatly from the same routines that were performed years before. Dislikes interruptions and surprises. Any deviation from his habits, for whatever reason, will more than likely frustrate him. His daily actions are almost wholly predictable. Seen by others as "set in his ways" or as a "creature of habit." Does not take kindly to suggestions that there is a better way of getting something done. Most of his actions are characterized by a high degree of certainty.

Adjectives: Habitual, methodical, predictable, systematic.

THE SAFEGUARDER

Thinks and acts cautiously. Takes great pains not to do something he will later regret. Looks before he leaps. Doesn't like surprises. Always on his guard. Like a well-armed sentry, ensures that no one will slip past and take advantage of him. Chooses his steps carefully, lest he make a wrong move. Before doing anything of importance, observes the way the wind blows, notices how the land lies, checks his getaway possibilities, and triple-checks the route to be taken. Tries to determine if there is anything hiding behind the rocks or just over the hill. His motto: An ounce of prevention is worth a pound of cure. Always ready to sound the alarm.

Adjectives: apprehensive, cagey, careful, cautious, chary, circumspect, discreet, judicious, leery, politic, preventive, prudent, pussyfooting, suspicious, unadventurous, unenterprising, wary.

THE SCOUNDREL

The Immoralist at his worst. Not only wants what someone else has but will use every underhanded method available to get it. Finds death and destruction enormously satisfying, especially when it comes from his own hands. Amuses himself with thoughts on how to bring the most harm with the least effort. Measures his success in terms of how much trouble he can bring to others. Does the exact opposite of everything that the Ten Commandments says one should do and not do. Feels no allegiance toward anyone at any time.

May also be called: blackguard, destroyer, evildoer, reptile, scum of the earth, skunk.

Adjectives: abominable, awful, baneful, base, contemptible, corrupted, deplorable, despicable, detestable, disgraceful, disreputable, evil, ignoble, infamous, inglorious, injurious, mistrusted, poisonous, scandalous, shameful, vile, unregretful, unrepentant.

THE SENTIMENTALIST

Romances the past instead of the future. Glorifies a stretch of time, a romantic rendezvous, a place that has become idealized in the mind. Talks about the "good ol' days." Reminisces about someone or a pet that died. Collects mementos that reinforce his romantic memory of someone or something; guilty of trying to keep a memory alive. Thumbs through old photographs, yellowed letters, childhood diaries in a drawer. Suspicious of change and thinks that something good may have been lost because of it.

May also be called: antiquarian.

Adjectives: emotional, maudlin, mushy, nostalgic, old fashioned, reminiscent, romantic.

THE SKEPTIC

Looks at practically everything with distrust, sometimes even questioning what he sees with his own eyes. Demands proof, then looks at the evidence with suspicion. Verification is his by-word. Difficult to persuade. Sniffs for implausibilities. Finds enjoyment in discrediting the irrefutable. Takes things with a grain of salt. Attracted to contradictions. Raises the question that believers don't want asked. Likes shooting holes through dogma, knocking the bottom out of iron-clad opinions.

May also be called: atheist, doubting Thomas, heretic, infidel.

Adjectives: atheistic, disbelieving, dubious, incredulous, irreligious, mistrustful, suspecting, unconvinced, ungullible, world-weary.

THE SLOB

Clutter follows him wherever he goes. Lacks a sense of order in all things he does or wears, finding no more annoyance in the heaps and scatterings of mounting odds and ends than he would in an untied shoestring. Burrows through a mess as if he were born to it. No appreciation of symmetry, harmony, or a straight line. A maestro of chaos. Always hunting for something and, when all else fails, accuses others of not bringing something back. Widely accepted procedures (administrative, etc.) make no impression. Efforts to bring some sense of order to his life are only met with wide-eyed incomprehension. His puts things out of sight, out of mind. Forgets that the devil is always in the details.

May also be called: frump, litterbug, slummock.

Adjectives: careless, disarranged, disheveled, disorderly, disorganized, disregardful, frowzy, frumpish, haphazard, messy, negligent, rumpled, slatternly, slipshod, sloppy, slovenly, unconscientious, undisciplined, unkempt, unmethodical, unparticular, unsystematic, untidy.

THE SMILER

Claims the ground between extrovert and introvert, in that he does not boldly insert himself into the company of others, yet is quite hospitable when approached. Engages in idle chit-chat. Extends sincere compliments. Pays attention to what others have to say. Has a smile for everyone, as well as a "thank you," a "good morning" and a "see you tomorrow." The soul of courtesy. But nothing much of consequence may fall from his lips, for he does not want to say something offensive or to seem out of step with others. May be heard to say, "Whatever the rest of you want to do is okay with me." A Mona Lisa. If he was a dog, his tail would be wagging for no apparent reason.

Adjectives: charming, cheerful, congenial, considerate, convivial, engaging, friendly, genial, good-natured, good-tempered, gracious, lighthearted, mannerly, pert, pleasant, respectful, sociable, sunny.

THE SNITCH

Exposes that which would otherwise remain hidden. Tells one or more secrets to one or more people. Confesses his complicity. Acknowledges what others have always suspected was true. Unmasks a lie that has deceived a great many. Tells the truth under pressure. Fear of recrimination forces him to insinuate rather than boldly attest. Wittingly or unwittingly betrays a confidence, spills the beans, brings something into the light. Becomes a witness against someone.

May also be called: betrayer, blabber, fingerpointer, informer, revealer, snitch, squealer, stool pigeon, tattler.

Adjectives: confessional, enlightening, informative.

THE SNOB

Looks for things that set people apart rather than what binds them. A creator of monetary, religious, geographical, or racial divisions and barriers.

Looks at himself as being better than someone else. Ability to understand the lifestyle of another group is practically nonexistent. Separates, isolates, shuts out, rejects, excludes. Fond of pecking orders, color-line barriers, and class structures. Abhors the notion that he should try to mix with those who are not in his so-called class. Appalled when he learns that he too is not welcome within a group into which he thought he had access.

May also be called: bigot, highbrow, high-hatter, illiberal, prig, racist, segregationist.

Adjectives: aloof, arrogant, biased, bigoted, class-conscious, contemptuous, disdainful, disrespectful, haughty, high-hatted, high-nosed, hoity-toity, imperious, intolerant, lordly, narrow-minded, partial, prejudiced, scornful, small-minded, snob, snooty, standoffish, stuck-up, supercilious, unindulgent, unsympathetic, uppity.

THE SOFTY

Inclined to weep for those who experience misfortune. Deeply touched by stories that have either happy or sad endings. Has the ability to mentally put himself in the other fellow's shoes, and thus feel the gladness or sorrow that abounds in that person's soul. Wears his heart on his sleeve. His emotions can be played like a stringed instrument. Falls for any sob story that comes down the pike. Swells with pity when a living thing suffers. Wishes he could stop others' pain and make their misfortune go away. Understands misery without being in its grip. Has a reservoir of tears that is easily tapped. A desire to help is ever-present. Feels guilty because he was spared the misfortune he sees, and he also feels guilty because he is glad that he was.

May also be called: bleeding heart, soft touch.

Adjectives: affectionate, commiserative, compassionate, concerned, condolent, emotional, empathetic, kindhearted, merciful, openhearted, sensitive, softhearted, soulful, sympathetic, tenderhearted.

THE SOPHISTICATE

Attracted to what is viewed as the world's more elevated features, among which may include any of the artistic attractions — that is, fine literature, classical music, great architecture, the ballet, paintings, etc. Has a deep appreciation for those gifts bestowed by nature. Has an intelligence that enables him to grasp at least some of the complex refinements that comprise those things he admires. Views with scorn those things that fail to fall within those areas he so admires.

May also be called: high-hat.

Adjectives: cultivated, cultured, educated, erudite, genteel, high-class, learned, polished, refined, well-bred, well-mannered, well-read.

THE SPENDTHRIFT

Has never owned a dollar that he didn't want to spend on himself or someone else. Has no serious attachment to money; sees it merely as a means of exchange for something he wants far more. Fritters away his paycheck on things that are not important. Does not save for that so-called rainy day. His motto: Easy come, easy go. Squanders what he has, as if plenty more were coming. In a burst of senseless generosity, may be heard to say, "Hang the expense."

May also be called: prodigal, wastrel.

Adjectives: dissipative, extravagant, improvident, incontinent, profligate, unrestrained, thriftless, uneconomical, unthrifty, wasteful.

THE STOIC

Happiness and sadness do not register on his face, but rather are buried in his heart. He is a closed book, an indecipherable inscription. Feels it is unbecoming to show how he feels about something. Meets pleasantness and unpleasantness as if they were only strangers passing through. Never shows nervousness or even a residue of doubt. Without complaint, does what must be done. Sometimes he acts as if he didn't care about the outcome, when in fact the exact opposite may be true. Takes things as they come. All of his emotions seem to be in perfect equilibrium. In comparison to others, he sometimes appears to be a steel bar standing in a plate of spaghetti.

May also be called: cool customer, man of iron.

Adjectives: calm, cool, coolheaded, enduring, even-tempered, forbearant, imperturbable, level-headed, long-suffering, patient, persevering, poised, self-confident, self-controlled, serene, steady, steel-nerved, stoical, strong-nerved, uncomplaining, unexcitable, unshrinking.

THE STONE

Can look unblinkingly at someone's misery and feel nothing, as if his soul were encased in an impenetrable shell; but, by the same token, neither does he extract pleasure from observing someone's misfortune. Nothing really plays on his heart strings. Has no tears to spare. Compassion does not fog up his observations. Able to look at the saddest of scenes without ever becoming emotionally involved. Perplexed by sympathy, the idea of guilt. Views misfortune as a fact of life, not an occasion for commiseration. His own experiences have blunted his feelings.

Adjectives: callous, cold-hearted, detached, dispassionate, frigid, hardened, hard-hearted, impassive, indifferent, objective, thick-skinned, uncompassionate, unconcerned, unemotional, unfeeling, unmoved, unsympathetic.

THE SUPPORTER

Will not abandon a friend, lover, or family member, or even those whom, from afar, he supports for some reason — even when it may be far more convenient to do otherwise. Commitments are never shallow, but are rather deeply embedded and verge on permanence. Remains faithful long after everyone else has given up. Stands as the one person you can call when you are in trouble, no matter if it is the middle of the night. Does not engage in second-guessing. The pillar one leans upon. Quick to lend a hand, provide aide, take someone's side, go to bat for, and offer words of encouragement. Remains by one's side during times of trouble. A constant companion, a faithful friend. Intensely loyal. Displays understanding when almost no one else will. Comes when called; stays after everyone else has gone. Forever plays second fiddle.

May also be called: advocate, backer, buddy, chum, collaborator, colleague, companion, comrade, crony, friend, man Friday, partner, patron, right-hand man, sidekick, teammate, upholder.

Adjectives: complimentary, constant, faithful, helpful, loyal, persevering, steadfast, sympathetic, trustworthy, understanding, unfaltering, unhesitating.

THE TAKER

Seizes that which does not belong to him, or he readily accepts whatever is offered to him without ever giving thought to repayment.

As one who pounces upon that which he believes he requires, he will resort to whatever means necessary to gain it. Has the patience to lie in wait for an interminable length of time. Sees possession as 99-percent ownership. If he wants men, he will commandeer them; if he wants land, he will annex it; if he wants money, he will steal it; whatever it is that entices him, he does not allow morality or any hindrance to deter him. If his taking impoverishes another, so be it. His mind is totally focused upon the prize to be had rather than upon the person who currently holds it. When he sees an opportunity, has no compunction about overcharging. More than happy to bleed one dry.

As the receiver of that which is kindly given, the words "thank you" rarely form on his lips; if they do, they are laden with insincerity. He will continue to accept whatever someone continues to give; there is no point when he says, "Enough!" Neither guilt nor gratitude can find a home in his heart. Easily forgets the benefits he has received.

May also be called: bloodsucker, buccaneer, extortionist, ingrate, looter, pirate, plagiarizer, plunderer, poacher, privateer, profiteer, robber, thief, vulture.

Adjectives: cutthroat, larcenous, light-fingered, plunderous, predatory, thievish, unappreciative, ungrateful, unthankful.

The Traitor

Cannot be counted upon to stand by his promises. Mouths loyalty, but is not committed. Sells himself to the highest bidder. Able to withdraw from an allegiance with no compunction. When it is convenient for him to do so, disavows any warm association with those whom he once claimed to support. Switches religion, politics, principles, and friendships as easily as he might change shoes. Goes the way the wind blows.

May also be called: apostate, backslider, betrayer, deserter, double-dealer, rat, renegade, scab, snake in the grass, turncoat, turntail.

Adjectives: bolter, disloyal, false, faithless, traitorous, treacherous, treasonous, two-faced, unfaithful, untrue.

The Vacillator

Wavers between what he thinks he should do and not do. Lacks core convictions. Subject to frequent mind changes and attitude reversals, without ever being sure he is committed to the right course. Often does not know which way to turn. Highly persuadable. Usually attracted to the last argument he hears on a matter. Cursed by the fact that he often sees the merit regarding both sides of an argument. Blows hot and cold; hems and haws; flip-flops on any issue at almost any time. Once he makes up his mind to do something, immediately wonders if he is not making a mistake. Has as many phases as the moon. Grows dilemmas in his mind as if they were grass. Acts as though he had two minds, one being contrary to the other and causing his thoughts to teeter-totter. Tends to delay taking action until the very last minute.

May also be called: chameleon, rolling stone, weather vane.

Adjectives: capricious, desultory, elastic, erratic, fickle, flighty, fluctuating, hesitant, inconstant, indecisive, irresolute, pliable, shilly-shallying, uncertain, unconfident, unreliable, weak-willed, willy-nilly, wishy-washy.

The Vegetator

Life is marked by a distinct passivity and quite likely attended by daily monotony that does not seem pervasive. To quote a cliché: snug as a bug in a rug. More wealth, status, or achievement would not render greater satisfaction; ambition, therefore, is at a treading-water stage. Content with the way things are, barring perhaps a few minor irritations that the world always manages to impose upon the living. Healthy, worry-free, and not burdened with any meaningful regrets or pangs of conscience. Faces the future without reservations or anxiety. Entertains a rather casual optimism.

Adjectives: blissful, comfortable, complacent, contented, cozy, happy, pleased, relaxed, satisfied, unbothered, undisturbed, untroubled.

THE VETERAN

Highly experienced in a particular area. Seen as the "old hand"—the person who has been around, who has been through it all before, who has seen it all, who knows how to do it, who's aware of what all the little secrets are. Knows the ropes, the ins and outs, and the little shortcuts that make things easier. The one person to turn to when you get stuck. Not born yesterday. Knows where the bodies are buried. Able to find and solve the problem, cut through all the red tape. Nothing gets past him.

May also be called: handyman, Jack-of-all-trades, old soldier, old timer.

Adjectives: accomplished, adept, crackerjack, masterful, practiced, skillful, versatile.

THE VISIONARY

Sees those things that could be, but which may never be. Within that mountainous terrain of the mind, searches for some gossamer stones and an acre upon which to build. Loses all sense of time and place. Juggles wishes. Fabricates notions. Journeys into places that have never been seen outside the circumference of his mind. Has a round-trip ticket to Utopia. Sees the creation before it is created. Hears the sounds before there are words or music.

May also be called: idealist, innovator, inventor, romantic.

Adjectives: absent-minded, creative, dreamy-eyed, fanciful, imaginative, impractical, ingenious, inventive, museful, notional, oblivious, preoccupied, unrealistic, woolgathering.

THE WARRIOR
(*See also* the Authoritarian, the Intimidator)

The Warrior does not try to make others fearful of him. While he is quick to fight, he does it to protect what is important to him. He is not, at heart, an aggressor; he is, for example, the athlete who must win, the debater who must prevail, the businessman who fends off a takeover of his company, the attorney who defends his client—a rival to be reckoned with in a specific area. Strong-willed, but doesn't flaunt it. Picks his quarrels carefully, and, when he does, fights tenaciously to achieve his desired end. At a moment's notice, and either for himself or on behalf of another, will utter a challenge and cross swords with anyone. Engages in a nonphysical assault upon those who wish to deny him entry, who use him as a target for mockery, or who see him as being unimportant.

May also be called: advocate, combatant, competitor, defender, guard, knight-errant.

Adjectives: combative, competitive, contentious, guarded, hostile, strong-willed.

THE WINNER
(See also the Luminary)

Has achieved a recognizable level of success, which may be discerned by the amount of money, property, fame, or achievement that is attributed to him. Has made a so-called noise in the world or has, as they say, made the grade. Born under a lucky star or with a golden touch. Stands at the top of his profession. A voice to be reckoned with. One of the privileged few. Has the upper hand, the advantage, the best of all possible worlds. Has made a killing, won the day, brought home the bacon. Rich as Rockefeller. Has done all right for himself.

May also be called: capitalist, champion, conquering hero, man of means, money-maker, mover and shaker, nabob, plutocrat, tycoon.

Adjectives: accomplished, comfortable, famous, opulent, prosperous, rich, smug, solvent, triumphant, wealthy, well-fixed, well-heeled.

THE YAWNER
(See also the Disregarder)

Different from the Disregarder in that he lacks all curiosity regarding virtually everything. Yawns though life, for there is nothing that particularly interests him. Enthusiasm is so shallow as to be nonexistent. Dwells perpetually within indifference. Plods along like a horse pulling a milk wagon, not thinking about where he has been, where he is going, or what is taking place around him. Questions do not take shape within him.

Adjectives: blasé, bored, indifferent, uninquisitive, uninterested, unquestioning.

11. Does the Character Have a Nickname?

There are literally thousands of nickname possibilities, and it would be far beyond the scope of this book to even begin to list them all. Instead, the emphasis here is placed on the *kinds* of nicknames available, thus allowing a writer to use his or her own imagination in determining what best suits the character in question.

Giving a character a nickname sometimes allows the writer to specifically or implicitly explore another dimension of the story — namely, the attitude of the individual who first hung the nickname on the character, as well as the group that continues to employ it. It is unlikely, for example, that a fat person would call another fat person Fatso. Nor would one Mexican immigrant lay the nickname Mexie on one of his countrymen, even if he didn't like him. Thus, at the core of some nicknames, particularly those that pinpoint the physical appearance or nationality of another, there may exist a thinly veiled prejudice, or a lack of understanding, or perhaps a streak of cruelty. Possibly all three.

On still another plane, some nicknames give the writer a good opportunity to quickly delve into the character's self-assessment. For example, if a character likes being called Ace, why is that? Is he a fighter pilot? A card shark? Does the name enhance the image that he has of himself? But suppose the character hates being called Rooster or Bubbles. Does he accept the handle graciously and feel it's not worth fighting about, or do rivulets of anger run through him each time the name is spoken? In short, does the nickname create a glow inside the character because it fits the profile he has of himself, or does it crack against his ears like an ugly snake whip?

Thus, in selecting a nickname, the writer may find it to his advantage to weigh the motives of the nickname-giver against the reaction of the nickname-wearer.

AMERICAN WEST

Writers frequently use nicknames when they develop stories that take place in America's Wild West. Of course, there is no restriction against using a western-sounding name in a modern story. But in doing so, it is important for an author to keep in mind that readers and moviegoers have long since become conditioned to associate such names with a certain degree of recklessness and free-spiritedness — no matter who they belong to. For example:

Places
Abilene, Arizona, Cheyenne, Dakota, Durango, Yellowstone.

Animals
Bronco, Bucktail, Buffalo, Diamondback, Doggie, Grizzly.

Indian
Birdsong, Blue Fox, Crowfoot, Dark Wing, Eagle Wing, Lightfoot.

Other
Banjo, Buckskin, Cactus, Colt, Giddyup, Saddlebags.

ANIMAL

Nicknames that are taken from the names of animals can serve many descriptive purposes. Some examples:

Appearance: *Ape*	Grace: *Butterfly*	Neck: *Goose*
Voice: *Frog*	Awkwardness: *Camel*	Agility: *Monkey*
Size: *Chigger*	Quickness: *Cobra*	Gait: *Duck*
Color: *Crow*	Slowness: *Snail*	Danger: *Fang*
Greed: *Buzzard*	Silence: *Clam*	Tenacity: *Bulldog*

AUTOMOBILE

Nicknames related to the automobile need not always appear in stories where people own, drive, or fix cars, but it certainly helps. For example, it would make little sense to use the nickname "Greasepit" in a story about landed gentry in antebellum South Carolina. That said, here are just a few nickname possibilities that fall in this category:

Type of Car
Chevy, Hatchback, Hot Rod, Jeep.

Noise
Beep, Blowout, Honk, Screech.

Parts
Bumper, Hub Cap, Lugnut, Wheels.

Other
Oil Can, Roadrunner, Cabby, Lube.

AVIATION

As with auto-related nicknames, those associated with the field of aviation need not always appear in stories where people fly airplanes. For instance, the nickname "Bomber" could be applied to a chief executive officer of a company who has a reputation for suddenly obliterating entire departments with the stroke of his pen. Here are just a few examples of nicknames that are related to the field of aviation:

Bomber	Sonic	Solo	Rocket
Cockpit	Sky King	Tail Spin	Wings
Glider	Runway	May Day	Chute

COMMON

Common nicknames have been used so often over the years that they have since lost any special meaning they might have once held — if in fact they ever had any — and, in terms of impact, they are closely related to those that are simply derivative of first names. Thus, a writer can usually attach such a nickname to a character without worrying about whether it will add anything positive or negative. Among the names that fit comfortably in this group are *Babe, Buddy, Buster, Corky, Dixie,* and *Skip.*

"CUTE"

A "cute" nickname is often given to a character who seems to have a bubbly nature and who lacks any great depth of intellect. Of all the different kinds of nicknames that can be given a character, those in the "cute" category are perhaps the most stereotypical; moreover, they are almost always applied to females, owing perhaps to male chauvinism. They are syrupy and convey the idea that the character has little substance. Possibilities include the following:

Bambi	Cookie	Moofy	Snooky	Tickles
Binky	Cuddles	Mookie	Snowflake	Tittles
Bubbles	Dumplin'	Mooshy	Snuffy	Topsy
Buffy	Fluffy	Muffy	Snuggles	Tuffy
Bunny	Giggles	Poopsie	Sugarfoot	Tweetie
Buttercup	Googie	Precious	Sweet Pea	Twinkie
Chickie	Goo-Goo	Puddles	Tabby	Twinkle
Coo-Coo	Gooky	Punkin'	Taffy	Wiggles

DERIVATIVES

Nicknames that are derived from first names are, of course, the most common. Charles becomes *Chuck*, for example, and Elizabeth becomes *Lizzy*. While such names impart an unmistakable informality and folksiness, they are incapable of adding anything special to a character. They are generic and can usually be adapted to fit hero and villain alike. Lizzy can be a wholesome, freckle-faced girl next door, or the mean-spirited daughter who uses an ax to chop up her parents.

DESCRIPTIVE

A nickname can be used to provide a one- or two-word physical description of the character. It may also describe a particular habit or an item with which the character becomes associated.

Descriptive Feature
Fatso, Little Bit, Knuckleface, Bones.

Descriptive Habit
Smoke, Toothpick, Whiskey, Blackjack.

Descriptive Item
Cap, Rings, G-String, Suitcase.

FAMOUS PERSON

When a character is given the nickname of a famous person, it always comes from the mouth of another character. More often than not, it will be used quite sparingly, or just once. Sometimes, though, the characters in a story will use the nickname often as a way of showing their respect for the admired traits of another. Here are three examples:
Affection: "Whatcha readin' now, *Shakespeare*?"
Respect: "Let's ask *Socrates*. He knows everything."
Derision: "Heard some talk that you're gonna lead us to the Promised Land. That right, *Moses*?"

FOOD

A food-related nickname provides a writer with considerable flexibility in relation to the image he wants to convey. Someone who eats a lot could be nicknamed *Burp*, someone who prefers junk food might be called *Snacks*, and so on. Just a few of the possibilities include the following:

Beans	Crackers	Meatball	Potluck	Spoons
Biscuit	Crumbs	Meatloaf	Pretzel	Spud
Chili Dog	Cupcake	Munchy	Puddin'	Taco
Chowder	Gumdrop	Nibbles	Rib Eye	T-Bone
Cornbread	Kiwi	Noodles	Shortcake	Wishbone
Corncob	Lollipop	Pickles	Soupy	
Crableg	Lunchbox	Popcorn	Sparerib	

However, the food-related nickname may have absolutely nothing to do with what a particular character likes to eat. For example, a character with red hair could be nicknamed *Carrots*; someone from the Far East might be nicknamed *Chopstick*; a so-called hillbilly could be nicknamed *Hambone*. If associated with water, the nickname might be *Crawfish*. An overweight person could be nicknamed *Lard*.

GAMES AND SPORTS

While it's not a hard and fast rule, nicknames associated with games and sports are generally reserved for characters associated with those activities. There are certain terms in each game or sport that lend themselves well to nicknames, with baseball and football possibly leading the pack. (Nicknames pertaining to football often have a heavy connection to the military as well.) Here are some nicknames that could be used for fictional characters who are either interested in sports or participate in them.

Baseball:
Blooper, Dugout, Hummer, Lefty, LoBall, Pick-off, Pop-Up, Shutout, Slider, Slugger, Spitter, Fungo.

Football:
Blitz, Coach, Fumbles, Hut-Hut, Kicker, Touchdown.

Basketball:
Hoop, Swish.

Other:
Ace, Bunker, Homestretch, Jock, Jumper, K.O., Knuckles, Legs, Ping-Pong, Racer, Ring Side, Rink, Shot-Put, Sidepockets, Skater, Spokes, Surfboard, Tee-Shot, Ten Pin, Trotter.

GEOGRAPHIC
(*See also* Nationalities)

If a writer chooses a nickname that links a fictional character to a specific locale, it may or may not have any significance to the story. For example, in the motion picture *Raiders of the Lost Ark*, audiences were not told why the adventurous main character was called *Indiana Jones*. The nickname simply had a lyrical ring to it and it was easy to remember. Some nations, cities, American states, regions, streets, and special areas lend themselves well to nicknames — though certainly not all of them. For instance:

Country:
Burma wore a pair of boots that everyone talked about, made from the hide of an alligator he had killed when it swallowed one of his chickens.

State:
It was a gunfight that *Montana* wanted no part of.

Region:
Slowly, from his sleeve, *Sahara* removed a long-bladed knife.

City:
There in the corner sat *Jericho*, hunched over a dirty glass and a half-bottle of wine.

The shortened names of geographical locations may also be adopted for nicknames. For example:

State:
When Joe looked at *'Bama*, they started to laugh at the same time.

City:
Frisco had the upper hand and he knew it.

Some geographically related nicknames can stand alone; others, however, sound better when they are linked to another name. For example:

First Name:
After he won the football game, they began calling him *Broadway Joe*.

Last Name:
Mountain Miller could shoot the eye out of a squirrel fifty yards away.

Combination:
The only person who stood in his way was *Minnesota Fats*.

INITIALS

Before deciding to use initials for a character's nickname, a writer should consider whether the initials are going to be used extensively throughout the story. If so, they will frequently stand alone — that is, they will not always be joined to a surname — and, therefore, the combined sound of the two letters must fall easily from one's tongue. The combinations most easily spoken include the following:

B.B.	D.C.	G.G.	K.C.	O.J.	T.J.
B.J.	D.D.	J.B.	K.K.	P.C.	T.T.
C.C.	D.J.	J.J.	K.O.	T.C.	Z.Z.

Other initials sound better when they precede a character's last name, although they can occasionally stand alone. Example: "*J.W. Butts* will be the movie's producer."

MILITARY

In the hit motion picture *M*A*S*H*, as well as in the long-running television series that followed, several characters were known by their nicknames, *e.g., Hawkeye* and *Trapper*. But only one of the key characters had a nickname that could be seen as military-related: that was *Radar*, who served as the all-knowing but still rather naïve assistant to the unit commander. A few other typical nickname possibilities that may have a military connection include the following:

Bazooka	Bunker	Scud	Sonar	Torpedo
Bombshell	Gunboat	Scuttlebutt	Tank	
Boots	Sarge	Shine	Taps	

MR. OR MISS

A writer can use a nickname beginning with "Mr." or "Miss" to quickly nail a specific skill, failing, or some other trait into the reader's mind. Such a name is more likely to be used when the writer first introduces the character, and it is rarely referred to again. Should the a nickname appear in the story after that, it will usually be uttered by another character, and usually in a derogatory manner. Here are three examples:

Mr. Arbitrator:
This nickname could imply that the character is skilled at settling differences between people with conflicting viewpoints and purposes. On the other hand, it could also be a nickname given facetiously to a no-nonsense tough guy whose idea of "arbitration" is to yank two enemies across a table until their noses touch, thus getting them to agree on what they thought they never would.

Miss Goody Two-Shoes:
A writer might apply this nickname to a character when it is necessary to quickly establish a sanctimonious image.

Mr. Automatic:
This was the nickname given to Luke Appling, the all-star shortstop who played for the Chicago White Sox. So superior were his fielding skills that practically anything he could reach with his glove was an automatic out. Nicknames that denote a skill are often comprised of adjectives.

MUSIC

In choosing a nickname linked to the field of music, the author must decide whether the name in some way reflects that particular character's interest or activity in music, or some other personal characteristic. Among the great many options that are available, here is just a small fraction:

BeBop	Drummer	Juke Box	Tango
Bluenote	Hi-fi	Melody	Tape Deck
Boogie	Hoofer	Piccolo	Tempo
Crooner	Jazz	Sax	Tin Pan
Dancer	Jingle	Shimmy	Tunes
Ditty	Jitterbug	Spinner	Whistler
Downbeat	Jive	Sticks	Yodel

NATIONALITIES

In selecting a nationality for a nickname, it will perhaps be important that no other character in the story should hail from the same area. It is worth remembering, too, that nicknames may reveal the prejudices of the nickname-giver. Among the possibilities — some of which are offensive — include Aussie, Brit, Chink, Cockney, Dago, Dutch, English, Fin, Frenchie, Irish, Kraut, Limey, Mex, Mexie, Scottie, Shamrock, Swede, Turk, Yank.

NAVAL

In selecting a "naval" nickname, an author may choose one that pertains to an entire ship, part of a ship, or something else that is water-related. For example:

Brig	Hawse	Rudder	Sea Horse	Spars	Windjammer
Clipper	Jigger	Schooner	Seaweed	Steamboat	
Dock	Ram	Scooter	Skiff	Tanker	
Hatch	Rigger	Scull	Sloop	Wharf	

OLD

Nicknames beginning with "old" are similar to those that begin with "Mr." or "Miss." The author usually uses them just once, when first introducing the character, for the purpose of establishing some image in the reader's mind. If used afterwards, the use will be sparing. Three examples:

Old Reliable:
A good nickname to use for a character who can always be counted upon when the going gets rough, or when someone is needed in the clutch.

Ol' Blood and Guts:
A nickname such as this could be applied, for example, to a general who has a habit of sending his men into battle with little planning and no regard for their safety.

Old Pinchface:
This could immediately depict a character's unsociability, someone in the story who could be misanthropic, pitiless, contentious, and so forth.

PRECEDING PROPER NAME

Some nicknames are effective only when they precede a proper name. *Babyface* Nelson and *Pretty Boy* Floyd were two of America's most notorious criminals. However, if you drop the proper name that follows either of them, the nickname sounds awkward. A nickname that is dependent upon a proper name for its existence can be an adjective, a noun, or an adjective-noun combination. Examples:

Adjective
Fearless Fosdick, *Hardhearted* Hannah, *Honest* Abe, *Shoeless* Joe Jackson.

Noun
Calamity Jane, *Homerun* Baker, *Honeysuckle* Rose.

Adjective-Noun
Cool Papa Hines, *Hot Lips* Houlihan, *Red Dog* Rumble, *Blue Eyes* Billy.

STRANGE AND EXOTIC

A strange or exotic nickname may evoke a faraway place or distant fantasy; or it may provide no link to anything that is instantly recognizable. Indeed, a writer may create one by simply arranging letters in a way that provides some special sound, one that seems uniquely suitable for a character he or she has in mind. A writer can also turn familiar utterances into exotic nicknames, *Abracadabra* being one of them. Here are just a few of the countless options a writer has at his or her disposal regarding the selection of a strange or exotic nickname:

Alabaster	Ditto	Jiffy	Poof	Snook
Applejack	Doke	Jinx	Potsie	Snoot
Arrow	Dong	Jipper	Poucho	Snout
Beezer	DooDah	Jolt	Pucker	Spree
Bingo	Dusky	Juju	Puff	Spurlock
Blackstone	Dustwind	Jumbiliah	Quick	Sputz
Blaze	Ember	Jupiter	Rambler	Swoop
Blur	Fireball	Kickapoo	Rango	Swoosh
Boffo	Firebolt	Kiki	Rasco	Swoozie
Bolt	Fizz	Koko	Raven	Tangerine
Breezy	Fleece	Krone	Razzle	Tarf
Briny	Flook	Lava	Rizzy	Tass
Buckhorn	Foto	Lavender	Roo	Tawny
Bupp	Furf	Leek	Rub-a-Dub	Thunderfoot
Burgundy	Glaze	Loo	Sable	Thunderheart
Butterwing	Glory	Madeira	Sapphire	Thunderstroke
Caboodle	Gog	Mahogany	Sark	Ting
Calico	Gong	Marigold	Scuff	Torch
Calypso	Gonzo	Misk	Sess	Touchstone
Cameroon	Gooch	Mog	Shadrack	Trig
Capricorn	Gossamer	Mojo	Shalimar	Trinity
Chantilly	Graywing	Mombo	Sha-Zam	Troon
Chestnut	Groot	Moonbeam	Shoke	Tweedledee
Chiffon	Gypsy	Moonglow	Shoo	Tweedledum
Chime	Hiccup	Mootzie	Silky	Vista
Cinnamon	Hickory	Mungo	Silverado	Weez
Clarion	Hippity	Nighthorse	Silverleaf	Whisper
Clopper	Hojo	Nuff	Sizzle	Whitehorn
Cobalt	Hoochee	Oogie	Skadoo	Whizzer
Coo-Coo	Hoodoo	Orchid	Skat	Yago
Coosh	Hush	Paffy	Skib	Yahoo
Cottonfoot	Iggy	Palamar	Skink	Yaz
Crispy	Imoo	Panky	Slade	Yellow Wing
Cymbal	Indigo	Peekaboo	Slappy	Yellowhammer
Dambi	Jade	Pidge	Slewfoot	Yogo
Dazz	Jangle	Piff	Sligo	Yoho
Dewdrop	Jart	Pojo	Sloo	Yorky
Diggity	Java	Poke	Sneezer	Yo-Yo

Zang	Zazz	Zing	Zoar	Zoot
Zap	Zepher	Zinger	Zook	Zuzu
Zart	Ziggy	Zip	Zookie	

"THE"

The rules that apply to a nickname using "the" are quite similar to those using "Mr.," "Miss," or "Old" — that is, it is usually used by the author just once, and, more often than not, when the character first enters the story. It serves to provide descriptive information that helps to establish some image in the reader's mind. In using such a nickname, the most common practice is to insert it between the first and last name of the character, or after the character's full name. In either case, it should be encased in quotation marks and the word "the" should be capitalized:

Charles "The Muckraker" Williams
Charles Williams, "The Muckraker"

But if the nickname follows the character's first name, and the last name is omitted, "the" is not capitalized and the quotation marks are dropped:

Prufo the Magnificent

Sometimes, however, such a nickname may actually be substituted for the character's real name throughout most of the story, particularly when it comes to villains. Indeed, in some stories where an effort is made to evoke an emotion — say, fear — with a mere mention of the nickname, there may be little need to mention the character's proper name at all. For example, if a character was introduced in this manner, using the nickname throughout the story could possibly be all that is necessary:

> Everyone in town knew who the *Annihilator* was. They had seen him grow up, watched him bully the other kids, steal money in broad daylight and brag about it. The way they saw it, he was a thug from the moment he was born. As for the sheriff, he was scared to death of him. So when Max Harper hired him to collect debts, the *Annihilator* soon assumed an air of importance formerly reserved for members of the Gestapo and similar notorious notables.

Also, the word "the" in some characters' nicknames may be followed by "Mr.," "Miss," or "Old." Two real-life examples are Bette Midler ("The Divine Miss M") and Joe Nuxall, one of the radio announcers for the Cincinnati Reds ("The Old Lefthander").

There are, of course, literally hundreds of nickname possibilities that can be linked with the word "the" and most are nouns. Among them include the following:

Accountant	Bulldozer	Demon	Iron Man
Administrator	Butcher	Devil	Jackal
Agitator	Cannibal	Dragon	Jawbreaker
Ambassador	Capitulator	Elder Statesman	Kingmaker
Apprehender	Chameleon	Emperor	Little Shepherd
Arranger	Chancellor	Engineer	Magnificent
Avenger	Chopper	Eradicator	Man-Eater
Barbarian	Claw	Executioner	Mechanic
Blade	Cleaver	Exterminator	Minuteman
Bodysnatcher	Collaborator	Fixer	Pirate
Brain	Computer	Gladiator	Princess
Breaker	Conqueror	Globetrotter	Shark
Broker	Crepehanger	Hammer	Smasher
Broom	Crusader	Hangman	Spoiler
Bruiser	Crusher	Iceman	Vulture
Buccaneer	Defender	Iron Duke	Warrior

TRADES

The area of construction is rich with nickname possibilities. But many can be found in other fields of labor as well. Here, for instance, are just a few:

Blacktop	Greaser	Rivet	Spade
Blowtorch	Grip	Sash	Striker
Corkscrew	Hammer	Shaker	Tar Pit
Digger	Jigsaw	Shingle	Trench
Drag	Pitchfork	Sixpenny	Trucker
Driller	Pumper	Skid	
Dumper	Ripsaw	Sledge	

VILLAINOUS

The best nicknames for villains are often those that immediately convey some hint of danger. Here are just a few that could possibly fill that function.

Blood	Fist	Skunk	Snatch	Stinger
Brimstone	Gash	Slash	Sniper	Stone
Bruiser	Knucklenose	Slicer	Snort	Strangler
Carve	Knuckles	Slick	Snot	Switchblade
Crush	Masher	Smack	Spike	Wart
Cutter	Scar	Smash	Spook	Weasel
Darkwing	Shooter	Snake	Squint	
Fingers	Skull	Snapper	Stabber	

WEATHER-RELATED

Weather-type nicknames, depending upon the one chosen, can convey a positive, negative, or neutral image to the reader or viewer. Some of these include:

Cyclone	Lightning	Sled	Snow
Misty	Raindrop	Sleet	Snowball
Muddy	Shiver	Slosh	Sprinkle

12. What Is the Character's Job?

Choosing the right kind of job for a fictional character can be just as important as selecting a name. The reader or viewer must be immediately convinced that "yes, that's the kind of thing that person might do." True, the character may be inept at discharging the responsibilities of that job — God knows that happens in real life with extraordinary frequency (for example, the son of a business owner may be totally unsuited for the managerial position his father has given him) — but that won't matter as long as the reader or viewer regards the match-up between character and job as plausible. Conversely, any kind of work that does not seem to fit the character will make it all the more difficult for the author to establish that character's credibility.

What follows is only a partial list of jobs that you may wish to review before assigning a character a line of work. The jobs are divided into major categories. (One of those categories is crime; it's not the kind of work one would find advertised in the help-wanted pages, but it still represents a means by which some characters acquire money.)

AGRICULTURE

beekeeper	farmhand	sharecropper
cattle rancher	field worker	sheep rancher
cowboy	migrant worker	shepherd
crop duster	pig farmer	tobacco farmer
dairyman	plantation owner	wheat farmer
farmer	rancher	

ANIMALS

blacksmith	elephant trainer	hunter
broncobuster	game warden	kennel owner
cat breeder	horse breeder	pet groomer
dog breeder	horse trader	veterinarian
dog trainer	horse trainer	

BEAUTY/FASHION

barber
beautician
coiffeur-coiffeuse
cosmetician
diet workshop
  counselor

dress designer
facial massager
fashion buyer
hairdresser
hatmaker
manicurist

masseur/masseuse
model
pedicurist
perfumer
tanning bed operator
wigmaker

BUSINESS

accountant
accounts payable clerk
accounts receivable
  clerk
activity manager
administrative aide
auditor
bank examiner
bank manager
bank teller
banker
benefits manager
billing clerk
bookkeeper
branch manager
broker
buyer
claims adjuster
client service rep
comptroller (controller)
contractor
copier operator
credit analyst

credit manager
customer support rep.
document manager
economist
exporter
factory owner
financial analyst
financial planner
financier
importer
industrialist
internal auditor
investment advisor
loan officer
mailroom clerk
market research analyst
office manager
payroll manager
pension administrator
personnel assistant
personnel manager
president
promotions coordinator

public relations rep
receptionist
records administrator
regional administrator
regional manager
researcher
sales manager
sales rep
secretary
stockbroker
switchboard operator
systems administrator
tax accountant
trader
typist
underwriter
vice president
warranty supervisor
wholesaler
workers' compensation
  rep

CRAFTS AND TRADES

appliance repairman
auto repairman
baker
barrelmaker
basketmaker

beermaker
beltmaker
boatwright
bookbinder
bootblack

bootmaker
bottlemaker
brewmaster
bricklayer
brickmaker

bronzesmith
broommaker
builder
bulldozer operator
butcher
cabinetmaker
cable installer
calligrapher
candlemaker
candymaker
carpenter
carpet cleaner
carpet layer
chainmaker
chimney sweep
cigarmaker
clock repairman
clocksmith
clothworker
coal miner
cobbler
coffin-maker
computer repairman
cooper
copier repairman
coppersmith
crane operator
demolitionist
diemaker
dishwasher repairman
ditchdigger
dollmaker
draftsman
dressmaker
driveway sealer
drywall hanger
electrician

engraver
furnace repairman
garbage collector
gardener
gas fitter
general contractor
glass blower
glassmaker
glazier
goldsmith
gunsmith
handyman
house painter
ironsmith
ironworker
janitor
junkman
laborer
landscaper
lathe operator
leathermaker
lineman
locksmith
lumberjack
machinist
maintenance man
mapmaker
mason
mechanic
metalworker
miller
milliner
millwright
paper hanger
paving contractor
plasterer
plumber

printer
puttier
remodeler
roofer
rope maker
saddle maker
sausage maker
seamstress
shoe repairman
shoemaker
silversmith
spinner
spot welder
steam fitter
steelworker
steeplejack
stonemason
tailor
tanner
tattoo artist
telephone repairman
television repairman
tentmaker
tinker
tinsmith
truck driver
typesetter
upholsterer
watch repairman
watchmaker
waterproofer
weaver
welder
wine maker
woodworker
wrecker

CREATIVE ARTS

architect
biographer

book editor
book publisher

caricaturist
cartoonist

carver
choreographer
composer
copywriter
engraver
etcher
graphic designer

historian
ice sculptor
illustrator
interior designer
novelist
painter
photographer

playwright
poet
screenwriter
sculptor
short-story writer
sign painter
speechwriter

CRIME

bank robber
bookie
bootlegger
burglar
con artist
counterfeiter
drug dealer
embezzler
extortionist
fence

forger
highwayman
hijacker
holdup man
housebreaker
kidnapper
loan shark
money launderer
moonshiner
numbers runner

pickpocket
pimp
pirate
prostitute
purse snatcher
racketeer
rapist
safecracker
smuggler
thief

DEATH

cemetery lot salesman
coroner
cremator
death notice writer
embalmer

executioner
funeral director
gravedigger
hangman
hearse driver

medical examiner
mortician
pathologist

EDUCATION

assistant dean
career counselor
civics teacher
college president
dean
dorm supervisor

English teacher
foreign language teacher
geometry teacher
headmaster
history teacher
librarian

lunchroom cook
math teacher
music teacher
phys. ed. instructor
professor
school principal

ENTERTAINMENT

acrobat
actor

announcer
ballet dancer

band leader
banjo player

barker
bassoonist
blues singer
booking agent
broadcaster
cameraman
casting director
cellist
choirmaster
chorus boy/girl
clarinetist
clown
comedian
concertinist
conductor
contortionist
costume designer
country singer
cyclist
director (film or stage)
disk jockey
drummer
emcee

female impersonator
fiddler
film editor
folk singer
gag writer
game show host
go-go girl
guitarist
harmonica player
hypnotist
jazz singer
juggler
lion tamer
magician
mime
oboist
opera singer
organist
pianist
pop singer
press agent
producer
program director

rock singer
saxophonist
screenwriter
set designer
showgirl
sound man
sound-effects man
stage manager
stiltwalker
stripper
talent agent
talk-show host
tap dancer
theater owner
theatrical agent
tightrope walker
trapeze artist
trombonist
trumpeter
vaudevillian
ventriloquist
violinist
xylophonist

GOVERNMENT

ambassador
assemblyman
attaché
attorney-general
campaign manager
censor
census taker
chancellor
chargé d'affaires
chief of staff
CIA agent
city councilman
city manager
consul
councilman
emissary

emperor
envoy
FBI agent
floor leader
governor
intelligence officer
mayor
minister
party whip
poll taker
postal inspector
postmaster general
premier
president
prime minister
propagandist

sec. of agriculture
sec. of commerce
sec. of defense
sec. of education
sec. of health and
    human services
sec. of interior
sec. of labor
sec. of treasury
secret agent
state legislator
tax assessor
tax collector
translator
U.N. ambassador
U.S. representative

| U.S. senator | vice chairman | vice governor |
| vice president | vice consul | |

HOTEL, RESTAURANT AND CLUB

banquet manager	cook's helper	headwaiter
bartender	counter person	host/hostess
bellhop	country club manager	hotel manager
bouncer	dining room supervisor	landscaper
busboy	dishwasher	maître d'
carhop	doorman	motel owner
cashier	elevator operator	porter
chambermaid	food server	restaurant manager
charwoman	front-desk clerk	valet
chef	gift shop clerk	waiter/waitress
cook	golf pro	

JOURNALISM

book reviewer	gossip columnist	proofreader
columnist	investigative reporter	science writer
copy reader	magazine publisher	society columnist
drama critic	movie critic	sportswriter
editor	news anchor	TV critic
food columnist	news reporter	typesetter
foreign correspondent	newspaper publisher	war correspondent
ghost writer	pamphlet publisher	

LAW

bailiff	divorce attorney	police commissioner
bankruptcy attorney	jailer	police dispatcher
bondsman	judge	prison guard
business attorney	law clerk	probation officer
constable	malpractice attorney	prosecutor
court reporter	paralegal	public defender
criminal attorney	parole officer	sheriff
deputy	patent attorney	tax attorney
detective	patrolman	warden
district attorney	personal injury attorney	

MANUFACTURING

assembly-line worker	mechanic	receiving clerk
binder	metalworker	riveter
dispatcher	night watchman	security guard
dock worker	operations manager	shipping clerk
expeditor	order filler	supervisor
foreman	packer	timekeeper
forklift operator	plant manager	tool and die maker
foundryman	process clerk	transportation manager
inspector	production control	truck driver
inventory clerk	production manager	warehouse supervisor
janitor	quality control	warehouseman
job coordinator	inspector	watchman
machinist	raw materials mgr.	welder

MARITIME

bargeman	deep-sea diver	navigator
boatswain	dock worker	pilot
boatwright	ferryman	roustabout
buccaneer	fisherman	sailor
cabin boy	gondolier	shipmaster
captain	helmsman	steward
commissary	longshoreman	whaler
deck hand	mess steward	

MEDICAL/HEALING

abortionist	dietician	hygienist
ambulance driver	dermatologist	immunologist
anesthetist	diagnostic technician	laboratory manager
audiologist	doctor	medical transcriptionist
biologist	druggist	midwife
cardiologist	ear-nose-throat	neurologist
child psychiatrist	specialist	nurse's aide
chiropodist	faith healer	nursing director
chiropractor	geriatric specialist	nutritionist
dental assistant	gerontologist	obstetrician
dental hygienist	gynecologist	occupational therapist
dental surgeon	homeopath	oculist
dentist	hospital director	optician

optometrist
orderly
orthodontist
osteopath
outpatient supervisor
paramedic
pediatrician
phlebotomist
physical therapist
physician

physiologist
physiotherapist
plastic surgeon
podiatrist
practical nurse
psychiatrist
psychologist
radiologist
radiotherapist
registered nurse

sexologist
speech pathologist
speech therapist
surgeon
veterinarian
wet nurse
witch doctor
X-ray technician

MISCELLANY

aluminum siding
  salesman
Bible salesman
blackjack dealer
bookie
box office attendant
concession attendant
delicatessen owner
diamond merchant
floorwalker
forest ranger
fundraiser

gatekeeper
handwriting analyst
insurance investigator
insurance salesman
junk dealer
labor organizer
lighthouseman
lobbyist
minister
nun
nurseryman
pawnbroker

pool shark
priest
promoter
publicist
rabbi
ragman
roulette wheel operator
security guard
telephone solicitor
ticket agent
toll booth operator
tree surgeon

RETAIL STORE

buyer
cashier
department manager

display designer
sales clerk
shop owner

stock clerk
window dresser

...where one of the following is sold:

air conditioners	automobiles	building materials	cosmetics
antiques	baby products	burglar alarms	doors
appliances	bakery goods	cameras	draperies
aquariums	beds	carpeting	exercise equipment
art supplies	bicycles	clothes	fencing
artwork	boats	coins	fire alarms
auto mufflers	books	computers	flags

flowers	hearing aids	motorcycles	tile
food	jewelry	musical instruments	tires
furniture	kitchen cabinets	office furniture	tobacco
furs	lawn care	office supplies	toys
gasoline	light fixtures	pagers	trailers
glassware	linoleum	paint	trucks
groceries	liquor	party supplies	uniforms
guns	luggage	refrigerators	vacuum cleaners
gutters	mattresses	software	water heaters
hardware	mobile homes	sporting goods	wedding supplies
health food	monuments	swimming pools	windows

SERVICE

apartment manager	domestic	letter carrier
appraiser	elevator operator	librarian
astrologer	employment agent	lifeguard
auctioneer	escort	maid
baby sitter	exterminator	marriage broker
bill collector	fireman	marriage counselor
bodyguard	fortune teller	milkman
bridal consultant	fumigator	nanny
butler	furniture mover	poll-taker
career counselor	garbage man	property manager
caretaker	gardener	rainmaker
caterer	gas man	real estate agent
credit counselor	groundskeeper	résumé writer
cruise consultant	house cleaner	social worker
custodian	housekeeper	telephone operator
dating consultant	iceman	tour guide
day care worker	laundromat manager	tow service operator
delivery person	lawn care professional	trail guide

TECHNICAL

aeronautical engineer	astronomer	botanist
agricultural engineer	astrophysicist	bridge engineer
anthropologist	automotive engineer	CAD/CAM operator
archaeologist	biochemist	chemical engineer
architectural engineer	biologist	chemist
astrochemist	biophysicist	circuit designer

civil engineer
climatologist
cloud-seeder
communications
   engineer
computer consultant
computer engineer
computer operator
computer programmer
construction engineer
controls engineer
customer engineer
data entry specialist
design engineer
development engineer
diesel engineer
digital engineer
ecologist
electrical engineer
electronic engineer
enzymologist
experimental engineer
field engineer
geographer
geological engineer
geologist

geophysicist
highway engineer
HVAC engineer
hydraulic engineer
industrial engineer
information engineer
inorganic
laboratory technician
liaison engineer
loss prevention
   engineer
maintenance technician
marine engineer
mechanical engineer
metallurgical engineer
meteorologist
mill engineer
mining engineer
network engineer
organic chemist
package consultant
physicist
plant engineer
process control
   engineer
product engineer

programmer-analyst
quality control engineer
radar engineer
radiation physicist
radiobiologist
radiochemist
refrigeration engineer
research assistant
research engineer
rocket engineer
safety engineer
sanitary engineer
servo engineer
software analyst
software engineer
structural engineer
support engineer
systems engineer
technical writer
telephone engineer
textile engineer
tool engineer
transportation engineer
value engineer
wastewater engineer

Transportation

air cargo pilot
air traffic controller
astronaut
baggage handler
brakeman
busdriver
cabdriver
chauffeur
conductor

co-pilot
flight attendant
ground crewman
jet pilot
P.A. announcer
radar technician
redcap
skycap
stationmaster

stewardess
stoker
stunt pilot
subway conductor
switchman
terminal manager
ticket-taker

13. Will the Character Face
a Nonhuman Adversary?

The introduction of an adversary can establish fertile ground for exploring the nature of at least one character in the story. That character may be the hero or heroine, or it may not. In any event, the presence of an adversary gives the writer an excellent opportunity to explore just how far one character can be pushed before he rebels, or tries to negotiate, or asks for help, or becomes angry, or runs away, or just gives up and accepts what he feels he cannot change.

The adversary does not have to be human. Some adversaries cannot even be seen; some cannot be heard. Nevertheless, they can bring danger, or cause hardship, or instill fear, worry, or discontent. Some of them can take on an importance that makes them the principal villain — the movie *Jaws* represents one scary example, because a giant shark had developed a taste for humans and it was the constant threat of that creature on the screen that kept moviegoers on the edge of their seats. For the most part, however, nonhuman adversaries play a *subsidiary role* within a story, and only occasionally do they become full-fledged villains.

In selecting a nonhuman adversary, the writer is faced with such questions as these:

Will the nonhuman adversary serve as a temporary plot driver, or will it remain throughout most of the story?

What effect will it have on at least one of the characters in the story?

What will it force the character to do?

The purpose of this chapter is to present a brief profile of some nonhuman adversaries, the use of which might allow the reader or viewer to see the nature of a character in bold relief.

ANIMALS

Hollywood has been the unqualified master in developing animal adversaries to scare the pants off us. We have seen heroes and heroines threatened by killer bees, attacked by elephant-sized ants, stalked by tigers, circled by giant sea creatures, victimized by thousands of birds, and chased by saliva-dripping wolves, just to name a few. The animal world is rich with potential adversaries, should the writer come to the conclusion that all of the human types have been exhausted (a misconception, surely).

Aside from outrageous examples like giant ants and murderous sharks, some excellent adversaries exist in the animal world, with the power to test the endurance and mental agility of human beings in a story. Turning from the monstrous to the mundane, what if a farmer keeps losing chickens to a fox that he can never seem to catch? Or what if his crops are being devoured by grasshoppers because he doesn't have the money for insecticide? What if it is discovered that the beloved park pigeons of a small midwestern town are carrying a disease that is deadly to humans? What if the neighbors are afraid to pass in front of someone's house because of a dog that likes to chase them? What if someone finds out that his house is being slowly eaten away by termites? And if the appearance of one cockroach disperses the guests at a well-planned party, will this initiate a war between the hostess and those critters that are crawling inside the walls of her house? Finally, it would be hard to convince a prisoner who is driven to despair by bedbugs that he is not the victim of nonhuman adversaries.

ATTITUDE OF AN AGE

All of the following traits are associated with human beings: strictness, leniency, neutrality, appeasement, ignorance, indifference, secrecy, violence, and wastefulness. As seen in the abstract, however, any one of these traits can serve as the signature of a time period. A character may look at the broad-based immorality that is taking place around him and see it as highly destructive to all the traditions his country holds dear. In his eyes, at least, that immorality would appear as a nonhuman adversary, even though human beings are the ones who are causing it. Again, the character would see immorality as an abstract, rather than identifying one or more individuals as the responsible parties. Indeed, whenever a character believes that the attitude of an age is a threat to the future, that attitude is a nonhuman adversary. While the character may be helpless in his effort to do anything about it, his ability at least to see what is happening gives him an edge over those who are blind to the presence of the enemy.

BLIGHT

A character who lives in high-income suburbia would never know blight as a nonhuman adversary, but one who resides in a neighborhood that is changing for the worse certainly might. Someone who once loved his tree-lined city street, his well-kept apartment building, and all the quaint shops that used to dot his surrounding landscape might well be dismayed to see the encroachment of blight. When building after building becomes boarded up, when graffiti offends the eye, when the departures of the shopkeepers seem to multiply, when the streets develop potholes and the signs turn rusty, and when the crime rate increases, what effect might all this have on the character? And what about the landlord's investment as property values continue to decline? As a nonhuman adversary, blight can steadily approach and threaten a place that a character calls home.

CHANGE

When a fundamental change occurs in an established social, business, governmental, or educational structure, that change becomes a nonhuman adversary in the mind of a person who is far from ready to accept it. For example, the livelihood of the typewriter repairman was suddenly threatened by the advent of the computer revolution, just as candlemakers stood defenseless as light bulbs made them expendable. And small shopkeepers all over America have gone down swinging as they fought their elimination at the hands of huge shopping malls.

As a nonhuman adversary, change can come in the form of a modification, transformation, innovation, conversion, reformation, nonviolent revolution, reversal, restoration, an increase or decrease, or a separation. Whatever its particular nature may be, and whether or not it is first seen as a harmless trend that will eventually go away, it upsets our comfortable view of our world, our habit of believing that things will remain as they are. Each new trend threatens the status quo. New ideas saw away at the underpinnings of well-established standards. Questions chip away at long-held wisdom.

For the fictional character, the situation is no different. While he or she may sometimes identify someone who is responsible for the change, for the most part that change will be faceless and will often first seem to be a harmless trend that suddenly appears overnight. It is only later, when this nonhuman adversary becomes too big to ignore, that a character will either marshal his forces to resist it or surrender to the inevitable.

CONFINEMENT

To appreciate the concept of confinement as a nonhuman adversary, one need not restrict one's view to the obvious, *i.e.*, imprisonment within a jail cell. Since confinement is the antithesis of freedom, there are many other examples, but they are more subtle. For example, consider the individual who feels trapped in a marriage. Even though that person's mate may be thoroughly loving and attentive — which, incidentally, the recipient may see as suffocating — and even though no bars or fences stand in the way of departure, that person may be obligated to remain with the spouse for any number of reasons, with children being just one of the possibilities. The enemy is not the spouse; instead, it is the inability to be free. Like the prisoner who sits behind bars, that individual may have no one to blame but himself for his predicament.

Confinement may appear as a nonhuman adversary when a worker feels trapped in a job that he hates; when a soldier is unable to leave the military until he is discharged; or even when, say, a city housewife is forced to move with her husband to the wide open spaces out West and she can no longer visit her neighbors, spend time in the shops, or hear the familiar voices of the street vendors.

DISASTER

This category of nonhuman adversaries provides the writer with several options. In the area of geological disturbance, for example, earthquakes and volcanic eruptions are by far the most obvious. Landslides and tidal waves are also excellent possibilities. To date, no one has ever written a fictional account of the earth suddenly shifting on its axis. Not only would such an event cause damage far beyond anyone's imagination, but the ensuing tidal waves would reshape the land mass on the globe as well. In time, though, someone will tell such a story.

Because of the devastation that occurs as a result of a great geological disturbance — if it isn't great, it may have no value as an adversary — things like earthquakes and volcanic eruptions almost always take place near the end of the story. Indeed, this type of nonhuman adversary requires the writer to be especially skilled in the craft of leading up to the inevitable, for the reader or viewer must continually be made aware that something dreadful is likely to happen. Prior to the devastation, the writer should take advantage of the opportunity to develop his human protagonists and antagonists, among whom there may be a scientist or a prophet, trying to warn others of the impending disaster. Of course, no one pays any mind. Then, at the proper moment in the story, the nonhuman adversary is unleashed, allowing the author to depict great panic, great heroism, and perhaps a smug "I told you so."

Nongeological disasters would include such things as a bridge collapsing or a dam bursting, as opposed to those disasters that may have a human cause, such as plane crashes and shipwrecks, even though any of these may come about as the result of bad weather. Again, what human reactions does the tragedy trigger? How does the nonhuman adversary bring the traits of a character into sharp focus?

DISEASE

Disease as a nonhuman adversary has long been a familiar story-making tool. It, too, can be used as either a plot driver or as a backdrop to a story. In the first instance, for example, the disease may be employed as an epidemic, which the hero or heroine may be trying to stop from spreading. People are warned, become infected, and try desperately to escape. The authorities show a lack of imagination, and an abundance of red tape ties everyone's hands. There is a race against time. And so on. All of it is a bit hackneyed, of course, but a good writer can make it entertaining reading or viewing nonetheless.

However, to qualify as a nonhuman adversary, a disease need not threaten a whole city or an entire nation. Setting aside the obvious threat posed by such infectious diseases as yellow fever, tuberculosis, AIDS, cholera, meningitis, smallpox, Bubonic plague, syphilis, typhoid, and leprosy, there are other ways to use disease as a threat. If a child comes down with chicken pox the day before the family takes a vacation, isn't that a nonhuman adversary, since it disrupts everyone's plans? If a character wakes up with laryngitis, how will he deliver a very important speech to the stockholders? What does the woman do when she finds out her boyfriend has gonorrhea? Will a case of the mumps mean that a man will no longer be able to bear children? What will the character do if he develops one of the following: heart disease, cancer, Bright's disease, Lou Gehrig's disease, Parkinson's disease, or leukemia?

When a character in the story is physically threatened by a disease, it gives the writer an opportunity to explore the manner in which the victim handles the misfortune, and how it affects his family, friends, and the other people with whom he comes into contact.

DISORDER

For the organized individual, combatting general disorder is tantamount to fighting grizzled, ill-shod rebels who, instead of aligning themselves in parade-like fashion where they might be leveled with a single cannon shot, jump out of alleyways firing and take pot-shots from rooftops. Disorder becomes a nonhuman adversary when the contributors to it are many in number and are essentially faceless — that is, when the blame for the mess cannot be laid upon any one person's shoulders. Yes, things are indeed strewn about, but who scattered them? Yes, procedures are in a total shambles, but who is to blame? Yes, there is lawlessness, but who is at fault? This nonhuman adversary is a thing out of harmony; it trips over its own devices. It is chaos, it is carelessness, it is freedom run amok. It impedes the success of getting even the smallest thing done; big things are out of the question.

GHOSTS AND DEMONS

Authors frequently create ghosts and demons to tell a spine-tingling story. To qualify as a nonhuman adversary, however, a ghost cannot simply be mischievous; instead, it will have to frighten the characters in the plot and possibly even endanger at least one of them in some way. A friendly sort like Casper the Friendly Ghost will not do. If the ghost has the ability to do some extraordinary things, so much the better; readers and viewers often enjoy seeing the unbelievable made believable.

Rod Serling, the creator of the widely acclaimed television series *The Twilight Zone*, was highly skilled at fashioning demons out of inanimate objects, including automobiles, a ventriloquist's dummy, and so on. Also, movies have been produced in which the hero or heroine is terrorized by one or more poltergeists.

HARD TIMES

As a nonhuman adversary, "hard times" can serve as a backdrop in a story or suddenly become a plot driver; but in the latter instance hardship will usually need a particular related event to trigger it. If, for example, hard times caused a little girl to steal bread from the kitchen of an aristocrat and she is killed for it, a town that is suffering from lack of food could erupt into wide-ranging anger. While the conditions that typify hard times may, in fact, have been generated and perpetrated by human beings, as a nonhuman adversary hard times will generally take on a life of its own and become a rather broad menace to the general population. The sweeping presence of hardship will be seen in every aspect of daily life.

Hard times might easily include poverty, famine, economic depression, war, and repression, but any period that is essentially negative may serve as a nonhuman adversary, *e.g.,* the Age of Disillusionment, the Age of Cynicism, the Age of Ignorance, the Age of Anxiety, the Great Depression, etc. While essentially faceless, a period of hard times is usually highly destructive in one form or another. Institutions can become dramatically altered; governments can be capsized; and the entire social structure can be realigned. It is a time when the people become severely disadvantaged and their restlessness boils. In his novel *A Tale of Two Cities*, Charles Dickens expertly wove in the element of hard times as his characters displayed love, courage, and nobility during a time when the French, in an anti-royalist frenzy, were beheading people in a blood lust.

As a nonhuman adversary, hard times will cause some characters to search for food, work, or justice — and perhaps all three at once. Hard times may bring out the best in them, or the worst.

THE LAW

Laws are generated by human beings, and apart from widely accepted conventions, most have at least one author who others can point to as being responsible. Formal laws usually outlive their originators by a great many years; indeed, some of them last several centuries, perhaps for the entire life of a nation. The longer they exist, the less likely it becomes that the authors will be remembered, and the more likely that the law will be seen not as a creation of humans, but as a restrictive power in its own right — that is, a nonhuman adversary to those who disagree with it.

For example, very few can trace the actual birth of Prohibition in America. While some may know that it was established by the eighteenth amendment to the Constitution in 1919, few people attach any faces or names to the passage of this amendment. Most people see Prohibition as simply a faceless power that attempted (unsuccessfully) to stop the production and sale of alcohol. The subsequent revolt against this law, this nonhuman adversary, led to passage of the twenty-first amendment 14 years later.

Is there a law, on or off the books, that one of your characters views as adversarial? How has it affected him or someone he knows, and what action does it prompt him to take? Will he purposely break the law? Or try to change it, perhaps, by campaigning against it?

MEDICAL DISORDER

As nonhuman adversaries, some medical disorders need a classification separate from disease. They may be genetic in nature, or they may be only temporary inconveniences associated with perhaps a particular lifestyle or a character's age. Take the latter instance: A teenager would certainly view acne as a terrible adversary, for it disrupts the physical image he would like to convey to the opposite sex. Each pimple is a wound suffered, and the mirror reflects the losing battle. Likewise, constipation and malnutrition may represent temporary conditions, but they arise out of deprivation.

Some of the more serious medical disorders would include arthritis, cerebral palsy, high blood pressure, asthma, cataracts, anemia, varicose veins, neuritis, ulcers, and diabetes. Whether a disorder runs in the family or is a result of the way the character conducts his life is something for the creative writer to decide.

Usually a character with a medical disorder must endure the hardship that accompanies it. Sometimes that comes in the form of chronic pain, and the character's ability to cope with this nonstop attack upon the body constitutes a dimension that will set him apart from all the others in the story.

MONOTONY

Monotony is a nonhuman adversary that slowly grinds away our energy on a daily basis. Struggle against its demands as we often do, it is nevertheless true that an overwhelming number of us can be counted among its victims. We march to the tick-tock of clocks, by doing certain things at certain times, as well as in certain ways. We take the same bus or drive the same way to work each day. From one desk to another we shuffle stacks of paper, each stack hauntingly similar to the ones preceding and following it. We watch the same television programs and listen to variations of the same conversations concerning the weather, the children, rising prices, and last night's sports news. A fictional character who is perceptive may well see his life as some sort of assembly line, in which, one way or another, he keeps adding the same parts to the engine of his life. To a character who is less perceptive, the frustration may be nameless but quite palpable. The question is, what will this monotony cause either character to do?

OLD AGE

Old age is, of course, a human trait; however, some of the things that accompany old age have an adversarial nature. For those who have crossed the broad waters from youth to old age and found themselves miraculously turned into elders on the far shore, the gratitude they feel for having made it that far may be diluted by the losses they have experienced along the way. Gone is the glowing skin that once had never known a wrinkle or a brown blotch. Gone is the eyesight that was once so keen. And gone, too, is the elasticity of the bones that used to bounce without breaking. These losses, and others like them, represent the wounds suffered in a battle with old age — an adversary who simply never loses. This adversary laughs at the individual who, refusing to admit defeat, tries to recapture the look of youth through exercise, facelifts, tonics, and clothes to dazzle the eye.

PHYSICAL IMPAIRMENT

Here the nonhuman adversary takes away what once belonged to the character. He who could see is now blind; or he who could hear is now deaf; or he who could walk is now crippled. Such a character must be differentiated from those born blind, deaf, or crippled, for in this case the impairment is an affliction to which the character is unaccustomed. The presence of any of these nonhuman adversaries places an enormous burden upon the character, for he suddenly finds himself deprived of a precious gift that he once took for granted. How will the character struggle to regain at least some of the ground he has lost? What victories might he achieve in utter darkness? What can he gain from the silence around him? What insight will become his in a wheelchair? Or might he be defeated by this nonhuman adversary and allow his will to shrivel and die?

THE "SYSTEM"

The so-called system, which practically everyone complains about, contains an assortment of nonhuman adversaries. While the system is in fact generated by humans, it is seen as self-perpetuating. Three of the prime candidates from this adversarial category include the following: (1) a bureaucracy, which attends every form of government on earth and is restrictive and frustrating in countless annoying ways to those who like swift action; (2) a chain of command — sometimes known as the "pecking order" — which occurs in the military, the corporate structure, and in many organizations, and which is comprised of layer upon layer of jealously guarded fiefdoms that one bypasses at one's peril; (3) a social order, in which one is assigned a place commensurate with one's ancestry, financial clout, skin color, education, or religion, or some combination thereof. There are of course other systems that are just as intimidating.

And woe indeed to that character who dares to buck the system, simply because he is weary of mountains of paperwork and snail-paced programs, or because he is tired of going through channels, or because he no longer wants to be excluded because of who he is.

TIME

Whenever a character in a story must do something within a certain time frame, *e.g.*, deliver the ransom money before noon, or perhaps be at a certain place before the clock strikes a specific hour, then time itself becomes a nonhuman adversary. Moreover, if time is to be used as an adversary, then it probably goes without saying that the writer must place obstacles in the path of the hero or heroine. One cannot make the reader or viewer squirm in his chair if everything goes according to plan. A race against the clock can rivet the reader's attention to the page and glue the theater-goer to the edge of his seat.

THE UNKNOWN

When a fictional character feels some degree of inexplicable dread about what the future may hold, he is experiencing the presence of a nonhuman adversary, nameless though it may be. He may believe that danger is just around the corner, yet he may not be able to define exactly what form it will take. He may feel that he is going to lose something of vital interest, though just what it is he really can't say. But it would be a mistake to assume that this character is a good candidate for psychoanalysis. He is not someone who makes mountains out of molehills and sees dragons lurking behind every tree. He is not a worrywart. What he feels instinctively but is unable to verbalize is a result of things he has seen and heard — pieces of a puzzle he has been putting together. He is trying to assemble a picture of the unknown, a shadowy thing that will burst fully featured upon the scene only when some momentous event takes place in the world.

This nonhuman adversary haunts the investor who, because of the most infinitesimal indicators, somehow senses great danger ahead in a stock market that is rushing to new heights. It presents itself to that person who knows that a war is coming but can tell neither when it will start nor who will initiate it. It dwells in the room with the child who knows his parents are terribly unhappy; it lurks in the minds of those who are afraid of losing their jobs and wonder what they will do; it is a phantom that, sometimes inexplicably, threatens one's sense of well-being.

WEATHER

Bad weather provides an author with an excellent opportunity to place his or her characters in extreme conditions that are beyond their control and, as a result, give them the chance to show their courage, cowardice, inventiveness, impatience, and so on. Even fog can be an adversary: In mystery stories, for example, it can prevent the protagonist from seeing the murderer's face, and on the high seas it can make the navigation of ships quite treacherous.

As a nonhuman adversary, bad weather can be a subsidiary antagonist or a plot driver. In the motion picture *Key Largo*, it served a subsidiary role: The hurricane did not supersede the conflict between the protagonist and the antagonist. In another story, bad weather might accentuate the human conflict in such a way that it actually helps bring it to a head. For weather as a plot driver, consider John Steinbeck's *The Grapes of Wrath*: Here a relentless drought was the villain, causing the Joad family as well as thousands of other Oklahoma farmers to give up their land and head for California. Thus the weather was a plot driver because it precipitated action.

Besides fog, hurricanes, and drought, other nonhuman adversaries in this category would include extreme cold, floods, tornadoes, blistering heat, blizzards, and even high humidity. High humidity? Yes; anyone who has lived in an unairconditioned city apartment during 100+ degree weather would easily recognize it as a brutal adversary that can make tempers snap like lightning bolts.

14. What Plot Drivers Will Affect the Character?

A plot driver is a device that causes the reader or viewer to ask, "What's going to happen next?" It is the banana peel that causes the status quo to lose its footing. Sometimes a writer needs only one plot driver to sustain a story, other times he or she needs more; sometimes one plot driver will beget another plot driver, which will beget another, and so on. The purpose, of course, is to generate action — mental or physical, or both — and propel the story forward, even if only inch by inch.

Plot drivers *create* reactions; rarely will you find one that has an emotional base. There are some internal and external traits that seemingly have the power to be listed as plot drivers — among the prime examples would certainly be jealousy, envy, resentment, courage, and cowardice — but the fact of the matter is, all of these traits tend to be reactive; their presence usually depends upon something else that happens in the story. For instance, a character does not suddenly *decide* to display jealousy or cowardice for the purpose of causing complications. The emotion surfaces because of what the character sees or hears — or at least thinks he sees or hears. Whatever he believes has happened, that is the actual plot driver, even if his belief is mistaken.

Nevertheless, you may see at least a couple of plot drivers listed in this chapter that could easily be seen as reactive. **Kindness** and **unkindness** come immediately to mind. In this chapter, however, an act of kindness or unkindness is seen not from the point of view of the person displaying it, but from the viewpoint of the individual who is at the receiving end.

Some plot drivers take place before a story even begins. Close to the beginning of *Hamlet*, for example, we learn that two plot drivers have already occurred: the death of the prince's father and the marriage of his mother to his uncle. The next plot driver occurs during the actual story and falls into the arrival category, for the ghost of Hamlet's dead father appears before him and reveals that he was murdered by his uncle.

The best kind of plot driver illuminates one or more of a character's internal traits, his strengths or weaknesses, his likes or dislikes, his wants or needs, or his fears. We learn some of these things when a character is faced with a dilemma, something unexpected, the emergence of danger, something he doesn't like, or one of any number of things that forces him to take action.

The purpose of this chapter is not to supply the writer with a list of every plot driver imaginable — there are literally thousands — but rather to present at least most of the major *categories*, allowing the writer to quickly isolate one or two options for his or her particular story. From that point on, the specifics are entirely dependent upon the author's creative intelligence and lie well beyond the scope of his book.

As you review this section, you will see that adversity is the granddaddy of all plot drivers. Of the 49 plot-driver categories listed in this chapter, almost two-thirds of them fall into adversity's camp; of the rest, a good percentage could become adversarial in nature as well. A tale filled with nothing but sweetness and light is invariably boring and not worth telling. Even in fairy tales there are dragons and villains.

ACCUSATION

If a character is charged with misconduct, how will he react if he is innocent? If guilty? Who will or will not believe the accusation? Does it come in the form of an insinuation, or is it boldly stated? What are the possible repercussions? Does the accusation threaten to destroy a reputation? Disgrace a family? Lead to the loss of friends? Place the character's livelihood in jeopardy? Is the character being used as a scapegoat for someone else?

ACQUISITION

What has been acquired, who acquired it, and what are the potential repercussions? Could the acquisition have an adverse effect on others in the story? To get it, did a character make a trade, borrow money, negotiate, barter, win a bet, inherit it, sell something else, make a bid, or speculate? How long has he wanted it? Does he view it as an investment? If so, in what way?

AGREEMENT

What is the nature of the agreement? For example, will two characters agree to marry? To divorce? To separate? Will one of the characters agree to join a group? Accompany someone? Collaborate, cooperate, compromise, or conspire with another? Will he sign an agreement or petition? Will he come to an understanding with someone? For whatever reason, has he decided to side with another character? Has he become a part of an alliance or partnership? Is the agreement an act of submission — that is, does the character capitulate, surrender, consent, yield, conform? How will others in the story react to the agreement, and where will this agreement lead?

ARRIVAL

Is the arrival a surprise? A welcome event? Something that has long been dreaded? For the character who is arriving, is it a homecoming, a visit, a chance to gain a sanctuary, an opportunity to get a new start? Does the arrival appear in the form of a ghost? How does the arrival of someone alter the course of the plot? How are others in the story affected?

ASSIGNMENT

Who has given the character an assignment, and what is he expected to accomplish? Is the character in the government or in private enterprise? Does he accept the appointment with alacrity, dread, or indifference? Who in the story resents the assignment, and why? If enemies are to be found, what will they do to undermine the character's efforts?

BAD LUCK

In what way does bad luck play a part in the story? At the most inopportune moment, is there a power outage, a sudden storm, a flat tire, a loss of records, a computer glitch? Or one of hundreds of other possibilities? And what is delayed or stopped by this stroke of bad luck? What happens as a result?

BIRTH

How does the birth of a child affect the plot? Does it, for instance, provide an unwelcome heir to the throne? Does it alter the way a character views his responsibilities? Does the birth draw the in-laws closer, or drive them farther away? Does the child bind the parents as a unit or insert a wedge between them? Was the birth wanted or not wanted?

CHANGE

What is the nature of the change that takes place? Is it, for example, a modification, transformation, innovation, conversion, reversal, restoration, increase, decrease, addition, decline, improvement, cessation, dismantlement, withdrawal, disbandment, elimination, or separation? Is it a long-lasting trend, a fad that will quickly come and go, or possibly a worrisome political or religious movement? Who stands to benefit from the change, and who doesn't? Who is against the change, and who isn't? After the change takes effect, what happens as a result?

CONCEALMENT

What is being hidden, why is it being done, and who is doing the concealing? Is it something tangible (buried treasure, important papers, a murder weapon), or is it intangible, such as the real truth of the matter? Who stands to gain or lose by hiding it? Who would, or would not, benefit by finding what or where it is? To what lengths will the character go to suppress, obscure, or disguise it?

CRIME

How will a crime change the structure of the plot? If someone is robbed, beaten, raped, murdered, tortured, or abducted, will the character seek revenge on his own terms? Or will that character, instead, let it become a matter for the justice system to settle? Will the character retreat psychologically? Will friends or family, or both, take action? How will it change the perpetrator's future actions, and will he become hunted in a way he never had been before?

DEATH

How does the death of someone in the story serve as a plot driver? Does the death occur as the result of accident, murder, suicide, execution, or natural causes? How will the other characters react to that person's demise? The plots of the classic motion pictures *Citizen Kane* and *Sunset Blvd.* are actually launched by death scenes: In *Citizen Kane*, the last word of the main character ("Rosebud") launches a reporter's investigation; in *Sunset Blvd.*, a body is seen floating face down in a swimming pool, and the voice of the deceased begins to tell the moviegoer why it happened.

DEBT

Does the character have a financial or moral obligation? To whom is the debt owed, how did it happen, and is the lender still alive? What sacrifices must be made? If gratitude defines the debt, what steps will the character take to repay the kindness he feels bound to honor? Has the giver ever expressed a desire to be compensated? Or is the debt, perhaps, embedded in guilt — that is, has the character done something for which he now feels ashamed and wishes to gain atonement? What will he do to make amends? If the debt is one of conscience, can it actually be paid in full, or is it seemingly a lifetime burden? Or does the character assume a burden of debt when, in fact, it is not rightfully his to shoulder, as in the classic film *It's a Wonderful Life*?

DECEPTION

Who is the one being deceived, and why? And what is the nature of the deception? Is it a deliberate lie? A misrepresentation? A disguise to protect a true identity? Perhaps a form of hypocrisy or a well-planned fraud? Does the character deceive for the purpose of self-gain or self-protection? What will happen if the deception is uncovered?

DEMAND

What does one character demand of another? The truth, perhaps? Possibly repayment? Maybe an opportunity to be heard? The recognition of a rightful claim? Whatever the demand might be, how will the other character respond to the demand? Will he acquiesce? Refuse its legitimacy? Ignore it altogether? What will happen if the demand is not satisfied? Or what if it is?

DEPARTURE

Who in the story departs, and who is left behind? What will be the nature of the departure? For example, will the character desert a friend? Renege on a promise? Back away from a belief once fervently held? Abandon his spouse and children? Spurn a way of life? Become an emigrant or defect to another country? Break a habit? Leave something undone? Withdraw the support he once pledged? Escape from a place where he was held against his will? Move from a town where he had long lived? Disappear and not be heard from again? Embark on an adventure?

Does he depart with regret? Is he afraid? Does he run toward something or away from something?

DEPRIVATION

Does the character deprive himself, or does someone else prevent him from having something? If the former, does he decide to go on a diet or a fast? Swear off sex? Never take another drink of liquor? Not use his credit card? Become penny-wise and not pound-foolish? But if the deprivation comes at the hands of someone else, what is it that he is not permitted to do? In either case, will he somehow find a way to circumvent the deprivation? And whether he does or doesn't, what are the repercussions?

DESIRE

Of all the plot-driving categories, this is certainly the broadest, for it encompasses all those things that characters want, *e.g.*, justice, affection, freedom, power, success, money, recognition, and so on. This plot driver may appear at the very beginning of the story — a character's lust for power, for example, should be displayed at the outset — or at some point after the story begins, a good example being when one character falls in love with another and desires the affection to be returned in kind. One of the most important questions for the author to ask is this: Who in the story stands in the way of the character's desire, and why?

DISAGREEMENT

What precipitated the conflict, and who are the characters who disagree? Following the disagreement, what will the participants do? Who, if anyone, attempts to intervene? What are the viewpoints of those who cannot agree, and what does each of them expect to lose through compromise? Does one of the characters frame the disagreement as an act of defiance? Is one character's stubbornness and rigidity seen by another as disobedience, a challenge to his authority, an act of insubordination?

DISASTER

This is one of Hollywood's favorite plot-driving devices. For example, a skyscraper will suddenly catch fire, a mine will cave in, a ship will begin to sink, a volcano will erupt, tornadoes will sweep across the terrain, an earthquake will strike, a nuclear meltdown will take place, a bus will lose its brakes on a steep hill, an infectious disease will threaten an entire population, or the hero or heroine will unexpectedly be thrown in the middle of a blizzard or flood. The melody of plot is transformed into a symphony of action, and a race against time is almost always a factor. Quick decisions have to be made, and heroism is displayed. On the other hand, a disaster may serve as a relentless and seemingly never-ending backdrop, one that might force the characters to give up and move away. A good example can be found in John Steinbeck's novel *The Grapes of Wrath*. In that story, a disastrous drought forces the Joad family to leave their parched land in Oklahoma and head for California.

DISCONTENT

Discontent is a plot driver that usually takes a little time to come to a boil. But the questions rarely change. What are the things contributing to the character's unhappiness? Can he identify any of them by name, or do they all combine and nibble away at him? At what point will his discontent become so weighty that it will force him to do something? What action will he take if he is in the grip of dissatisfaction, sadness, premonition, disillusionment, or self-reproach? And will he in turn surprise himself? Perhaps perplex others?

DISCOVERY

Does the character uncover something that alters his conviction or lifestyle? Is it a tangible discovery in that he finds something of value, *e.g.,* money, a diary, a piece of evidence? Or does he come across something that is intangible — that is, is he told something that he did not know, or does he see something happening with his own eyes? Does he recognize someone who tries to avoid him? Stumble upon something that is rather surprising? Detect that which is hidden? Does he receive information by way of a telegram, a handwritten message, or an inscription that few even knew existed? Whatever the discovery may be, how does it drive the plot? Who gains? Who loses?

DISLOYALTY

Toward whom does the character become disloyal, and why? Is it an act of marital infidelity? Has he turned against a group to whom he once pledged his allegiance? Has he betrayed a friend's confidence? Committed an act of treason? What will be the repercussions?

ENTICEMENT

Who entices whom, and what is the nature of the enticement? Is it an invitation? A bribe? An offer that's hard to pass up? A sexual seduction? If the enticement is successful, what will one character gain and the other lose? What will be the repercussions?

FAILURE

If a character fails to do something, is it because he forgot, was perhaps blasé, or was unable to achieve what he set out to do? If the last, did another character work to stop him, or was he lacking in something he needed to succeed? What will be the repercussions of this failure? Does the failure follow a boast or an unreal expectation? Does the failure affect only one person, or does it involve others as well? How deep is the disappointment? Does it affect the reputation of the person who failed?

FREEDOM

If a character is given his freedom, what will he do with it? And from what is he being freed? Is he being released from prison? Is he given an opportunity to leave a country or neighborhood that has deprived him? Is he provided with some kind of authorization? Allowed to do something that he was never permitted to do before? Who objects to his freedom, and what will that character do?

GOOD FORTUNE

Will a character's good fortune swell him with confidence and prompt him to seek even more, and, by possibly overextending himself, cause adversity to pounce and devour? Or is the emphasis, instead, upon the resentment others feel toward the character who is enjoying that good fortune? How might one character's prosperity, promotion, victory, fame, popularity, prestige, or happiness bore holes into another's ego, and how might the latter retaliate?

HUMILIATION

Was the humiliation intentional; that is, did one or more characters set out to make someone else a laughing stock? Or is the humiliation self-imposed, following a failure? What course will this embarrassment take? For example, will the character shrink from others, even though his words or deeds may have been perfectly innocent, or will he harbor a desire for revenge?

IDEA

If a character comes up with a fresh idea (which might also be called a plot, master plan, scheme, solution, or proposal), how will the acceptance and implementation of that idea change the course of the story? Who stands to benefit from its success, and who can be projected as the loser?

INFORMATION

How does the introduction of information cause things to happen in the story? Does one of the characters, for example, act on a rumor or form an opinion based on a piece of gossip? Does he receive a report? Get a scoop or good tip on something? Is an announcement made by a company or a government? Does a radio or television station bring a late news flash? Is there an article in a newspaper or magazine that sheds new light? Or does someone in the story suddenly display honesty? And in that moment of candor, is something confirmed? A confession made? Evidence supplied?

INJUSTICE

If an injustice occurs in the story, what is its nature, who was the implementer and victim, and what action will be taken in response? Who seeks justice, and is the perpetrator aware of what he has done? If he is or isn't, what is the nature of his defense? What are the liabilities of righting a wrong or of letting things slide unattended? Who has been harmed by this injustice?

INTERVENTION

What will happen if a character decides to act as a mediator between two parties who cannot reach an agreement? Will he solve one problem, yet create another? Will he find himself taking sides? Will he solve the dispute or make things worse? And will anyone object to his intervention? Will he ever regret having become a go-between?

INTRUSION

This is a favorite plot driver for those who write comedy. Possibilities include the surprise of an unannounced visitor from out of town, the annoyance of in-laws, and the inconvenient meddling of the neighborhood gossip, all of which tend to make things happen, much to the displeasure of hero or heroine. An intrusion on a more serious level would be a police investigation, or perhaps a security check for a new job. Whatever the situation, how does the character handle the situation? What misunderstandings occur? Whose feelings get hurt? How does a seemingly harmless intrusion lead to a minefield of adversity?

KINDNESS

At whose hands does the character experience a kindness, and does it initiate a change in that character's direction? If a character's misery or misfortune is relieved, will he want to express his thanks in some way? Does he know from whom the kindness came? Would he be surprised if he knew the source? In what way does that act of altruism change the thinking of the person who received it? What are its long-range repercussions?

LOSS

Does the character lose something tangible or intangible, *e.g.*, youth, reputation, love, power? Can it be retrieved, or is it lost forever? If it can be regained, what steps will he take to repossess it? Is he at fault for the loss, or is someone else to blame? How does the loss place him at a disadvantage? What are the likely repercussions of the loss?

MARRIAGE

What is the nature of the marriage? Is it matrimony between two lovers? Is a partnership being formed? Are two groups or two lovers going into cahoots with each other? What exactly is being formed into one? What does this link-up mean to others? Who is for it and who is against it? What will be the aftereffects?

MISTAKE

Someone in the story makes an error. For example, a character may misconstrue what he saw or misunderstand what he heard; overestimate or underestimate someone or something; or possibly engage in a misidentification, misapplication, miscalculation, or misinterpretation. What will it cause him to do, and what effect will his mistake have on others?

NOSTALGIA

How will the character's sentiment cause him to take action? Does he set off to visit the place where he grew up? Where he gained the richest memories? Where he fought and survived a war? Where he experienced his greatest love? Where his life took a turn for the better? Does he write a book or letter? Make a long-overdue phone call? And how will his nostalgia be received?

OVERINDULGENCE

If a character overindulges himself — that is, if he should eat or drink too much, or gamble more than he should, or amuse himself in some activity far longer than reason would allow — what will happen as a result of it? And how does his overindulgence affect others?

PHYSICAL AFFLICTION

If a character suddenly becomes, say, crippled, disfigured, blind, deaf, or diseased, in what other way, besides the personal suffering, can the effects of that disability be felt? Will he, for example, lose his job? Will his friends shy away? Does the role of his spouse change dramatically? Are all his relationships altered? But what if the physical affliction is only temporary? What will be the ripple effect of amnesia, a backache, a toothache, or a broken limb? Or what will take place when the character suffers a stroke or a heart attack? What if he learns he is going bald or has become impotent?

PROVOCATION

To become provoked is to be stimulated into taking action. The question is, What will the action be? Will an argument ensue? Will a fight take place? And is it because a character reacts to being bullied or teased, or because he becomes annoyed at something that is not purposely directed toward him at all, such as loud music coming from another apartment? On the other hand, does he find himself in a situation in which he must contend with someone he does not like? Do their personalities conflict, and does that conflict cause them to squabble? Vow to get even? Feel forever estranged?

PUNISHMENT

How might an act of punishment alter the course of the story? Does it happen soon after the punishment, or is there a delayed reaction of several years? When a character is punished for something he did or did not do, upon whom does the burden of the reaction mainly rest — the punished, punisher, or someone else? Does the punishment, for instance, outrage the character's family or friends? Incense an entire nation? If the punishment is not physical, can it be seen as a chastisement? Social isolation? Confinement? Dismissal? Suspension?

REJECTION

Who experiences the rejection, and what will it cause the character to do? For example, what will happen if the character is segregated, expelled, discharged, evicted, banished, deported, exiled, blackballed, or banned? Does he feel rejected by the world in general? Is he excluded from a group of which he would like to be a part? Is he spurned by someone he loves? Has the job he wanted been given to someone else? Why has he become an outcast? Why is he shown a lack of respect, and how will he express his resentment? Or is the rejection framed as a boycott? Is there a social dividing line that says "Keep Out"? On the other hand, perhaps the story will focus on the individual who is doing the rejecting. If so, what will his hostility, disrespect, or aversion cause him to do?

RESOLUTION

What takes place in the story that instills resolve within a character? Does he, for example, give his word of honor? Pledge himself to something? Guarantee results? Make a general pronouncement to all, or take a silent oath? And what will he do to make his self-assertion more than just an idle promise?

SEARCH

What interests the character so much that it occupies almost all of his attention? Why does he feel a need to sift through the meaningless to get to the meaningful? To canvass, track down, explore, and analyze? To get to the bottom of something? What will he investigate? Who will he interrogate? And what will happen as a result of the search he leads? Does he conduct a search for the truth, or is it in fact a witch-hunt? Is he a prosecutor or persecutor?

SOCIAL UPHEAVAL

This kind of plot driver lies well beyond any one character's ability to do anything about it. If a revolution suddenly erupts, for example, his or her life will unavoidably be affected by it. The same is true if, say, there is a great depression, a radical political movement, or anything that tends to sweep the characters of the story along with it as if they were caught in the strong current of a river, forcing them to make decisions as a result of it.

SUPPORT

If one character decides to provide assistance to another, will he loan something? Use his influence on that character's behalf? Offer funding? Show him the wherewithal? Act as a sponsor? Provide guidance? Find him a job? Introduce him to the right people? Offer a little advice? And what will happen as a result of his support?

THEFT

There are all kinds of theft — *e.g.*, stealing money or possessions surreptitiously or through a clever swindle; kidnapping; land annexation; government seizure; plagiarization; and so forth — but its value to the story lies in what follows the theft. The author must decide whether to emphasize the character who stole, or the victim, or both. Does the theft cause anything else to happen? What characters are suddenly drawn together because of the theft?

THREAT

What danger does the character suddenly face? Is it he who is threatened, or a family member or friend? Does the character stand unprotected? Will he submit to demands in order to appease the person who threatens him? Or is the threat more general and the "villain" quite faceless? For instance, is his business on the rocks? Is his marriage unsteady? Are his children adrift and angry? Has someone been warned or given an ultimatum?

UNKINDNESS

What is the nature of the unkindness displayed? Is it, for example, ingratitude, malice, spite, cruelty, ridicule, acrimony, faultfinding, or inhospitality? And how does that heartlessness, that rudeness, that unfriendliness produce adversity, a desire to get even, or perhaps an enemy for life?

Index

abandoned 171
abandonment, fear of 105
abashed 18
abnormal 158
abominable 181
aboveboard 57
absent-minded 52, 187
absolute 40
absorbed 9, 51
absorbing 45
abstemious 77, 151
abstinent 13, 77, 151
abuser 165
accessories, like or dislike of 98
accident-prone 62, 153
acclaimed 42
accommodating 36
accommodator 147
accomplished 39, 42, 187, 188
accumulative 79
accusation 223
accuser 148
accusing 148
achievements 127
acquiescent 75, 148, 152
acquisition 223
acquisitive 25, 79, 166
acquisitor 166
acrimonious 21, 44, 149
acrobatic 62
action, self-assessment of 135
active 61
adamant 74
adaptable 74
addict 148
addlebrained 4
adept 39, 187
adjusted 70
admirable 19, 54
admiring 29
admonitory 169
adoring 29, 56
adrift 25
adroit 62
adulatory 43
adulterous 164

adventure 128; desire for 85
adventurer 148
adventurous 23, 64, 149
adversarial 73
adversaries, nonhuman 212–221
adversary 149
adversity, self-assessment of 135
advising 65
advisor 169
advisory 169
advocate 185, 187
affable 34, 159
affected 57, 66, 158, 163, 175
affecting 44
affection, desire for 86
affectionate 16, 183
affluent 42
afraid 24, 64, 174; see also fears
aggravated 14
aggravating 36
aggressive 73, 160, 162, 165
agile 62
agitated 14, 18, 29
agitative 44
agnostic 57, 118
agreeable 148, 159
agreement 223
agriculture, jobs in 202
aimless 25, 63, 167
alarmed 51
alarmist 174
alcoholic 157
alert 10, 23, 48, 64
alienated 70
all-knowing 3
alluring 45
almsgiver 160
aloof 10, 34, 66, 70, 167, 183
also-ran 168
altruist 170
altruistic 22, 27, 55, 79
amateur 149
amateurish 39

ambiguous 177
ambitious 25, 160
amenable 75
amiable 34, 159
amicable 159
amnesiac 52
amoral 20, 54, 164
amorous 13, 179
amusing 69
analytical 3, 164
analyzer 159, 164
anarchical 178
anarchist 165
angelic 172
angry 16
anguished 18, 31, 60
animals 212; jobs with 202; like or dislike of 98
annoyed 18
annoying 36
anonymous 42
antagonist 149
antagonistic 16, 73, 149, 178
anticipative 8, 11, 53, 171
antiquarian 181
antsy 29
anxious 18, 29, 69, 71, 163, 168
apathetic 10, 25, 69,72
apologetic 31, 179
apostate 186
appealing 45
appeased 17
appeaser 148
appeasing 72, 148
apple-polisher 152
appreciative 30
apprehensive 8, 12, 18, 24, 64, 71, 163, 168, 174, 180
approachable 34, 36, 159
arbiter 172
arbitrary 40, 68, 150
ardent 13, 71, 151
argumentative 73
aristocratic 38

aroused 14
arousing 44
arrival 224
arrogant 28, 183
art, like or dislike of 98
artful 57
Artful Dodger 155
artificial 57, 66, 156, 163, 175
artistic 8
artless 57, 67, 170
ascetic 13, 77, 151
ashamed 31, 60
asinine 49
aspersive 44
aspirant 160
aspiring 25, 160
assiduous 26, 63, 160, 162
assignment 224
assured 49
assuring 44
astrologist 176
astute 3,10, 48, 164
atheist 118, 181
atheistic 57, 181
athletic 62
atonement, desire for 86
attached 16
attentive 10, 36, 51
attitude of an age 213
attuned 70
audacious 23, 64, 75, 149, 153, 171
august 54
austere 68, 77
authoritarian 149
authoritative 40, 68
autocrat 150
autocratic 40, 68
autonomous 37
avaricious 27, 79
avenger 150
averse 16
avid 71
avoider 150
aware 10
awe-struck 29
awed 23

awful 181
awkward 62, 153

babbler 154
babbling 46
babe in the woods 157
back-scratcher 152
backbiter 155
backbiting 44, 155
backer 185
background 127–133
backslapper 152, 159
backslider 157, 186
backward 4
bad 55
bad luck 224
bad-tempered 73
bamboozler 155
baneful 55, 181
bankrupt 42, 168
barbarous 55, 73
barfly 157
barren 9, 81
base 20, 55, 164, 181
bashful 35, 67
beaten 42
beauty: desire for 86;
   jobs in 202; self-
   assessment of 136
befriender 160
begrudger 151
begrudging 16, 151
beholden 30
beliefs 116–123; core
   117; formal 117; informal 119; temporary
   116
believer 151, 157
believing 5, 31, 49
belittling 44, 155
belle of the ball 159
bellicose 73, 165
belligerent 73, 165, 178
bellyacher 161
bemoaning 47
bench warmer 167
benefactor 160
beneficent 22, 79
benevolent 22, 55, 79,
   160
besotted 157
bested 168
bestial 55
betrayer 182, 186
bewildered 18
bewitching 45
biased 7, 59, 183
big baby 174
big flop 168
big shot 168
big wheel 168
big-hearted 22, 27, 79,
   160
bigot 183

bigoted 7, 59, 183
bigwig 168
bilious 73
birdwitted 4
birth 224
bitchy 44, 47
bitter 21, 44
bizarre 158
blabber 182
black sheep 164
black-hearted 55
blackballed 171
blackguard 181
bland 46
blasé 10, 52, 66, 156, 188
blasphemous 57
bleeding heart 183
blessed 42
blight 213
blissful 17, 186
blithe 11, 69, 171
blockheaded 4, 49
blockish 49
bloodsucker 185
bloodsucking 41
bloodthirsty 22, 55
bloody 55
bloody-minded 22
blowhard 158
blue 69
bluenose 175
blundering 62
blunt 57
blustering 66
boaster 158
boastful 66, 158
bold 8,13, 23, 35, 64,
   149
bolstering 44
bolter 186
bombastic 66, 158
bon vivant 78
bondman 152
bonehead 166
boob 168
book-learned 149
bookish 43
boor 180
boorish 38
booster 176
bootlicker 151
bootlicking 43, 75
boozehound 157
boozer 157
bore 152
bored 10, 18, 52, 188
boring 46, 152
borrower 168
boss 150
bossy 40, 68, 150
bothered 18, 51, 168
bound 30
bounteous 79
bountiful 22, 79

bourgeois 38
braggart 158
brainless 4, 49
brainy 3, 48
brash 64, 73, 153
brave 24, 64, 149, 153
braveheart 152
brazen 64, 75, 153
bridled 13
bright 3, 48, 69
brilliant 3
broad-minded 7
broke 42
brooding 168, 173
browbeaten 75
browbeater 165
brusque 34
brutal 55
brutish 20, 55
buccaneer 185
buddy 185
buggy 158
bulldog 161
bullheaded 6, 161
bullish 11
bully 165
bumbling 62
bumpkin 180
bungler 153
bungling 62
buoyant 11, 17, 69, 171
business 203
businesslike 171
bustling 61, 162
busy 61
busybody 153
butterfingered 153
buttery 156

cagey 64, 180
cajoler 152
calculating 57
callous 21, 31, 61, 184
calm 14, 71, 184
calumnious 44
candid 57, 174
cantankerous 73, 161
capitalist 188
capitulative 152
capricious 63, 186
captious 12, 44
captivating 45
carefree 17, 69
careful 23, 64, 76, 180
careless 13, 64, 77, 165,
   170, 182
careworn 18, 69, 168
caring 16, 22, 36
carnal 13
carousing 179
carpetbagger 155
carping 44
case-hardened 21
castaway 171

castle-builder 157, 163
casual 35
cat's paw 151
causeless 25
caustic 44, 155
caution 157, 178
cautious 23, 50, 64, 172,
   180
caviling 44
celebrated 42
celebrations, like or dislike of 98
celibate 151
censorious 44, 155
cerebral 43
ceremonies, like or dis-
   like of 98
certain 5
chagrined 31, 60
challenging 50
chameleon 186
champion 188
chance-taking 64
change 214, 224; desire
   for 86; fear of 105;
   self-assessment of 136
changeable 26, 63
chaotic 77
character type 147–188
characteristics, like or
   dislike of 99
charismatic 45
charitable 22, 27, 79,
   160
charlatan 155, 163
charming 45, 182
chary 180
chaste 19
chatterbox 153
chatterer 154
chatty 46, 154
chauvinistic 151, 165
cheap 79, 166
cheat 155
cheeky 75
cheerful 11, 17, 60, 69,
   171, 182
cheerless 69, 168, 173
cheery 69
cherishing 16
cherubic 56
chicken 174
chicken-hearted 24, 64,
   174
childhood 128
children, self-assessment
   of 136
chilly 34
chipper 17, 69
chiseler 155
chivalrous 19, 64
choleric 14, 16, 73
chum 185
chummy 159

churlish 75
circumlocutory 46
circumspect 13, 23, 64, 180
civil 36, 156
class-conscious 30, 183
clear-cut 57
clear-sighted 48
clement 20, 22
clever 48, 156
clinging 166
clodhopper 153, 180
close-fisted 79
closed-minded 6, 74
close-mouthed 47, 154, 167
closefisted 166
clothes, like or dislike of 99
clownish 38
clumsy 62, 153
coarse 38, 180
cocksure 5, 49, 151
cocky 35, 158
cold 16, 34
cold-blooded 22
cold-hearted 22, 184
collaborative 37
collaborator 185
colleague 185
collected 14, 71
collector 166
comatose 61
combatant 187
combative 73, 165, 187
comfort, desire for 86
comfortable 17, 186, 188
comforting 36
comical 179
commanding 40, 44, 150
commendable 19, 54
commiserative 183
commitment, desire for 87
common 38, 170, 180
commonplace 9, 81, 170
communicative 46, 159
companion 185
companionable 34, 159
company man 169
compassionate 16, 20, 55, 183
compatible 70
compelling 44
competent 39
competitive 25, 37, 187
competitor 187
complacent 17, 70, 186
complainer 163
complaining 47, 161
complaisant 36, 75
compliant 74, 75, 148, 152

complimentary 43, 156, 185
composed 13, 71
compromising 37, 68, 74
compulsive 148
compunctious 31, 60
comrade 185
con man 155
concealer 154
concealing 154
concealment 224
conceited 28, 66, 158
concerned 18, 36, 51, 183
conciliator 172
conciliatory 21, 72
concupiscent 13
condemning 44
condescending 66
condolent 183
confessional 182
confident 5, 11, 35, 49, 151, 171
confinement 214
confining 174
conformable 75
conforming 9, 81
conformist 154
confounded 5, 18
confused 5,14, 18
congenial 34, 159, 182
congratulatory 43
conjectural 51
connected 15
conniving 57
conquered 168
conquering hero 188
conscience-stricken 31, 61, 179
conscienceless 54
conscientious 19, 55, 64, 76, 170, 173
conservative 64, 77, 78
considerate 20, 22, 36, 160, 182
consoling 36
constant 16, 19, 26, 59, 63, 162, 185
constrained 28, 35
constricted 35
contemplative 12, 164
contemptible 20, 55, 164, 181
contemptuous 30, 183
content 25
contented 17, 70, 186
contentious 25, 73, 162, 165, 178, 187
continent 77
contrary 73, 178
contributive 37
contributor 160
contrite 31, 60, 179

contriving 54
controlled 13, 35, 41
controlling 40
contumacious 75
conventional 9, 81, 154
conversational 46
convert 151
convinced 5, 49, 74, 151
convincing 44
convivial 69, 159, 182
cool 14, 16, 34, 71, 184
cool customer 184
coolheaded 14, 184
cooperative 37, 75
coquette 160
coquettish 160
cordial 16, 34, 159
correct 19, 35, 170
corrupt 20, 164
corrupted 181
corruptible 20, 54
corrupting 55
counselor 169
counterfeit 163, 175
courage: desire for 87; self-assessment of 137
courageous 24, 64, 153
courteous 75, 156
courtly 36, 38
covetous 27, 79, 151
coward 174
cowardly 24, 64, 174
cowering 75, 174
coy 66
cozy 186
crab 161
crabby 73, 161
crackerjack 187
crackpot 157
crafts & trades, jobs in 203
crafty 57
cranky 73, 161
crass 180
craven 24, 64, 174
creative 8, 187
creative arts, jobs in 204
creditable 54
credulous 49
crepehanger 173
crime: jobs in 205; as plot driver 225
criminal 54
cringing 75
critic 154
critical 44, 155
crony 185
crook 164
crooked 20, 57
cross 73
cross-examining 159
crotchety 73, 158
crude 180

cruel 22, 55
crusading 178
crushed 18
cultivated 38, 80, 183
cultured 38, 80, 183
cunning 3, 57, 156
curiosity 157
curious 9, 65, 153
curmudgeon 166
curmudgeonly 73
curt 73, 161
customs, like or dislike of 98
cutthroat 165, 185
cutting 44
cutup 178
cynical 12, 32, 173

dandified 66, 158, 175
dandy 158
daredevil 149
daring 8,13, 23, 64, 149, 153, 171
dastardly 24
daunted 5, 18
dauntless 24, 64, 149, 153
dawdler 155
dawdling 61, 155
daydreamer 157
daydreaming 51
deadbeat 152
deadly 55
death: fear of 105; jobs in 205; as plot driver 225
debased 55
debauched 13, 20, 54, 157, 164
debonair 69
debt 225
debtor 168
decadent 164
deceitful 20, 57, 163
deceivable 31, 157
deceiver 155
decent 19, 55, 170
deceptions 225
decided 26, 49
decorated 42
dedicated 16, 59, 63
defamatory 44, 155
defeated 12, 18, 42, 168
defeatist 173
defender 177, 187
defenseless 40
deferential 29, 67, 75, 152
defiant 75, 171
deficient 39
defiling 55
deft 62
degenerate 164
degraded 54

deist 118
dejected 12, 18, 69, 169
deleterious 55
deliberate 64
deliberative 12, 164
delicate 38
delighted 17, 45
deludable 31, 157
delusive 156
demand 226
demanding 68, 150
demented 177
demonstrative 35
denigratory 44
dense 4, 166
denunciatory 44, 148, 155
departure 226
dependable 19, 59
dependent 41
deplorable 181
depraved 55
deprecating 44
depressed 18, 69, 169
deprivation 226
deprived 42
deranged 177
derisive 44, 75
derogatory 44
deserter 186
desire 226
desirous 25, 160
desolate 18
despairing 12, 18, 69, 173
desperado 164
despicable 20, 55, 164, 181
despondent 12, 18, 69, 169, 173
despotic 40, 68, 150
destitute 42, 168
destroyer 181
destruction: desire for 87; fear of 106
destructive 148
desultory 25, 63, 186
detached 6,10, 35, 52, 66, 70, 184
detail-minded 76
determined 25, 26, 63, 160, 161
detestable 181
detested 54
detractive 44
devil-may-care 23, 64
devilish 22, 55, 80
devious 57
devoted 16, 56, 59, 151
devotee 151
devotional 56
devout 56, 151
dexterous 62
diabolical 22, 55

dictator 150
dictatorial 40, 68, 150
didactic 46
die-hard 161
diffident 28, 50
dignified 19, 38, 54
dignitary 168
digressive 46
dilatory 61
diligent 26, 64, 76, 160, 162
dillydallier 167
diplomat 156
diplomatic 36, 173
direct 35, 57, 174
disadvantaged 42
disaffected 18, 70
disagreeable 73
disagreement 227
disappointed 18
disapprobatory 155
disapproved 171
disarranged 182
disaster 215, 227
disbelieving 32, 50, 57, 181
discarded 171
discerning 3, 48, 164
disciple 151
disciplined 76, 173
discomposed 18, 51
disconcerted 51
disconnected 10, 15, 173
disconsolate 12, 69, 169, 173
discontent 227
discontented 18, 70, 169
discordant 178
discouraged 12, 18, 69, 169
discouraging 45
discourteous 36
discovery 227; fear of 106
discreditable 54
discredited 54
discrediting 44
discreet 13, 23, 36, 64, 156, 180
discriminating 48, 59
discriminatory 148
discursive 46, 175
disdained 171
disdainful 28, 30, 75, 183
disease 215
disenchanted 169
disenfranchised 40
disengaged 10, 70
disgraceful 54, 181
disgruntled 70, 169
disguised 57
disgusted 18
disheartened 12, 18

disheveled 182
dishonest 20, 57, 58, 156, 164
dishonor, fear of 106
dishonorable 20
disillusioned 169
disingenuous 57
disinterested 10
disloyal 20, 60, 186
disloyalty 228
disobedient 75, 178
disobliging 36
disorder 216
disorderly 77, 182
disorganized 77, 182
disowned 171
disparager 155
disparaging 44
dispassionate 7, 13, 52, 71, 184
dispirited 12, 169
displeased 18, 70
disputatious 50, 73
disquieted 14, 18, 29, 51, 71, 169
disregarder 156
disregardful 11, 30, 156, 170, 178, 182
disreputable 54, 164, 181
disrespectful 30, 75, 183
dissatisfied 18, 70, 169
dissembling 57
dissident 70, 75
dissipated 54
dissipater 156
dissipating 78
dissipative 184
dissolute 55
dissonant 75
dissuadable 74
dissuasive 45, 176
distant 16, 35, 167
distinguished 42, 168
distracted 156
distraught 14
distressed 51, 60, 69
distressing 165
distrustful 32, 50, 64
disturbed 14, 51
disunited 70
divinatory 53, 176
diviner 176
dizzy 4
do-gooder 170
docile 75, 148, 152
dogged 26, 63, 162
dogmatic 6, 49, 74, 151
dogmatist 151
doleful 18, 69, 169, 173
doltish 4, 49, 166
dominant 40
dominated 40, 75
domineering 40, 68, 150
donor 160

dopey 4, 49, 166
doting 16
double-crossing 57, 156
double-dealer 186
double-dealing 156, 163, 164
double-faced 57
doubtful 5, 26, 50, 174
doubting 32, 50
doubting Thomas 181
doughty 153
dour 18, 69
down-and-out 168
down-and-outer 168
down-at-the-heels 168
down-to-earth 9, 50, 67, 81, 178
downcast 18, 69
downhearted 12, 173
downtrodden 42
Draconian 68
dramatic 66, 175
drastic 68
dreamer 157, 163
dreamy 8, 51
dreamy-eyed 163, 187
dreary 69, 152, 154, 169
dressy 175
drink, like or dislike of 100
droll 69
drowsy 61
drug addict 157
drunkard 157
dry 152
dualist 118
dubious 50, 181
dull 4, 9, 49, 152
dull-witted 4, 49, 166
dumb 4, 49, 166
dunce 166
dupable 31
dupe 157, 151
duplicitous 57
dutiful 19, 59, 170
duty, self-assessment of 137
duty-bound 19, 59, 170
dynamic 40
dynamo 160, 162

eager 13, 71, 160
eager beaver 160, 162
earnest 71
easy mark 157
easygoing 68, 71, 148
eavesdropper 159
ebullient 71
eccentric 157, 171
economical 77, 158
economizer 158
ecstatic 17
edgy 29, 71
educated 43, 183

education 128; jobs in 205; self-assessment of 137
effervescent 69
efficacious 50
efficient 39, 76, 171
effusive 52
egocentric 28, 158
egotist 158
egotistic 28, 66
elastic 62, 186
elated 17
electrifying 45
elegant 38
elevated 19, 54
elfish 80
eloquent 44, 175
elusive 151
embarrassed 18, 31, 60
embittered 21, 150
eminent 42, 168
emotional 13, 15, 181, 183
empathetic 20, 183
empiricist 118
empty-headed 4, 49, 166
emulative 9, 25, 81
enamored 16
enchanting 45
encouraged 11, 171
encouraging 44
enduring 26, 184
enemy 149
energetic 61, 160, 162
engaged 9, 51
engaging 182
engrossed 51
engrossing 45
enigmatic 177
enlightened 43
enlightening 44, 169, 182
enraged 16
enslaved 152
enterprising 8, 23, 61, 160, 162
entertaining 45, 159
entertainment: jobs in 205; like or dislike of 99
enthralling 45
enthusiastic 9,11,13, 71, 160, 171
enticement 228
enticing 45, 176
entranced 17
entrancing 45
entrenched 161
envenomed 21
envious 27, 151
Epicurean 78
equable 14
equality, desire for 87

equitable 6, 19, 59
erratic 60, 63, 158, 186
erudite 43, 183
esteemed 42
esteeming 29
estimable 19, 54
estranged 70
ethical 19, 55, 174, 178
evasion, desire for 88
evasive 57, 151, 154, 177
even-tempered 14, 72, 184
evenhanded 19, 59
evil 22, 55, 181
evildoer 181
exacting 68, 76, 150, 171, 173
exaggerative 66, 148, 156
exalted 54
examinational 164
examiner 159, 164
examining 9, 65
exasperated 18
exasperating 165
excellent 19, 55, 172
excitable 14, 71, 162
exciting 44
exemplary 19, 54
exhibitionist 158
exhilarated 17
expectant 53, 171
expectations, self-assessment of 137
experienced 39
expert 39
exploitable 31, 157
exploitative 55
exploration, like or dislike of 100
exploratory 23, 159, 164
explorer 158
explosive 73, 162
extemporaneous 8
external traits 33–82
extolling 43
extortionist 185
extravagant 22, 66, 79, 184
extremism 122
extrovert 159
extroverted 35
exuberant 69, 71
exultant 17

facile 62
facilitating 156
factional 59
failed 42
failure 129, 168; fear of 107; as plot driver 228; self-assessment of 138
faint-hearted 24, 63, 65, 174

fair 59
fair-minded 6, 59, 173
fair-weathered 60
fair-weather flatterer 152
faithful 16, 19, 59, 185
faithless 57, 60, 186
fake 163, 175
faker 155
false 20, 57, 186
false-hearted 20, 156
faltering 63
fame, self-assessment of 138
fanatic 151
fanatical 7, 151
fanciful 8, 51, 187
farseeing 53
farsighted 53, 176
fascinated 9
fascinating 45
fashion, jobs in 203
fast-moving 61
fastidious 66, 173
fasting 77, 151
fatigued 61, 155
fault-finding 44
faultfinder 155
faultless 19
fawner 152
fawning 43, 75, 152
fearful 18, 24, 64, 174
fearless 23, 64, 149
fears 104–115
featherbrained 4, 166
feckless 61
feeble-minded 49
feisty 73
felicitous 69
fence-straddler 156
ferocious 55, 73
fervent 13, 71
fevered 13
fickle 60, 63, 186
fidgety 29, 71
fiendish 22, 55
fierce 22, 73
fiery 13, 73
financially embarrassed 168
fine 19
fine lady 175
fingerpointer 182
finicky 173
finished 38
fire-eater 149, 162
firm 6, 68, 161
first-rate 54, 172
first-rater 170
fitful 71
fixated 63

fixed 5, 26, 63, 74, 161
flagging 61
flake 157
flaky 158
flamboyant 66
flashy 66, 158, 175
flat 152
flattering 43, 152, 156
flawless 172
flexible 6, 62, 63, 68, 74
flighty 186
flimflammer 155
flirt 159
flirtatious 160
florid 66
flourishing 42
flowery 175
fluctuating 26, 63, 186
flunky 152, 168
flush 42
flustered 14
focused 25, 63
foe 149
folksy 34, 36
follower 151
fond 16
food, like or dislike of 100
fool 151
foolable 157
foolhardy 64, 153
foolish 4, 49, 166
foot-dragger 155
footman 152
fop 158, 175
foppish 175
forbearant 148, 184
forbearing 7, 28, 48, 68
forbidding 68, 150
forceful 40, 44, 150, 175
forecaster 176
foreknowing 8, 53, 176
foreseeing 53, 176
foresighted 8, 53
forgetful 30, 52, 170
forgetfulness, desire for 88
forgiving 21, 68, 160
forlorn 169
formal 35, 80
forsaken 171
forthright 57, 174
fortunate 42
fortune-teller 176
forward 35
forward-looking 11, 171
four-flusher 155, 163, 175
foxy 57, 156
fraidycat 174
frank 57
fraternal 34
fraternizing 159

fraud 155, 175
fraudulent 57, 156
free liver 157
free-speaking 57
free-thinking 6
free-wheeling 80
freedom: desire for 88;
  as plot driver 228;
  self-assessment of 138
freeloader 152
freeloading 41
frenzied 61
fretful 18, 29, 70, 163
friend 185
friendly 159, 182
friendship, self-assess-
  ment of 139
frigid 13, 184
frisky 61, 71
frivolous 63
frolicsome 80, 179
frowzy 182
frugal 79, 158
frump 182
frumpish 182
frustrated 18, 70
fuddlebrained 4
fuddy-duddy 173
fulfilled 70
fumbling 62
fuming 14, 16
fun-loving 80
funereal 12, 161, 173
furious 16
fussbudget 171, 173
fussy 76, 171

gabber 154
gabby 46, 154
gadfly 159
gallant 24, 66, 153
galling 165
galvanizing 44
gambler 149
game 23, 153
garish 66
garrulous 46, 154
gasbag 154
gassy 154
gaudy 175
gay 17, 69
generous 21, 27, 55, 79,
  160
genial 34, 182
genteel 38, 80, 183
gentle 72, 75
gentlemanly 80
ghosts and demons 216
gifted 8, 39
giver 160
giving 27, 79
glad 17
gladsome 69
gleeful 17, 69

glib 46, 154, 156
gloomy 12, 18, 69, 169,
  173
glorified 42
glorifying 43
glowering 34
glowing 69
glum 12, 18, 69, 169, 173
glutton 157
gluttonous 27, 78, 157
go-between 172
go-getter 160, 162
goading 44
goal-deficient 25
goal-oriented 25
godly 56
gofer 152
gold digger 160
goldbricker 155
good 19, 55, 170, 172
good-for-nothing 54,
  167
good fortune 228
good health, desire for
  89
good-humored 72
good luck, desire for 89
good-natured 22, 55,
  72, 182
Good Samaritan 160
good-tempered 72, 182
goody-goody 163, 175
goody-two-shoes 175
goof off 155
goon 165
gossip 153, 154
gossipy 46
governed 41
government, jobs in
  206
grabby 79
graceful 38, 62
graceless 38, 62
gracious 22, 36, 148,
  156, 160, 182
grand 38, 54
grandiloquent 66
grandiose 66, 158
grandstander 158
grandstanding 175
grasping 27, 79, 166
grateful 30
gratified 17, 30
grave 69, 169
greasy 156
great-hearted 24
greedy 27, 79
green 39, 157
greenhorn 149, 157
gregarious 34, 159
grief-stricken 18
grieved 179
griever 160
grieving 161

grim 69
griping 47
gripped 51
gritless 24, 64, 174
gritty 24, 64, 153
grouch 161
grouchy 73, 161
grouser 161
grousing 47
groveling 75, 152
grudgeful 21, 149, 150
grudging 27, 79, 166
gruff 161
grumbler 161
grumbling 47, 73, 161
grumpy 161
guard 187
guarded 13, 23, 35, 47,
  64, 187
guardian 177
guarding 78, 174
guiding 78
guileful 20, 57, 156
guileless 57, 157, 170,
  174
guilt-ridden 31, 60
guiltless 31
guilty 31, 179
gullible 31, 49, 157
gushy 46
gutsy 23, 64
gypster 155

habits 126
Habitual 180
hail-fellow 34
hair-splitting 177
half-hearted 26, 71
half-witted 49
hammy 66
handy 39
handyman 187
hanger-on 152
haphazard 182
hapless 42
happiness, self-assess-
  ment of 139
happy 17, 69, 186
happy-go-lucky 69
harasser 165
hard 68
hard-fisted 79
hard-hearted 21, 184
hard-shelled 6
hard times 217
hard worker 162
hard-working 61
hardened 6, 21, 61, 184
hardhead 161
hardheaded 6, 74
hardy 23, 64
harm, fear of 107
harmful 55
harmonious 37, 159

harsh 22, 36, 68
hasty 13, 64, 165
hate-filled 16
haughty 34, 66, 158, 183
haunted 51
have-not 168
hawker 176
hayseed 180
headmaster 150
headstrong 6, 74, 161
health, self-assessment
  of 140
heart-broken 18
heart-stricken 179
heartened 11
heartless 21, 22, 55
heartsick 169
hearty 13, 34, 69
heathen 57
heavy-footed 62
heavy-handed 62, 153
heavy-hearted 18, 31,
  60, 69, 169, 179
heckler 165
hedonist 157
hedonistic 78
heedful 10, 64
heedless 11, 13, 52, 64,
  156, 165, 170
heinous 55
hell, fear of 107
help, desire for 89
helper 160
helpful 22, 36, 185
henpecked 75
henpecker 155
heretic 181
heretical 57
hero 153
heroic 24, 64, 149, 153
heroine 153
hesitant 5, 23, 26, 63,
  65, 174, 186
hick 180
hickish 38, 180
hidebound 7
high and mighty 158
highbred 80
highbrow 43, 183
high-class 183
highfalutin 66, 175
high-flown 66
high-handed 40, 68
high-hat 183
high-hatted 66, 158, 183
high-hatter 183
high-living 78
high-minded 19, 55, 178
high-nosed 158, 183
high-powered 40
high-principled 170, 178
high-reaching 160
high-sounding 66, 175
high-spirited 17, 69, 71

high-strung 14, 29, 71
high-toned 158, 175
highly-polished 172
histrionic 66
hit-or-miss 170
hoarding 79
hoggish 27, 79, 166
hoity-toity 66, 158, 183
holier-than-thou 57, 66
holy terror 162
home, self-assessment of 140
homesick 15
homey 34
honest 19, 57
honey-mouthed 156
honeyed 43
honorable 19, 54, 170, 174
honored 42
hoodlum 164, 165
hooligan 165
hopeful 11, 171
horny 13
horrible 55
horse trader 156
hospitable 34, 159
hostile 16, 22, 34, 149, 178, 187
hot-blooded 13
hot-tempered 73, 162
hotel, restaurant, jobs in 207
hothead 161
hound 162
household, like or dis-like of 100
huckster 176
humane 20, 55
humanist 118
humble 28, 67, 165
humdrum 46
humdrummer 154
humiliated 18, 31
humiliation 229
humorous 69
hurried 162
hurt 18
hurtful 44, 55, 165
hustler 160, 162
hypercritical 44, 155, 173
hypersensitive 73
hypochondriac 163
hypocrite 156, 163
hypocritical 57, 156, 163

idea: fear of 108; as plot driver 229
idealist 163, 187
idealistic 51
ideological 49
idle 61, 167
idler 167

idolatrous 29, 56
ignoble 20, 55, 164, 181
ignominious 55
ignorant 166
ignorant 4, 43, 166
ill-adjusted 70
ill-behaved 38
ill-bred 38
ill-disposed 16, 22
ill-famed 54
ill-fated 42
ill-humored 161
illiberal 7, 78, 166, 183
ill-intentioned 22
illiterate 43, 166, 180
ill-mannered 38, 180
ill-matched 169
ill-natured 22, 161
illogical 45
ill-starred 42
ill-tempered 73
illustrious 19, 42, 168
imaginary invalid 163
imaginative 8, 81, 148, 187
imbecilic 49
imitative 9, 81, 154
immersed 9, 51
immoderate 78
immodest 28
immoral 20, 55, 164
immoralist 163
immovable 6, 161
imp 178
impartial 6, 59, 173
impassioned 13, 44, 71
impassive 14, 184
impatient 29, 64, 162
impenetrable 6
impenitent 31, 61
imperial 54
imperious 28, 40, 68, 150, 183
impertinent 75
imperturbable 14, 28, 71, 184
impetuous 13, 64, 149, 165
impious 57
impish 80
implacable 21, 74
impolite 36
important 42, 168
impostor 156, 163, 175
impoverished 42
impractical 51, 163, 187
impressionable 6
impressive 44
improper 20
improvident 64, 78, 184
improvisational 8
imprudent 13, 64, 73, 75
impugning 44

impulsive 13, 64, 149, 165
impure 20
inaccessible 34, 165, 167
inaccurate 77
inactive 61, 167
inartificial 67
inattentive 11, 52, 156, 170
incautious 13, 153
incendiary 44
incensed 16
incitive 44
incognizant 43
incompatible 70
incompetent 39
incompliant 74, 178
inconsiderate 21, 36
inconsistent 77
inconsolable 173
inconspicuous 67
inconstant 60, 186
incontinent 184
incorruptible 19, 55
incredulous 32, 181
incriminatory 148
incurious 10, 66
indebted 30
indecent 20, 54, 180
indecisive 5, 26, 186
indefatigable 26, 63, 161, 162
indefinite 5, 177
indelicate 38
independent 41, 167
indestructible 40
indifferent 10, 15, 30, 66, 71, 156, 184, 188
indigent 42, 168
indignant 16
indiscreet 57
indiscriminate 59
indistinct 177
individualism, self-assessment of 140
individualistic 37, 41
indocile 161
indolent 61, 167
indomitable 23, 161
indubious 31
indulgent 21, 28, 68, 148
industrious 61, 160, 162
ineffectual 40
inefficient 39, 77
inelastic 6
inelegant 38
inept 39, 62, 149
inequitable 59
inert 61
inexperienced 39, 149
inexpert 39
inexpressive 45
infamous 54, 181
inferior 40, 54

infidel 181
inflamed 14, 16
inflammatory 44
inflated 66, 158
inflexible 6, 62, 68, 74, 150, 161
influenceable 6
influential 40, 44
informal 35, 67
information 229
informational 46
informative 46, 149, 182
informer 182
infuriated 16
ingenious 8, 31, 39, 187
ingenuous 49, 57, 157
inglorious 181
ingrate 185
ingratiating 34, 152
inharmonious 169
inhibited 13, 35
inhospitable 34, 35, 37, 161
inhuman 22, 55
inhumane 55
inimical 16, 73, 149
iniquitous 55, 164
injudicious 64
injurious 44, 55, 181
injustice: fear of 108; as plot driver 229
inner-directed 41
innocent 31, 49, 157
innovative 8
innovator 187
inquiring 9, 65, 159
inquisitive 9, 65, 153, 159
inquisitorial 65
insane 177
insecure 18
insensitive 21, 52
insidious 22, 156
insightful 8
insignificant 40, 43, 170
insincere 57, 156, 163
insipid 152
insistent 150
insolent 75, 158
insolvent 42
insouciant 69
inspectional 164
inspector 159
inspired 160
inspiring 44
instigative 44
instructive 46, 169
instructor 169
insubordinate 75, 178
insufferable 161
insulting 155
insurgent 178
insurgent 75
insurrectionary 178

insurrectionist 178
intellectual 43, 48, 164
intelligent 3, 48
intemperate 78, 79, 157
intense 13, 71
intercessionary 173
interested 9, 51
interesting 45
interfering 65
intermediary 172
internal traits 3–32
interrogative 153, 159
interrogative 9, 65
interrogatory 164
intervention 229
intimidated 23
intimidating 165
intimidator 164
intolerant 7, 29, 183
intractable 6, 74, 161
intransigent 6, 68, 74
intrepid 24, 64, 149, 153
intrigued 9
introvert 164
introverted 35
intrusion 230
intrusive 65, 159
intuitive 8, 53, 176
inventive 8, 39, 187
inventor 187
investigative 9, 164
investigator 159
invidious 22
invincible 40
involved 9, 51
invulnerable 40
irascible 73, 162
irate 16
irksome 152
iron-willed 26
ironfisted 40
irreligious 57, 181
irreproachable 55, 172
irresistible 45
irresolute 5, 26, 50, 63,
    186
irresponsible 60, 63
irreverent 30, 57, 75
irritable 73
irritated 16, 19
irritating 161, 165

Jack-of-all-trades 187
jaded 10
jaundiced 7
jaunty 11, 17, 69
jaw-box 154
jealous 32, 174
jealousy, fear of 109
jellyfish 174
jingoistic 165
jinxed 168
jittery 24, 29, 71
jobs 202–211

jocular 69
John or Jane Doe 170
jolly 17, 69, 159
journalism, jobs in 207
jovial 69
joyful 17, 69
joyless 69, 173
joyous 69
jubilant 17
judgmental 178
judicious 13, 23, 36, 64,
    156, 164, 180
jumper 164
jumpy 29, 71
just 19, 59
justice, desire for 89

keen 10, 48
keen-witted 3
keeper 165
killjoy 173
kind 22, 55
kind-hearted 22, 36,
    160, 183
kindness 230
kinglike 150
klutzy 62
knave 178
knavish 20
knee-knocker 174
knight-errant 187
knightly 19, 153
know-it-all 158
know-nothing 166, 180
knowing 48
knowledge, desire for
    89
knowledgeable 43
kowtowing 75

lackadaisical 156
lackey 152
lackluster 69
laconian 166
laconic 47, 167
ladies' man 160
ladylike 80
laggard 155, 167
lamenter 161
lamenting 47, 161
languid 61
languorous 61, 167
larcenous 185
large-hearted 22, 79
lascivious 13, 78
laudable 19
laudatory 43
lavish 79
law 217; jobs in 207
law-abiding 75
lawless 75
lawyer 176
lax 68, 148
lazy 61

lazybones 155
leaden 69
lean-witted 4
learned 43, 183
lecherous 13, 54
lecturer 175
leech 152
leechlike 41
leery 23, 32, 50, 64, 180
left-handed 62, 153
leisure, desire for 90
leisurely 167
lender 160
lenient 7, 20, 28, 68, 148
lethargic 25, 61, 155
lettered 43
level-headed 14, 184
lewd 54, 78
liar 156
libelous 44
liberal 7, 21, 79, 160
liberal-minded 27
licentious 13, 54, 78, 157
licked 168
lickerish 54
lifeless 61
light-fingered 185
light-footed 62
light-hearted 11, 17, 69,
    182
lightsome 17, 69
likes and dislikes 97–
    103
lily-livered 24, 64, 174
limber 62
lingering 155
lionhearted 24, 64, 153
lionized 42
lissome 62
listless 61, 155
literary 43
literate 43
lithe 62
lithesome 62
litterbug 182
lively 61
loaded 42
loafing 61
lofty 19, 54
logical 3, 44, 164
logician 164
loitering 155
loneliness, fear of 109
loner 167
long-faced 169
longing 15
long-sighted 53
long-suffering 7, 28, 48,
    148, 184
long-winded 46, 175
loose 20, 62, 164
loose-jointed 62
looter 185
loquacious 46, 154

lordly 28, 68, 183
loser 167
loss 230
lost 164
lost soul 164
loutish 38, 180
love 129
lovelorn
loving 16
low-born 38
lowbrow 180
low-minded 20
low-spirited 12, 18, 69,
    173
loyal 16, 19, 59, 185
loyalty, desire for 90
luck, self-assessment of
    41
luckless 42
lucky 42
lugubrious 12
lumbering 62
luminary 168
lumpish 49, 155
lush 157
lustful 13, 78
lying 57
lyrical 175

Machiavellian 156
machinelike 9, 81
mad 16
madcap 23, 149
magisterial 66, 150
magnanimous 7, 22, 54,
    79, 160
magnate 168
magnetic 45
magnificent 172
magpie 154
majestic 54, 175
maladjusted 70
maladroit 62, 149
malcontent 70, 168
maleficent 55
malevolent 22–23, 55
malicious 55, 149
maligning 22, 44, 155
malingerer 155
malingering 61
malleable 74
man about town 175
man Friday 185
man in the street 170
man of action 162
man of few words 167
man of iron 184
man of means 188
manipulated 41
manipulative 44, 156,
    169
mannered 66, 175
mannerist 175
mannerly 182

manufacturing, jobs in 208
maritime, jobs in 208
marriage 129; fear of 109; as plot driver 230; self-assessment of 141
martyr 169
masher 160
masquerader 175
masterful 40, 187
masterly 39
materialist 118
materialistic 50
maternal 16, 78
matter-of-fact 174, 178
maudlin 181
mealy-mouthed 43, 152, 156, 163
mean 7, 27, 55, 79
mean-spirited 20, 22, 55
mechanical 9, 81
meddlesome 9, 65, 159
mediator 173
mediatory 37, 173
medical disorder 218
medical/healing, jobs in 208
meditative 12
meek 75, 148, 152, 165
melancholic 18, 69, 169
melancholy 173
melodramatic 66, 175
memoried 52
memoryless 52
mendacious 57
mentor 169
mercenary 20, 79
merciful 20, 55, 183
merciless 21, 55, 165
mercurial 63, 73
meritorious 19, 54
merry 17, 69
mesmerizing 45
messenger 176
messy 77, 182
methodical 76, 171, 180
meticulous 64, 76, 173
mettlesome 23, 149, 153
middleman 173
mighty 40
mild 72
militant 73
militarist 165
militaristic 73, 165
military 130
milksop 174
mindful 10, 22, 64
mindless 4, 49
ministering 152
mirthful 17, 69
mirthless 69
misanthropic 12, 22, 161

mischief-loving 80
mischief-maker 178
mischievous 80, 178
miscreant 55
miser 166
miserable 18, 69, 169, 173, 179
miserly 27, 79, 166
misfit 169
misfortune 130; desire for 90
misinformed 148
mistake 230
mistaken 148
mistrusted 181
mistrustful 32, 181
mixer 159
mocking 36
moderate 13, 72
moderator 173
modest 28, 67, 165
mogul 168
mollified 17
mollifying 72
monarchial 150
money 131; desire for 90
moneyed 42
money-grubber 166
moneygrubbing 79, 166
money-maker 188
monkish 13
monopolistic 79, 166, 174
monopolizer 166
monotonous 152
monotony 218
monstrous 55
mooching 41
moody 69, 169, 173
moonraker 157
moonstruck 51
moping 169
moral 172
moral leader 178
moralist 169
moralistic 19, 55, 66
morality, self-assessment of 141
moronic 49
morose 18, 69
mortified 18, 31, 60
mothering 78
motivated 25, 160
motivating 44
mourner 161
mournful 18, 69, 161, 173
mousy 165
movable 6
mover and shaker 188
moving 44
muckraker 155
muddleheaded 166

mudslinger 155
mulish 74
mundane 9, 50, 81
munificent 22, 27, 79, 160
murderous 22, 55
museful 12, 187
mushy 181
music, like or dislike of 100
mutineer 178
myopic 8
mystic 118
mystical 8

nabob 188
nag 155
nagging 36, 44, 155
naïve 31, 49, 157
nap-taker 155
narcissistic 28, 66
narrow-minded 7, 183
nasty 22, 36, 44
nationalistic 151
natural 67
naturalist 118
nature, like or dislike of 100
naughty 80, 178
neat 76
neat freak 171
needs 83–95
needy 42, 168
ne'er-do-well 61, 167
nefarious 55
neglecter 170
neglectful 11, 52, 64
negligent 77, 156, 167, 170, 182
negotiator 173
neighborly 34, 159
neophytic 39
nerveless 153
nervous 14, 24, 29, 71
neurotic 163
neutral 6, 59, 156, 173
nicknames 189–201; American West 189; animal 190; automobile 190; aviation 191; common 191; "cute" 191; derivatives 192; descriptive 192; famous person 192; food 192; games & sports 193; geographic 193; initials 194; military 195; "Mr." or "Miss" 195; music 196; nationalities 196; naval 197; "old" 197; preceding proper name 197; strange & exotic 197; "The" 199;

trades 200; villainous 200; weather-related 201
niggardly 79, 166
nimble 62
nitpicking 44, 76
noble 54
noble-minded 19
nobody 170
nominalist 118
nonaggressive 167, 172
nonaligned 41
nonathletic competition, like or dislike of 100–101
nonchalant 10, 52, 71, 156
noncombatant 173
noncombative 72, 172
noncommunicative 47
noncompetitive 37
noncompliant 75
nonconforming 8
nonconformist 157, 170
nonconfrontational 172
nondescript 42
nonextravagant 77
nonindulgent 13, 77
nonintellectual 49
noninterfering 148
nonmaternal 79
no-nonsense 68
nonpartisan 6, 7, 59, 172, 173
nonpaternal 79
nonplayful 80
nonresistant 75
nonspeculative 64
nonviolent 72
nostalgia 230
nostalgic 15, 52, 181
nosy 9, 65, 153, 159
notable 42, 168
noteworthy 54
notional 8, 187
notorious 54
noxious 55
nurturing 16

oafish 4, 153, 166
obdurate 68, 74
obedient 75, 152
obeisant 29, 152
objective 6, 59, 184
obligated 30
obliging 36, 75, 148
oblivious 11, 20, 52, 156, 187
obnoxious 155, 161
obscene 164
obsequious 43, 75, 152
observant 10
obsessed 178
obstinate 6, 26, 74, 161

obstructed 168
obtrusive 65
obtuse 4, 49
occupied 51
oddball 157
oddballish 171
oddity 157
odious 54
offended 18
offensive 155, 161
office stuff, like or dis-
　like of 101
officious 65, 159
oily 163
old age 219
old fashioned 181
old soldier 187
old timer 187
omens, fear of 100
omnipotent 40, 150
omniscient 3
one in a million 172
one-sided 7, 59
open 35, 57, 74
open-and-aboveboard
　174
open-eared 9
open-eyed 10
open-handed 22, 79,
　160
openhearted 183
open-minded 6, 74
opinionated 6
opportunity, self-assess-
　ment of 141
opposed 16
oppressive 40, 150
oppressor 150
optimist 171
optimistic 11, 171
opulent 188
oracle 176
oracular 53
oratorical 46
orderly 76, 171
ordinary 9, 81, 154, 170
organized 76
organizer 171
original 8
orthodox 154
ostentatious 66, 158, 175
out-of-step 70
outcast 171
outgoing 34, 35
outrageous 55
outspoken 57
outstanding 54
overbearing 40, 66, 68,
　150
overconfident 5, 66, 151
overcurious 65
overindulgence 230
overindulgent 157
overjoyed 17

overnice 163
overprecise 76
overrefined 163, 175
overweening 66
overwrought 51

pacific 14, 72, 172
pacified 17
pacifist 172, 173
painstaking 64, 76, 173
palmist 176
panicky 174
pantheist 119
paragon 170, 172
parasite 152
parasitic 41
pariah 171
parochial 7
parrotlike 9, 81
parsimonious 79, 166
partial 7, 59, 183
participatory 37
particular 76, 173
partisan 59
partner 185
party-goer 179
passionate 175
passive 28, 75, 148, 152
paternal 16, 78
patient 28, 48, 64, 184
patriot 151
patriotic 151
patron 185
patronizing 66
pauper 168
pauperized 168
peace, desire for 91
peaceable 72, 172, 173
peaceful 14, 71
peacekeeper 172
peacock 158
peculiar 158
pedantic 43, 66
peddler 176
pedestrian 9, 81
peevish 73
penitent 31, 60, 179
penniless 42, 168
penny-pinching 77, 79,
　158, 166
pensive 12, 69
penurious 79, 166
people, like or dislike of
　101
peppy 61, 162
perceptive 3,10, 48, 164
peremptory 40
perfection, desire for 91
perfectionist 173, 178
perfidious 20, 54, 164
perfunctory 77
perjurer 156
perky 61
permissive 7, 68, 74, 148

pernicious 22, 55
perplexing 177
persecutor 165
perseverance, self-
　assessment of 142
persevering 26, 63, 162,
　184, 185
persistent 26, 63
persnickety 173
perspicacious 8, 48
persuadable 6, 74
persuaded 5
persuasive 44, 176
pert 182
pertinacious 26
perturbed 14
perverse 74
perverted 55
pesky 36
pessimist 173
pessimistic 12
petitioner 176
petty 7, 20, 54, 79
petulant 73
Philadelphia lawyer 156
philanderer 160
philanthropic 79, 160
philanthropist 160
philosophical 3, 48, 164
phlegmatic 71
phobias 113; *see also*
　fears
phony 57, 66, 156, 163,
　175
phrasemonger 175
physical affliction 231
physical impairment
　219
picky 173
picture-straightener 171
pietistic 56, 66
piggish 27, 79, 157, 166
pighead 161
pigheaded 6, 161
pinchfist 166
pipedreamer 157
pirate 185
pitchman 176
pithy 47
pitiless 21, 68, 165
placated 17
placating 72, 148
places 131; like or dis-
　like of 102
placid 14, 71
plagiarizer 185
plagued 179
plain 67
plain dealer 173
plain-spoken 57, 67
plaintive 161
playful 80, 178, 179
pleasant 34, 182
pleased 17, 69, 186

pleasing 45
pleasurable 45
pleasure-seeking 78
pliable 75, 186
pliant 6, 68, 75, 152
plodding 62, 162
plot drivers 222–233
plotting 150
plucky 24, 64, 149, 153
plunderer 185
plunderous 79, 185
plutocrat 188
poacher 185
poised 14, 184
poisonous 181
polemic 73
polished 38, 66, 80, 156,
　183
polite 156
politic 23, 36, 64, 180
politician 156
politics 131; like or dis-
　like of 102
Pollyanna 171
poltroon 174
poltroonish 64
pompous 66, 158, 175
ponderous 12
pontificating 151
poor man 168
poor white trash 168
positive 5, 49, 151
positivist 119
possessions, self-assess-
　ment of 142
possessive 166, 175
possessor 166, 174
poverty, fear of 110
poverty-stricken 42, 168
power, desire for 91
powerful 40, 150
powerless 40
practical 50, 74
practical-minded 9, 178
practiced 39, 187
pragmatic 9, 50
pragmatist 119, 178
praise, desire for 91
praise-seeking 169
praiseworthy 19, 54
praising 43
prancing 66
prankish 80
prankster 178
prattler 154
preacher 175, 176, 178
preachy 46
precipitate 13
precise 64, 171
precognitive 53
precognizant 8, 53, 176
predaceous 55
predatory 79, 185
predictable 180

predictive 53, 176
predictor 176
predictory 53
predisposed 59
preeminent 42
preferential 59
prejudice, self-assessment of 143
prejudiced 7, 183
prejudicial 30, 59
premonitory 53
preoccupied 9, 187
presageful 53, 176
prescient 8, 53
preservation, desire for 92
pretender 175
pretentious 66, 156, 158, 175
prevaricator 156
prevention, desire for 92
preventive 180
prideful 28, 158
prig 158, 175, 183
priggish 7, 66
prim 66
primitive 38
princely 19
principled 19, 54, 174
prisoner 175
prissy 80
private 167
privateer 185
privileged 42
probing 9, 159
procedural 76
procrastinating 61
procrastinator 170
prodigal 79, 184
productive 61, 162
profane 57
professional 39, 43
proficient 39
profiteer 185
profligate 13, 55, 78, 164, 184
prognostic 53, 176
prognosticator 176
programmatic 9, 81
progressive 79
prohibitive 150
prolific 61
prolix 46
prominent 42, 168
promiscuous 20
promoter 176
promotive 176
proper 19, 54, 170
property, desire for 92
prophesier 176
prophet 176
prophetic 176
prosaic 9, 46, 50, 81, 152

prosperous 42, 188
protective 16, 78, 175
protector 177
protesting 47
proud 28
proverbs 121
provident 64
provincial 180
provocation 231
provocative 45, 176
provoking 165
prudent 23, 64, 77, 180
prudish 66, 175
prurient 13
prying 9, 65, 159
psychic 176
psycho 177
public-spirited 79
puckish 80
puffed up 158
pugnacious 73, 165, 178
punctilious 38, 66, 171, 173
punishment: fear of 110; as plot driver 231
punitive 68, 150
puppet master 150
pure 19, 54, 172
puritan 175
puritanical 19, 55, 66, 151, 175
purposeful 25, 26, 63, 160
purposeless 25, 27, 63, 167
pushover 157
pusillanimous 64, 75, 174
pussyfooting 180
putterer 167
puzzled 50

quack 156, 163
Quakerish 175
qualified 39
qualmish 24, 174
quarrelsome 73, 155, 162
queer 158
queer duck 157
querulous 44
questing 23
questioning 9, 32, 50, 159, 164
quibbler 177
quick 3, 48
quick-eyed 48
quick-moving 61
quick-tempered 14, 73, 162
quick-witted 3, 48
quiescent 61
quiet 47, 72
quixotic 64
quizzical 9

rabble-rousing 44
racist 183
radiant 69
radical 178
rambling 46
rambunctious 35
rampageous 162
rancorous 21, 44, 149, 150
rapacious 27, 55, 79
rascal 177
rascally 80, 178
rash 13, 23, 64, 153
rat 186
rational 3
rationalist 119
rattlebrained 4
raw 38, 149
reactionary 6
ready 10
realist 119, 178
realistic 9, 15, 50, 74
reasonable 3, 59, 74
reasoning 164
reassured 11
reassuring 44
rebel 178
rebellious 75, 178
recalcitrant 75, 161, 178
receptive 74
reckless 23, 64, 80, 170
reclusive 167
recognition, desire for 92
recollective 52
reconciled 70
recreant 64
recriminatory 148, 155
redundant 46
referee 173
refined 38, 80, 183
reflective 12, 52
reformer 178
regardful 16, 29
regretful 31, 60, 161, 179
regulated 41
rejected 171
rejection: fear of 111; as plot driver 232
relaxation, like or dislike of 102
relaxed 14, 17, 71, 186
relentless 63
reliable 59
relief, desire for 93
relieved 17
religious 56
reluctant 23, 174
reminiscent 52, 181
remiss 61, 77, 167
remorseful 31, 60
remote 70
removed 16
renegade 186

renounced 171
renowned 42
repentant 31, 60, 179
repenter 179
repetitious 46
repining 47
repressed 13, 35
repressive 68
reproachful 155
reprobate 164
reptile 181
reputable 54, 168, 170, 174
reputation 132; self-assessment of 143
researcher 159
resentful 21, 47, 149, 151
reserved 13, 35, 165, 167
resigned 48
resistant 161
resolute 26, 63, 74, 153, 161, 162
resolution 232
resolved 26
resourceful 8
respectful 19, 29, 36, 182
responsibility, desire for 93
responsive 6, 48, 74
restive 29, 71
restless 18, 29, 71, 169
restoration, fear of 111
restrained 13, 35, 41, 80, 165, 167
restricted 41
restrictive 175
retail store, jobs in 209
retaliatory 21, 148, 150
retentive 166
reticent 13, 23, 35, 47, 165
retiring 35, 67, 165
retributive 21, 150
retrospective 52
revealer 182
reveler 179
revengeful 21, 150
reverent 56, 151
reverential 29, 56
revolutionary 178
rewarded 17
rich 42, 188
ridiculing 44
righteous 19, 55
right-hand man 185
right-minded 19
rigid 6, 35, 62, 74, 161, 173
risk-taker 149
risk-taking 64
rivaling 37
robber 185
rogue 178

roguish 80
rolling stone 186
romance, self-assess-
    ment of 143
romantic 15, 51, 163,
    181, 187
rompish 179
rookie 149
rosy 11
rotten 55
rough 180
rounder 157
rowdy 73
royalistic 150
rube 149, 179
rude 36,73
rueful 31, 60, 179
ruffian 165, 180
ruinous 55
ruling 40, 150
ruminative 12
rumormonger 153
rumpled 182
run-of-the-mill 9, 81
rustic 38, 180
rut walker 180
ruthless 22, 55

sacrificial 160
sacrilegious 57
sad 18, 69, 161
sadistic 55
safeguarder 174, 180
safeguarding 78
safekeeper 177
sagacious 8, 48
saintly 56, 172
salacious 13, 55
salesman 176
sanctimonious 57, 66,
    163
sanguine 11, 17, 171
sap 157
sarcastic 36, 155
satisfied 17, 25, 49, 186
saucy 75
savage 22, 55
saving 77, 158
savvy 48
scab 186
scalawag 178
scamp 178
scandalmonger 153
scandalous 55, 164, 181
scared 24, 64
scaredy-cat 174
schemer 156
scheming 20, 57, 156
scholar 159
scholarly 43, 164
schooled 43
schoolmarmish 43
schoolmasterish 43
scoffing 44

scolding 155
scorned 171
scornful 30, 44, 183
scoundrel 180
scowling 161
scrappy 73, 162
screwball 157
scrimping 77, 166
scrupulous 19, 54, 64,
    74, 173
scrutinizing 65
scum of the earth 181
search 232
searching 9
secluded 167
second-rate 42, 54
second-rater 154
second-sighted 8, 176
secrecy, desire for 93
secretive 47, 154
sectarian 7, 59
secure 28
security: desire for 93;
    self-assessment of 144
sedate 14, 69, 71
seditionary 178
seditious 75
seductive 44, 176
sedulous 26, 63, 76
seeker 159, 164
seeker of justice 148
seer 176
segregationist 183
selective 76, 173
self-abnegating 77
self-absorbed 27
self-accusing 60, 179
self-applauding 158
self-assertive 35
self-assessment 134–146
self-assured 5
self-centered 27, 158
self-condemning 60,
    179
self-confident 5, 184
self-congratulatory 158
self-conscious 28, 67,
    165
self-controlled 13, 71,
    77, 151, 184
self-convicting 60
self-denying 13, 27, 77,
    151
self-deprecating 67
self-depreciative 28, 165
self-depriving 77, 158
self-devoted 158
self-disciplined 13, 77,
    178
self-effacing 67, 165
self-esteeming 28, 158
self-governing 13, 41,
    167
self-important 28, 66

self-indulgent 78, 157,
    164
self-inflated 158
self-interested 27
selfish 27, 79, 166, 175
selfless 22, 22
self-neglecting 77
self-possessed 14, 71
self-praising 158
self-promoting 176
self-protective 174
self-regulating 13
self-reliant 41, 167
self-reproachful 31, 60,
    179
self-restraining 77
self-restricting 77
self-righteous 7, 178
self-sacrificing 27, 77,
    158, 169
self-satisfied 17, 158
self-seeking 27
self-serving 54
self-sufficient 41
self-supporting 41
self-sustaining 41
self-taught 43
semi-literate 43
sensational 175
sensible 44
sensitive 36, 183
sensual 13, 157
sensualist 157
sententious 47
sentimental 15, 52
sentimentalist 181
separated 37
separation, fear of 111
serene 14, 17, 70, 71, 184
serf 152
serious 69
sermonizing 46
servant 152
service jobs 210
servile 75, 152
serving 152
set 74
severe 68
shady 54, 57
shaky 60
shallow 4, 49
shallow-brained 4
shamed 18
shamefaced 31
shameful 54, 181
shameless 28, 31, 55
sharp 3, 48, 73
sharp-sighted 48
sharp-witted 48
sharper 156
sheepish 31, 60
sheltering 16, 78, 177
shielding 177
shiftless 61, 167

shifty 57, 156
shilly-shallying 186
shortsighted 8, 53
short-tempered 73, 162
show-off 158
showy 66, 158, 175
shrewd 3, 48
shrinking 24, 67, 165
shy 67, 165
sidekick 185
side-stepping 57
silent 47, 167
silver-tongued 175
simple 49, 67
simple-hearted 31, 67
simple-minded 4, 49
Simple Simon 157
sincere 57, 174
sinful 55, 57, 164
single-minded 25
sinister 20, 55
sinless 172
sinner 164
skeleton at the feast 173
skeptic 181
skeptical 32, 50
skillful 39, 187
skinflint 166
skirt chaser 160
skittish 174
skittish 29, 64, 71, 174
skunk 164, 181
slack 61, 77
slanderer 155
slandering 155
slanderous 44
slapdash 77
slatternly 77, 182
slave 152
slave driver 150
slavish 152
slick 54, 156
slinky 174
slippery 151, 156
slipshod 170, 182
slob 181
sloppy 77, 182
slothful 61, 167
slovenly 77, 170, 182
slow 49, 61
slow-footed 155
slow-moving 61, 155
slow-paced 155
slowpoke 155
slow-witted 49, 166
sluggard 155
sluggish 61, 167
slummock 182
sly 57, 156
slyboots 156
small 7
small fry 170
small-minded 54, 183
small-time 170

smart 3, 48
smells, like or dislike of 102
smiler 182
smooth 71, 156
smooth-spoken 43
smooth-tongued 156, 163
smug 17, 188
snake in the grass 156, 186
snappish 73
snitch 182
snob 158, 182, 183
snobbish 7, 34, 66
snoopy 9, 65, 153, 159
snooty 66, 158, 183
snotty 66
sober 69
sober-faced 69
sociable 34, 159, 182
social upheaval 232
socializer 159
soft-hearted 20, 183
soft-soaper 152
soft touch 183
softy 183
solemn 12, 69, 169
solicitor 176
solicitous 16, 36
solitary 37
solvent 188
somber 18, 69, 173
somnambulant 155
somnolent 61
soothing 36
soothsayer 176
sophisticate 183
sophisticated 38
sophistication, desire for 94
soporific 61
sordid 54
sore 16
sorrowful 18, 69, 161, 173
sorrow-laden 179
sorrow-seeker 173
sorry 31, 60
sot 157
soulful 183
sour 34
sourpuss 161
sour-tempered 161
sovereign 41
sparing 77, 79, 158
sparkling 69
speculative 12, 23, 51, 64
speculator 149
speechmaker 175
speedy 162
spendthrift 79, 184
spineless 64

spirited 13, 23, 35, 61, 162
spiritless 12, 69
spiteful 21, 149
spitfire 162
splendid 54, 172
spoilsport 173
spokesman 173
sponger 152
sponging 41
spontaneous 13, 35, 80
sportive 179
sports, like or dislike of 103
spotless 172
sprightly 62, 69
spry 62
spunkless 24
spunky 24, 64, 149, 153
spurned 171
squandering 79
square-dealing 174
square-shooting 57
squealer 182
stability, desire for 94
stable 59
stagy 66, 175
staid 14, 18, 69
stalwart 24, 59, 64, 153
standoffish 167, 183
starched 35
starchy 66
starry-eyed 51, 163
staunch 19, 54, 59
steadfast 19, 26, 59, 185
steady 59, 63, 184
stealthy 57
steel-nerved 184
sterling 54
stern 22, 68, 150
stickler 173
stiff 62, 161
stiff-backed 6
stifling 175
stilted 66, 80
stimulating 45
stingy 27, 79, 166
stinting 79, 158
stirring 44
stodgy 152
stoic 184
stoical 48, 71, 184
stolid 4, 13, 49
stone 184
stone-broke 168
stone-hearted 21
stool pigeon 182
stormy 14, 73
story-telling 57
stout-hearted 24, 64, 149, 153
straight 57
straightforward 57, 174
straight-shooter 170

straight-shooting 174
strained 29
strait-laced 66, 175
strapped 168
strengths and weaknesses 125
strict 68, 150
stringent 68, 150
strong 40
strong-minded 26, 161
strong-nerved 184
strong-willed 26, 63, 161, 187
structured 171
strutful 158
stubborn 6, 74, 161
stuck-up 66, 158, 183
student 159
studious 43
stuffy 35, 152
stump speaker 176
stupid 4, 49, 166
suave 156
subdued 18, 35, 152
subjugated 40, 75, 152
sublime 19
submissive 75, 148, 152
subordinate 40
subservient 75, 152
subsidizer 160
success: desire for 94; fear of 112; self-assessment of 144
successful 42
sugary 43
suggestible 6
sulky 18, 69
sullen 18, 34
sunny 11, 17, 34, 69, 182
supercilious 66, 183
superexcellent 172
superficial 4, 163
superior 19, 40, 172
superiority: desire for 94; self-assessment of 145
superlative 54
supernaturalist 119
superstitious 151
supple 62
support 233
supporter 185
supportive 44
suppressive 175
supreme 40
sure 49, 151
sure-footed 62
surly 73
surreptitious 57
suspecting 32, 50, 181
suspicious 23, 32, 50, 167, 175, 180
swaggerer 158
swaggering 66, 158, 175

swayable 6
sweet-tongued 152
swellhead 158
swell-headed 158
swindler 156
swollen 66
sybaritic 78
sycophant 152
sycophantic 43, 75, 152
sympathetic 20, 55, 183, 185
systematic 76, 171, 180

taciturn 47, 167
tactful 36, 156
tactless 36
taker 185
talebearer 153
talebearing 46
talented 8, 39
talkative 46, 154
talker 154
tarnished 54
taskmaster 150
tattler 182
tattletale 153
taunting 36
taut 29
teacher 169
teammate 185
tearful 161
tease 178
technical jobs 210
tedious 46, 152
teetotaling 77
telepathic 53
temperamental 13, 71
temperate 13, 77, 151
tempestuous 73
tenacious 25, 26, 63, 161, 162, 166
tender 16, 55
tender-hearted 20, 36, 183
tense 14, 29, 71, 169
terrified 174
terrorist 165
terse 47, 167
testy 73, 161
tethered 13
thankful 30
theatrical 66, 158, 175
theist 119
theft: fear of 112; as plot driver 233
theoretical 51
thick 4, 49, 166
thick-headed 4, 49
thick-skinned 21, 72, 184
thick-witted 4, 49
thief 185
thievish 57, 185
thin-skinned 73, 161

thinker 164
third-rate 54
thorough 64, 76, 171
thoughtful 10, 12, 36
thoughtless 13, 36
threat 233
threatening 149
thriftless 79, 184
thrifty 77, 158
thrill-seeking 23
thrilling 45
thriving 42
thud 168
tidy 76, 171
tight 27, 79, 166
tightfisted 79
tight-lipped 47, 167
tightwad 166
time 220
timid 24, 64, 67, 75, 165
timorous 24, 64, 174
tippler 157
tireless 26, 63, 162
tiresome 46, 152
toadying 152
tolerant 7, 28, 68, 148
tongue-tied 45
top-lofty 66, 158
topnotcher 170
tormented 18, 31, 51, 60, 163, 169, 179
tormenting 165
tormentor 165
torpid 61
tortured 169
totalitarian 40, 68
touchy 73, 161
tough 68, 150, 161
tractable 75
traditionalist 154
trailblazer 149
trained 39, 43
traitor 186
traitorous 20, 60, 186
tranquil 14, 71
transcendent 55
transgressive 75
transparent 57
transportation, jobs in 211
transported 17
traveler 159
treacherous 20, 57, 156, 164, 186
treasonous 60, 186
treasuring 16
tremulous 24
trickster 156
tricky 57, 156
triumphant 17, 42, 188
troubled 14, 18, 51, 69, 70, 169
truckler 152
truckling 75, 152

truculent 22, 73
true 16, 19, 59
true-blue 16, 59
truehearted 19
trustful 31, 49, 151
trusting 49
trusting soul 151
trustworthy 19, 59, 185
truth, fear of 112
truth-loving 19
truthful 57, 174
truthfulness, desire for 95
truthless 156
turbulent 14, 71, 73, 162
turncoat 186
turning point 132
turntail 186
turtlelike 155
tutored 43
twitchy 71
two-faced 57, 156, 163, 186
two-timer 156
tycoon 168, 188
tyrannical 40, 68, 150
tyrant 150

ugly customer 165
umpire 173
unable 39
unaccommodating 36
unaccomplished 39, 42, 168
unacquainted 149
unadventurous 64, 174, 180
unaffected 67
unaffecting 45
unaffectionate 16–17
unafraid 23, 149
unaggressive 72
unalarmed 52
unalert 11
unallied 41
unalterable 6, 68
unambiguous 57
unambitious 25, 167
unanticipative 8, 53
unapologetic 61
unappealing 46
unappeasable 21
unappreciated 171
unappreciative 30, 185
unapproachable 34
unashamed 31, 61
unassailable 40
unassertive 75
unassuming 7, 35, 67, 157, 165
unathletic 62
unattached 41
unaware 11, 30, 53, 166
unbalanced 177

unbelieving 57
unbelligerent 72, 172
unbending 74, 161
unbenevolent 22
unbiased 7, 59, 74
unbigoted 7
unblemished 54
unbothered 52, 186
unbreakable 161
unburdened 71
uncaring 10, 16
uncertain 5, 26, 63, 186
unchangeable 6, 161
unchanging 63
uncharitable 22, 27, 79
unchaste 164
uncheerful 69, 169, 173
unchristian 57
uncivil 36
uncivilized 55, 180
unclean 164
uncollaborative 37
uncomfortable 18, 179
uncommendable 54
uncommitted 6, 59
uncommon 158
uncommunicative 165, 167
uncompanionable 167
uncompassionate 21, 184
uncompelling 45, 46
uncompetitive 25
uncomplaining 48, 184
uncomplimentary 44, 155
uncomposed 71
uncompromising 6, 26, 37, 68, 74, 161
unconcealed 57
unconcerned 10, 17, 25, 52, 66, 69, 71, 156, 184
unconfident 186
unconformable 158
uncongenial 34
unconquerable 40
unconscientious 164, 182
unconscious 11
unconsenting 75
unconstrained 41
uncontentious 72, 172
uncontrite 31
uncontrolled 78
unconventional 8, 158, 171
unconvinced 5, 50, 181
unconvincing 45
uncooperative 37
uncordial 34
uncorrupt 172
uncourageous 24, 174
uncouth 38, 180
uncreative 9, 81

uncritical 43, 48, 68, 156
unctuous 43, 152, 156
uncultivated 38
uncultured 180
undaring 9, 24, 81, 174
undaunted 24, 64, 149, 153
undeceptive 174
undecided 5, 26, 50, 63
undefiled 19, 55
undeliberate 165
undeliberative 13
undemonstrative 13, 35
undependable 20, 60
underhanded 20, 57, 156, 164
underprivileged 42
understanding 3, 7, 28, 48, 185
undetermined 5, 26
undeviating 63
undevout 57
undignified 54
undirected 63
undiscerning 4, 11, 49
undisciplined 13, 77, 78, 171, 182
undiscriminating 151
undisguised 57
undismayed 64
undistinguished 54
undisturbed 14, 52, 71, 186
undogmatic 6
undoubting 5, 31, 49, 151
undutiful 178
uneasy 23, 29, 51, 70, 169
uneconomical 184
uneducated 43, 166
unembarrassed 31, 61
unemotional 13, 15, 184
unenergetic 61
unengaged 52
unenlightened 43, 166
unenterprising 9, 81, 167, 180
unentertaining 152
unenthusiastic 156
unenticing 46
unequivocal 57
unethical 20, 54
unexacting 170
unexceptional 9, 81, 170
unexcitable 71, 184
unexciting 154
unexpectant 8, 53
unfailing 59, 63
unfair 59
unfaithful 20, 60, 186
unfaltering 26, 63, 185
unfanciful 9

unfearful 153
unfeeling 16, 21, 22, 36, 184
unfixed 5, 63
unflagging 63
unflappable 14, 71
unflattering 44
unflinching 24, 64, 153
unfocused 25
unforgiving 21
unfortunate 42
unfriendly 16, 34, 149, 161
unfrightened 23, 149
unfulfilled 70
ungainly 62, 153
ungenerous 79–80, 166, 175
ungenteel 180
ungenuine 156
ungodly 57
ungovernable 75
ungraceful 153
ungracious 161
ungrateful 30, 185
ungratified 70
ungregarious 165
unguarded 31, 49
ungullible 181
unhandy 62, 153
unhappy 18, 69, 70, 169
unhelpful 36
unheroic 24, 64, 174
unhesitant 64
unhesitating 162, 185
unholy 57
unhostile 172
unhurried 64
unimaginative 9, 81, 154, 178
unimpassioned 13
unimpeachable 19, 54
unimportant 42, 170
unimpressed 50
unimpressive 45
unindulgent 7, 29, 183
uninformed 43, 166
uninhibited 35, 80
uninquisitive 66, 188
uninspired 9, 81
uninspiring 45
uninstructed 43
unintellectual 43
unintelligent 4, 49, 166
uninterested 10, 16, 52, 66, 188
uninteresting 46, 66, 152
unintrusive 66
uninventive 9, 81
uninvited 171
uninvolved 10, 52
united 70
unjaundiced 7

unjust 20, 59
unkempt 180, 182
unkind 22, 36
unkindness 233
unknown 42, 220
unladylike 80
unlearned 43, 166, 180
unlettered 43
unloved 171
unlucky 42, 168
unmagnetic 46
unmalleable 6
unmanageable 75
unmerciful 22
unmethodical 77, 182
unmeticulous 170
unmindful 10, 11, 30, 52, 156
unmoneyed 168
unmotivated 25
unmoved 10, 71, 184
unnatural 158
unnoteworthy 170
unobservant 11, 156
unopinionated 6
unoriginal 9, 81, 154
unorthodox 8, 158, 171
unostentatious 67
unparticular 182
unperceptive 4, 8, 11
unpermissive 150
unpersuadable 6, 74
unpersuasive 45
unperturbed 52
unpleasant 73
unpliable 161
unpolished 38, 67, 180
unpractical 163
unpracticed 39
unprejudiced 7
unprepared 149, 156
unpretending 67
unpretentious 28, 67, 165, 174
unprincipled 20, 55, 164
unproductive 61, 155
unprosperous 168
unprotective 16, 79
unprovocative 45, 46
unpugnacious 172
unqualified 39, 149
unquestioning 31, 49, 66, 151, 188
unrealistic 51, 163, 187
unreasonable 7, 59, 74
unreasoning 166
unrecognized 42
unrefined 80, 180
unreflective 13
unregretful 31, 61, 181
unrelaxed 71
unrelenting 26, 161, 162
unreliable 60, 186
unreligious 57

unremembering 52
unremitting 63, 162
unremorseful 61
unrepentant 31, 61, 181
unresentful 21, 48
unreserved 35, 159
unresisting 75, 148
unresourceful 9, 81
unrestrained 35, 78, 80, 157, 184
unrevealing 47, 154
unrevengeful 21
unrighteous 57
unromantic 9, 15, 50, 178
unruffled 14, 48, 71
unruly 75
unsatisfied 70, 169
unschooled 39, 43
unscrupulous 20, 54, 164
unseasoned 39
unselfish 22, 27, 55, 79, 160
unsentimental 15, 178
unsettled 5, 26, 51
unsexual 13
unshakable 63
unshrinking 149, 184
unskillful 39, 149
unsociable 34, 161
unsoiled 172
unsophisticated 38, 157
unsorrowful 31
unsparing 68
unspeakable 55
unspiritual 57
unspoiled 19
unspontaneous 80
unstable 14, 60, 63, 73
unstinting 22, 79
unsubmissive 75, 161, 178
unsuccessful 42, 168
unsuited 169
unsullied 54, 172
unsure 5, 23, 50
unsuspecting 31, 53, 157
unsuspicious 49
unswerving 26, 59, 63, 162
unsympathetic 7, 21, 183, 184
unsystematic 182
untalented 39
untalkative 167
untaught 38
unthankful 185
unthinking 64, 165
unthrifty 184
untidy 77, 182
untimid 149, 153
untiring 63, 162
untouchable 171
untrained 39, 43

untried 149
untroubled 17, 31, 52, 61, 69, 186
untrue 186
untrustworthy 20, 60
untruthful 156
untutored 38
unusual 158
unvaliant 174
unvalorous 174
unvalued 171
unversed 43
unvigilant 11
unvirtuous 164
unwanted 171
unwarlike 72
unwary 11, 31, 49
unwatchful 156
unwavering 26, 59, 63
unwelcome 171
unwholesome 55
unwise 4
unworldly 31
unworried 69, 71
unworthy 54
unyielding 6, 26, 63, 68, 74, 161, 171
up-and-coming 160
upbeat 11
upholder 185
uplifting 44
uppish 66, 158
uppity 66, 183
upright 19, 54, 57
upset 14, 51
upstanding 19, 54, 170
uptight 29, 71
upward-looking 25, 160
urbane 38
utilitarian 50, 119

vacant 49
vacillating 5, 26, 63
vacillator 186
vacuous 4, 49, 166
vain 28, 158
vainglorious 28, 66, 158
valiant 24, 64, 149, 153
valorous 24, 64, 149, 153
vamp 160
vanquished 168
vassal 152
vaunting 66
vegetative 61
vegetator 186
venal 20, 57
venerable 54
venerating 56
vengeful 150
venomous 16
venturesome 23, 64, 149
venturous 64
veracious 19, 57, 174
verbose 46

versatile 39, 187
versed 39, 43
veteran 187
vexatious 161
vexed 18, 169
vicious 22, 55
Victorian 66
victorious 42
victory, desire for 95
vigilant 10, 23, 32, 64
vigorous 61
vile 22, 55, 164, 181
vilifying 44
villainous 55
vindicated 17
vindicator 150
vindictive 16, 21, 150
violence, fear of 113
violent 73
viperous 55
virginal 13
virtue, desire for 95
virtuous 19, 55, 56, 170, 172
virulent 16, 22
visionary 8, 51, 187
vitalist 119
vivacious 69, 159, 162
volatile 73
volcanic 162
vulgar 38
vulgarian 180
vulture 185
vying 37

wacky 158
waggish 69, 80, 179

Walter Mitty 157
wanton 20, 55, 164
wants and needs 83–95
warlike 73, 165
warm 16, 34
warm-blooded 13
warmonger 165
warrior 187
wary 10, 23, 32, 50, 64, 180
washout 168
waspish 73
wasteful 184
wastrel 184
watchful 10, 64, 175
wavering 24, 60, 63
wayward 54, 164
weak 40, 64
weak-hearted 64
weak-kneed 24, 64, 75, 174
weak-willed 26, 186
weakling 174
weaknesses 125
wealthy 42, 188
wearisome 46, 152
weary-footed 155
weather 221
weather vane 186
well-adjusted 70
well-balanced 70
well-behaved 80
well-bred 38, 183
well-disposed 72
well-educated 43, 164
well-fixed 42, 188
well-heeled 42, 188

well-informed 164
well-intentioned 160
well-known 42
well-mannered 80, 156, 183
well meaning 160
well-off 42
well-read 43, 164, 183
well-thought-of 168
well-to-do 42
well-trained 39
wet blanket 173
wheeler-dealer 176
whimsical 8, 51
whining 47
whipped 168
white feather 174
white-livered 24, 174
wholehearted 13
wholesome 19, 170
wicked 20, 22, 55, 164
willful 6
willing 74
willowy 62
willy-nilly 186
wily 156
windbag 154, 175
windy 46, 154
winner 188
winsome 69
wise 48
wishful 25, 160
wishy-washy 186
wistful 15, 169
witch-hunter 148
withdrawn 35, 70, 165
witless 4, 49

woebegone 31, 69
woeful 31, 169, 173
wolf in sheep's clothing 156
wolfish 27, 79
woodenheaded 4
woolgatherer 157
woolgathering 187
word 133
wordy 46
work, self-assessment of 145
workaholic 160, 162
world-weary 181
worried 18, 29, 69, 169
worrywart 173
worshipful 29, 56, 151
worthless 54
worthy 19, 54
wrathful 16
wretched 18, 54, 164, 169, 179

yawner 188
yearnful 160
yearning 15
yellow 24, 64, 174
yielding 75
yokel 149, 180
youth: desire for 95; self-assessment of 145

zealot 151
zealous 13, 151
zestful 23
zippy 61